KEY CONCEPTS IN LEISURE

Palgrave Key Concepts

Palgrave Key Concepts provide an accessible and comprehensive range of subject glossaries at undergraduate level. They are the ideal companion to a standard textbook, making them invaluable reading to students throughout their course of study, and especially useful as a revision aid.

Key Concepts in Accounting and Finance
Key Concepts in Business Practice
Key Concepts in Cultural Studies
Key Concepts in Drama and Performance
Key Concepts in e-Commerce
Key Concepts in Human Resource Management
Key Concepts in Information and Communication Technology
Key Concepts in International Business
Key Concepts in Language and Linguistics (second edition)
Key Concepts in Law
Key Concepts in Leisure
Key Concepts in Management
Key Concepts in Marketing
Key Concepts in Operations Management
Key Concepts in Politics
Key Concepts in Public Relations
Key Concepts in Psychology
Key Concepts in Social Research Methods
Key Concepts in Sociology
Key Concepts in Strategic Management
Key Concepts in Tourism

Palgrave Key Concepts: Literature
General Editors: John Peck and Martin Coyle

Key Concepts in Contemporary Literature
Key Concepts in Crime Fiction
Key Concepts in Medieval Literature
Key Concepts in Modernist Literature
Key Concepts in Postcolonial Literature
Key Concepts in Renaissance Literature
Key Concepts in Victorian Literature
Literary Terms and Criticism (third edition)

Further titles are in preparation
www.palgravekeyconcepts.com

Palgrave Key Concepts
Series Standing Order
ISBN 1–4039–3210–7
(*outside North America only*)

You can receive future titles in this series as they are published by placing a standing order. Please contact your bookseller or, in case of difficulty, write to us at the address below with your name and address, the title of the series and the ISBN quoted above.

Customer Services Department, Macmillan Distribution Ltd, Houndmills, Basingstoke, Hampshire RG21 6XS, England

Key Concepts in Leisure

Jonathan Sutherland and Diane Canwell

palgrave
macmillan

First published 2009 by
PALGRAVE MACMILLAN

Palgrave Macmillan in the UK is an imprint of Macmillan Publishers Limited, registered in England, company number 785998, of Houndmills, Basingstoke, Hampshire RG21 6XS.

Palgrave Macmillan in the US is a division of St Martin's Press LLC, 175 Fifth Avenue, New York, NY 10010.

Palgrave Macmillan is the global academic imprint of the above companies and has companies and representatives throughout the world.

Palgrave® and Macmillan® are registered trademarks in the United States, the United Kingdom, Europe and other countries.

ISBN 978–0–230–22428–5

This book is printed on paper suitable for recycling and made from fully managed and sustained forest sources. Logging, pulping and manufacturing processes are expected to conform to the environmental regulations of the country of origin.

A catalogue record for this book is available from the British Library.

A catalog record for this book is available from the Library of Congress.

10 9 8 7 6 5 4 3 2 1
18 17 16 15 14 13 12 11 10 09

Printed and bound in Great Britain by
CPI Antony Rowe, Chippenham and Eastbourne

Contents

Introduction

Originally, the study of leisure was restricted to looking at time that was spent by individuals outside the working environment. It was typified by examining the use of discretionary time and involvement in recreational activities. However, it has now become a far more structured academic discipline, which not only studies but analyses aspects of leisure. There is also a far more blurred boundary between leisure and work-related activities. Indeed, much of the study focuses on how work-related activities are actually integral parts of peoples' lives, contributing to their pleasure, motivation and well-being.

Strictly, the term 'leisure' refers to free time, using its roots in Latin and in old French. However, leisure, whilst having been perhaps restricted to the more fortunate classes in the past, became a far broader activity by the middle of the nineteenth century with the development of industrialised labour processes and a reduction in working hours.

It is also important to note that there are two other key types of leisure, which can be broadly described as either active or passive. It is at this point that leisure has crossover with many other social science disciplines. The study of active leisure investigates from low- to high-impact physical activities, encompassing all sports. That of passive leisure investigates activities that do not require any great mental or physical energy.

The study of leisure has now extended into other areas, which were once the preserve of disciplines such as sociology. Culture is an important aspect, as is class, consumption, motivation and aspects of the interface between leisure and society.

Leisure is a strong, vibrant and growing multidisciplinary study area, which has, over time, acquired an academic status to rival more traditional disciplines such as sociology and psychology.

The structure of the glossary

Every attempt has been made to include all of the key concepts in this discipline; taking into account currently used terminology and jargon common throughout the study of leisure around the world. As with any developing area of academic study, there are differing trends and perspectives and certainly the focus of study changes over time. It is important to note that leisure impinges upon allied disciplines, such as sociology, psychology, travel, tourism and sport. It is therefore incredibly difficult to set any hard and fast boundaries with regard to where the study of leisure ends and a new disciplinary area begins.

The key concepts have been arranged alphabetically in order to ensure that the reader can quickly find the term or entry of immediate interest. It is normally the case that a brief description of the term is presented, followed by a more expansive explanation.

The majority of the key concepts have the following in common:

- They may have a reference within the text to another key concept identified by a word or phrase that is in bold type – this should enable the reader to investigate a directly implicated key concept should they require clarification of the definition at that point.
- They may have a series of related key concepts which are featured at the end of the definition – this may allow the reader to continue their research and investigate subsidiary or allied key concepts.
- They may feature book or journal references – a vital feature for the reader to undertake follow-up research for more expansive explanations, often written by the originator or leading writer in that particular field of study.
- They may include website references – it is notoriously difficult to ensure that websites are still running at the time of going to print, let alone several months beyond that time, but in the majority of cases long-established websites have been selected or governmental websites that are unlikely to be closed or to have a major address change.

Glossary terms – a guide

Whilst the majority of the key concepts have an international flavour, readers are cautioned to ensure that they have accessed the legislation or organisations in particular, which refer to their native country. It was not possible to include the legislation of all countries and as a result the slant is very much towards the UK, Europe and the United States. The supporting website at www.palgrave.com will contain legislative entries for the majority of other major countries including Canada and Australia.

It is also often the case that there are terms which have no currency in a particular country, as they may be allied to specific legislation or organisational terms of another country; in these cases readers are cautioned to ensure that the description does not include a specific reference to such law, and not to assume in these cases that the key concept is a generic one and that it can be applied universally to the study of leisure.

In all cases, references to other books, journals and websites are based on the latest available information. It was not always possible to ensure that the key text or printed reference is in print, but most well-stocked college or university libraries should have access to the original materials. In the majority of cases, when generic leisure books have been referenced, these are, in the view of the writers, the best and most available additional reading texts.

A la carte

Translated from the French, this literally means 'from the menu'. The term indicates to the customers that each dish ordered will have a separate price. The term is also used in tour literature to indicate to the customer that a choice of options will be available.

ABTA

The Association of British Travel Agencies (ABTA) was formed in 1950 by 22 leading travel companies, and now represents over 5,500 travel agencies and 900 tour operations throughout the British Isles. ABTA is the principal trade association of travel agents and tour operators in the UK. Members range from small, specialist tour operators and independent travel agencies through to publicly-listed companies and household names; from call centres to internet booking services and high street shops. They all carry the ABTA logo, which means they offer choice, value, and high levels of service.

ABTA's main aims are to maintain high standards of trading practice for the benefit of its members, the travel industry at large, and the consumers that they serve, and to create as favourable a business climate as is possible for all its members.

The amalgamation of ABTA and the Federation of Tour Operators (FTO) on 1 July 2008 created a still more powerful and authoritative voice for the travel industry.

ABTA provides the following services:

- Financial protection in cases of failure of the travel company.
- A complaints procedure.
- Travel insurance.
- A code of conduct for its members to follow.
- Access to an independent arbitration scheme in the case of disputes.
- Access to a personal injury mediation scheme.

www.abta.com

Accommodation

When related to a package holiday, this term refers to a room, lodging, a suite of rooms or a dwelling place, which is offered to travellers in hotels, bed and breakfast establishments or on cruise ships. It is usually used for sleeping and the storage of property. In self-catering accommodation a kitchenette may also be included, which may contain a refrigerator, cooking rings, crockery, cutlery and utensils. Basically the term refers to any establishment that provides shelter and overnight accommodations to travellers.

Action learning

With the support of either peers or colleagues in a small group, this is a process by which a link is made between reflecting on past events, making sense of actions, and identifying actions or options that can be taken, or new ways of behaviour in relation to future events and activities. The participants need to be given time and space to develop a relationship between reflection and action, according to McGill and Brockbank (2003/2006). Typically, the groups (also referred to as sets) have five to seven members and need a facilitator to help establish ground rules. Each member presents an issue, a problem or concern that needs to be explored and understood. Sets often meet on a regular basis in order to develop strategies. Action learning can probably be attributed to Reg Revans, who developed the idea in the 1930s and went on to refine it over the next two decades, during work with the National Health Service and the National Coal Board. Revans wrote:

> The central idea of this approach to development, at all levels, in all cultures and for all purposes is, today, that of a set, or small group of comrades in adversity, striving to learn with and from each other as they confess failures and expand victories.

McGill and Brockbank further described it as:

> A continuing process of learning and reflection with the support of colleagues working on real issues. [It] can achieve improvement and transformation in a wide range of applications and disciplines including professional, training and other contexts.

The primary purpose of the process is to encourage individuals and the group as a whole to take an active stance toward problems and is often seen as a way of unblocking blockages.

McGill, Ian and Brockbank, Anne, *Action Learning Handbook*. Kogan Page, 2003/2006.
Revans, R. W., *ABC of Action Learning*. Lemos & Crane, 1998.

Active ageing

'Active ageing' is a relatively new definition of ageing. It aims to reflect both the desire and the ability of older members of the population to remain connected and engaged with a broad range of activities, including leisure, education and work. The approach supposes that life does not follow traditional stages (**age segregation**), running from education dominating childhood and adolescence, work dominating the early and middle adulthood, and retirement (and opportunities for additional leisure) in later adulthood. In effect, it suggests a far more **age integration** approach, where education, work and leisure occur across all stages of an individual's life.

See also **age integration, age segregation.**

McPherson, D. B., 'Leisure in Later Life', in G. Gross (ed.), *Encyclopedia of Recreation and Leisure in America*. Charles Scribner's Sons, 2004.

A

Active audience

This is a theory that is often applied to television audiences and suggests that audiences are not an undifferentiated mass of people, but a series of isolated individuals. Watching television is both a socially and a culturally informed activity and its central concern is the negotiation of meaning. Audiences are active in the sense that they view the television programmes on the basis of acquired cultural competences, integral parts of the context and their language and social relationships. It is a development of work suggested by Gramsci (1971) and developed by Hall (1981), focusing on the encoding and decoding model of communication. This proposes that messages conveyed to audiences have different meanings to readers, audiences and consumers, dependent upon their own criterion that determines their decoding of that message.

The term 'active audience' is also associated with **hermeneutics**, which challenges the concept that there is only one actual meaning associated with authorial intent. The audience approaches any information with a range of different expectations and anticipations, which are modified during their engagement. Reading, for example, is not merely the reproduction of textual meaning, but it actually produces new meaning in the minds of the readers. A text can guide the reader, but it cannot fix the meanings because it cannot anticipate the imagination of the reader.

See also **hermeneutics**.

Gramsci, A., *Selections from the Prison Notebooks*, ed. Q. Hoare and G. Nowell-Smith. Lawrence & Wishart, 1971.

Hall, S., *Culture, Media, Language*. Hutchinson, 1981.

Morley, D., *The Nationwide Audience*. British Film Institute, 1980.

Activity theory

Activity theory, as claimed by Burgess (1960), suggests that individuals can increase their satisfaction with life on retirement if they maintain a relatively active level of physical, social and intellectual pursuits. This reduces the sense of social isolation that many in older age groups can feel. In effect they replace their lost role in society with a new range of interests and activities.

Burgess, W., *Aging in Western Societies*. University of Chicago Press, 1960.

Adaptive cognition

This term is used to describe the practical aspects of mental function on problem solving and decision-making. It can also be applied to moral reasoning, social motivation and affection. It was first mentioned in a study by Blanchard-Fields and Chen (1996) which looked at the socio-cultural influences on cognitive functioning in older people.

See also **cognitive functioning**.

Blanchard-Fields, F. and Chen, Y., 'Adaptive Cognition and Aging', *American Behavioral Scientist*, 39:3 (1996), pp. 231–48.

Ad hoc group

The term can mean an existing collection of travellers, such as groups and travel clubs, whose members share a common interest or organisational affiliation.

A

Add-ons

These are additional items that can be purchased separately and included in a tour. They are optional tour features that are not included in the basic tour price, such as sightseeing excursions or special activities.

Affinity group

An organisation that has been formed for a specific purpose and subsequently sponsors group travel arrangements, for example, clubs, schools and trade associations. The groups of people who share the common hobby, interest or activity are united through regular participation in shared outings.

After departure charge

This term relates to charges incurred by a customer that do not appear on the guest's initial bill but are paid when they check out of a hotel, such as for telephone calls, newspapers or in some cases dining room, room service or bar charges.

Age integration

The degree to which a particular leisure activity or interest is considered to be intergenerational, either in terms of the extended family, or across society in general. It implies a degree of social and leisure involvement.

See also **age segregation.**

Atchley, R. C., 'Continuity Theory and the Evolution of Activity in Later Adulthood', in J. R. Kelly (ed.), *Activity and Aging: Staying Involved in Later Life.* Sage, 1993, pp. 5–16.

Age segregation

This is the study of the extent to which the elderly are either segregated or integrated into leisure activities that are more commonly associated with different age groups. Specific activities, leisure preferences and values undoubtedly change over time and some people make transitions as they age. However, some leisure activities are not seen as being intergenerational and there is an unseen bias against those who are considered to be too old to be following a particular leisure pursuit.

Atchley, R. C., 'Continuity Theory and the Evolution of Activity in Later Adulthood', in J. R. Kelly (ed.), *Activity and Aging: Staying Involved in Later Life.* Sage, 1993, pp. 5–16.

Agent

The term 'agent' relates to an individual or a business that has the power to act as the representative of another individual or business. In the leisure industry the term most frequently relates to a specific kind of agent, such as a travel agent. It is a legal relationship in which one person acts for another in a business dealing with a third party.

AIO variables

These are Activities, Interests and Opinions (AIO), which are used to measure and categorise customer lifestyles. Earlier leisure and recreation research tended to focus on differentiating groups by their recreational activities, focusing on preferences and demographic information. AIO looks at more fundamental lifestyle information, such as that carried out by Moore and Driver (2005) and Petrick (2002).

Moore, C. and Driver, E., *The Information Workplace Will Redefine the World of Work at Last.* Forrester, 2005.

Petrick, J. F., 'Development of a Multidimensional Scale for Measuring the Perceived Value of a Service', *Journal of Leisure Research*, 14:2 (2002), pp. 119–34.

Alienation

Originally a sociological term that implies a form of false consciousness (Lefebvre 1947), it is now more broadly used in leisure studies to explain a synthetic unreality. It suggests that the world is full of rationalised and bureaucratic procedures, with stable and secure social frameworks, and that individuals look for meaning. Dean MacCannell in *The Tourist* (1976) argued that the modern world appeared to be inauthentic and that tourism in particular was a fruitless search for the authentic and, in any case, it was a short-lived experience. It was an attempt to escape from true reality. The supposition was that tourists are cultural dupes; they are self-deceived and tourism provides for an intellectually challenged and culturally vacuous audience.

Cohen, S. and Taylor, L., *Escape Attempts.* Penguin, 1976.

Lefebvre, H., *Critique of Everyday Life*, Vol. 1. 1947; trans. John Moore, Verso Books, 1991.

MacCannell, D., *The Tourist: A New Theory of the Leisure Class.* Schocken Books, 1976.

Rojek, C., *Ways of Escape.* Macmillan, 1993.

All-inclusive

An all-inclusive package holiday is one where all components of the holiday are included in the price paid. The term 'inclusive' relates to flights, accommodation, transfers, meals and some drinks, although often these are restricted to soft drinks, wine and beer. The benefit of this type of holiday is that the customers are aware of the full cost of the holiday and do not have to make provision for spending money while at their destination, except of course for personal shopping.

Amenity package

Offering this type of package is often used to induce clients to book through a particular tour organisation or travel agency. For example, on a cruise a cluster of special features, such as complimentary excursions ashore, bar or boutique credit, or wine at dinner are offered to clients, usually as a bonus or additional feature.

A

Area of Outstanding Natural Beauty (AONB)

The Dower Report (1945) and the Hobhouse Report (1947) recommended that a number of the finest landscapes in England and Wales should be given special legal status to ensure their preservation 'for the nation's benefit'.

Landscapes of equal value were designated as either AONBs or National Parks as a result of differences in size, scale and aims. There are now 41 Areas of Outstanding Natural Beauty, with the primary purpose of:

- Conserving and enhancing the natural beauty of the landscape.
- Meeting the need for enjoyment of the countryside.
- Showing regard for those who live and work there.

AONB include hedgerows, spinneys and bluebell woods, heath, marsh, and meadow. The AONB status protects the examples of these that still remain today and conserves the landscape's survival for future generations.

Some AONBs are owned by public bodies, such as the Forestry Commission, or by conservation organisations such as the National Trust and County Wildlife Trusts. Other areas are owned by local authorities and government departments, like the Ministry of Defence. But much of the land within AONBs continues to function as traditional, farmed landscapes.

The Countryside Agency (CA) and the Countryside Council for Wales (CCW) are responsible for designating AONBs and advising on policies for their protection. They ensure that they are successfully conserved and enhanced. The overall responsibility of care is assumed by local authorities and the rural community. To encourage consistent policies and positive coordination, AONBs have undertaken the following actions:

- The formation of Joint Advisory Committees – representatives of the different local authorities, landowners, farmers, residents and conservation and informal recreation interests.
- The appointment of AONB officers to coordinate local management operation.
- The preparation of Statements of Intent (or Commitment) and Management Plans.

Grants for safeguarding traditional farmed landscapes within a number of AONBs are available through schemes run by the Department for the Environment, Food and Rural Affairs (DEFRA) and the Welsh Office.

AONB landscapes naturally attract visitors, and managing visitor numbers is a growing challenge in AONBs. Leaflets, trails and ranger services are provided to show visitors why the landscape is precious and how to protect it.

See also **National Parks Service, Countryside Agency (CA)** and **Countryside Council for Wales (CCW)**.

www.aonb.org.uk

A

Articulation

The term 'articulation' is an expression of ideology through social practice. Articulation is the realisation of patterns of human behaviour. Social practice confirms ideological patterning, such as when an individual without realising it replicates the values of a social group to which they are associated. It is also the means by which limitations to these patterns are exposed and acknowledged.

Harris, David, 'Articulation', in *The Handbook of Leisure Studies,* ed. Chris Rojek, Susan Shaw and A. J. Veal. Palgrave Macmillan, 2006, pp. 504–17.

ATOL

ATOL is a protection scheme for air holidays and flights managed by the Civil Aviation Authority (CAA). All tour operators and travel firms selling air holiday packages and flights in the UK are required by law to hold a licence called an Air Travel Organisers' Licence (ATOL).

ATOL protects a customer from losing money or being stranded abroad if the tour operator goes out of business, and gives refunds to those who find they can't travel, as well as arranging for people abroad to fly home.

See also **Civil Aviation Authority.**

www.atol.org.uk

Attraction

The term 'attraction' relates to an item of specific interest to travellers, such as natural wonders, Areas of Outstanding Natural Beauty, museums, theatres, manmade facilities and structures, entertainment venues, or sporting activities.

Attribution theory

Although there were several theories of attitudes tested and developed in the 1950s, it was not until the 1970s that attribution theory emerged to try to explain causal explanations that individuals give for the various events that they encounter and the effects that these have on their social behaviour.

Authenticity

In leisure, as well as in travel and tourism, the term 'authenticity' refers to customers' need to experience an authentic and fulfilling activity. The authentic experience will motivate the customer and shape their behaviour. Inauthentic experiences are thought to be unfulfilling, whilst authentic ones provide light relief from the boring and sometimes meaningless day-to-day life of the customer.

Daniel Boorstin (1961) termed inauthentic experiences as 'pseudo-events' because of their lack of representation of reality. His argument was that when people are unable to experience reality they turn to pseudo-events and often settle for meaningless, commercialised experiences.

Dean MacCannell (1976) believed that modern mass leisure is linked to the way in which people cope with modern society. He believed that work is becoming meaningless and that people gain their sense of identity from experiencing authentic leisure activities. MacCannell's work related to the authenticity of the setting, as well as the authenticity of the participants.

The level of authenticity of a leisure experience, it is argued, relates to the level of the understanding of the visitor. E. Cohen (1979) believed that the level of authenticity was linked to manipulation or staging by the leisure site. Different participants respond in different ways to the levels of authenticity and many are happy just to be experiencing the situation, regardless of the authentic nature of it.

Boorstin, Daniel, *The Image: A Guide to Pseudo-events in America.* Harper Row, 1961.
Cohen, E., 'A Phenomenology of Tourist Experience', *Sociology*, 13 (1979), pp. 179–201.

Gilmore, James H. and Pine, B. Joseph II, *Authenticity: What Consumers Really Want.* Harvard Business School, September 2007.

MacCannell, D., *The Tourist: A New Theory of the Leisure Class.* Schocken Books, 1976.

Axial constructs

Axial constructs concern the formal and informal institutions around which forms of leisure and practices emerge and develop. They are axial in as much as they are fundamental to the leisure actions and choices that individuals make and are fundamental to the development of those interests by the individual. They are constructs in as much as they refer to the principles and structures through which particular traditions of behaviour and social values are embedded (such as fashion choices, work and leisure activities, language and accent). They are also fundamental in terms of individuals' views of responsibility, social inclusion, quality and rights. In one sense they manufacture an individual's view of the world but they do not necessarily determine an individual's perspective, although they can encourage options and inclinations to follow particular leisure paths.

Bourdieu, P., *Outline of a Theory of Practice.* Cambridge University Press, 1977.

Bourdieu, P., *Distinction.* Routledge, 1984.

A

Baby boomers

This is a term used to describe individuals who were born during the post-Second World War 'baby boom' period (1946 to 1964). Many countries experienced an enormous spike in birth rates during this period, notably in the west and in Commonwealth countries such as Canada, Australia and New Zealand.

This group now, however, represents the ageing population and their sheer numbers are considered to be something of a challenge for leisure professionals. They will expect higher levels of education and health and should demand a greater availability of leisure activities. Predictions suggest that they will require more individualised activities, rather than group ones, as they are most closely associated with smaller groups and extended families. According to Adkins (1994) they will also focus on leisure programmes revolving around social interaction, nutrition, intergenerational exchange and stress reduction. There will be a major shift, according to Ziegler (2002), from games and activities most closely associated with senior citizens to workshops, night classes and weekend courses. This generation reflects the fact that the older population is becoming increasingly diverse in terms of its leisure demands. It also suggests:

- That a macro-solution regarding leisure policies will not necessarily work beyond providing active and health-enhancing activities.
- That publicity and promotion of subsidised facilities, programmes and activities, along with support, such as tax incentives, will be necessary.
- That micro-issues related to individual leisure preferences and needs will need to be considered and this will be the most challenging aspect.

Adkins, K. D., 'The Leisure of Aging: We've Only Just Begun', *Illinois Parks and Recreation* (November/December 1994), p. 30.

Ziegler, J., 'Recreating Retirement', *Parks and Recreation*, 37:10 (2002), p. 56.

Back haul

The term 'back haul' relates to the return movement of a means of transport which has provided a transport service in one direction. In other words, when an outbound shipment is delivered, instead of the means of transport returning home empty, a load is picked up from a destination near the final stop-off, allowing it to return full.

Back of house/back office

The term 'back of house' usually relates to the hospitality industry and distinguishes between the different areas of a restaurant, theatre or hotel. 'Back of house' is the area where, for example, the cooks and other support staff are based.

Usually this is a 'staff only' area and is the section of the restaurant or hotel in which food is stored and prepared. This area can also include rest rooms and changing areas for the staff. The staff in the back of house usually does not have direct contact with customers.

In the theatre the back of house is the off stage area. This is also off limits to customers.

See also **front of house/front office.**

Backpacker

A backpacker is someone who carries their own belongings and walks to their destination. The first backpackers were those who had no choice but to walk, as there was little choice of alternative transportation. Foresters, trappers and soldiers all had to carry their own food, clothes and equipment, but in the early twentieth century mountaineers also joined the backpacking society. They found it more convenient to carry their own belongings. The independence that this form of transport gave soon spread to those wishing to be more self-sufficient and free in their travels, and backpacking became more popular.

Backpacking experiences are often used for team building and interpersonal skill building because it increases self-esteem and confidence.

Back-to-back

This is the sequential booking of two different tours in order that the customer has a continuous journey. The term is also used to describe situations where one group arrives at a destination as another group leaves it, for example in package holidays.

Batch mode

Although this term is more closely associated with computer operations, in which a standard task or set of tasks is performed on a group of records, such as automatically updating databases rather than manually opening, editing and saving each one, it has leisure connotations.

It refers to the processing of a group of transactions at a single time. Each of the transactions is collected and processed at the end of each day or time period. They are processed against the master files and the master files are updated. A prime example would be updating customer files, or stock files, as orders are taken. At the end of each day a batch processing program will generate lists of required stock to be sent to customers, or to be reordered from suppliers. It would also generate invoices and management reports as part of the same process.

See also **elctronic ticketing.**

Behavioural models

Behavioural models have close associations with psychology and with business management. They look at how managers make decisions in conditions where there is uncertainty, or where they are operating without a full understanding of the situation or potential consequences, or without access to information.

Behaviour models of decision-making can be differentiated from more neoclassical approaches, which assume that decision-makers have access to all necessary information and that the decisions made are on a rational basis.

Mounir, R. and Tate, R., 'A Behavioural Model of Leisure Participation, based on Leisure Attitude, Motivation and Satisfaction', *Leisure Studies*, 12:1 (1993), pp. 61–70 (10).

Benchmark/benchmarking

Benchmarking is a process of identifying and learning from the best practices of similar activities being undertaken by other organisations. Benchmarking is used to:

- Improve the business's understanding of the external environment.
- Learn from the successes and failures of others.
- Identify and compare elements of a competitor's strategy.
- Learn best practices from any industry to apply to and improve your own internal processes.
- Minimise complacency; in other words, recognise that internal progress may not be apace with competitors.
- Learn to be creative or proactive and not reactive.

It is generally believed that there are five steps towards benchmarking:

1 Identifying what is to be benchmarked. As it is not possible to benchmark everything at once, benchmarking should be applied to the most critical areas. A detailed study and measurement should be undertaken in the selected areas to identify base data as well as ensuring managerial support and the involvement of staff within those areas.

2 Determining who to benchmark with. It is essential to determine which other organisations should be approached. Direct competitors are unlikely to be responsive, but non-direct competitors may be more willing to exchange information. Benchmarking candidates should encompass both small and large businesses, as well as those in the public or private sector.

3 Data collection. Face-to-face interviews and visits to other businesses often provide the best quality information. The correct questions need to be asked and cross-checked. Inaccuracy at this point may invalidate the whole process.

4 Data analysis. Meaningful comparisons need to be made between the business and the benchmarked organisation. Steps should be taken to identify dissimilar or divergent issues, as well as entrepreneurial or novel ideas.

5 Identifying and implementing proposals. Having identified desirable components, the business now needs to plan how these will be implemented, ensuring clear communication. Changes may require training and new criteria to be understood. There will be a period before full efficiency is achieved and a monitoring system needs to be implemented to provide feedback.

The benchmarking process may reveal more valuable information to a potential competitor than the business may receive from that competitor. It requires a fundamental trust which reflects the rights and legalities of both parties. There are key ethical aspects in relation to benchmarking:

- Dealing with individuals and organisations in an honest manner.
- Ensuring that other parties understand how information will be used.
- Promptly informing other parties if the use of information is to be changed.
- Ensuring that all activities are carried out with integrity.
- The establishment of precise ground rules if a competitor is used in the benchmarking process.

Bogan, Christopher E. and English, Michael J., *Benchmarking for Best Practices: How to Define, Locate and Emulate the Best in Business.* McGraw-Hill Education, 1994.

Bilateral agreement

A bilateral agreement is a series of treaties, exchanges, state visits and other agreements between two states, usually associated with political and cultural relations. Bilateralism has a greater flexibility than multilateral agreements, which can involve many states and is, of course, more flexible than unilateralism, when a single state acts on its own.

In the leisure context it can be a cultural exchange of ideas and a sharing of common or associated approaches. Equally, a provision by which individuals involved in sport, leisure and tourism may enter into networks for mutual benefit, such as air transport agreements.

The US routinely enters into bilateral agreements where both countries allow one another's airlines to enter each other's markets, and each will nominate designated airlines to serve one another's markets.

Biographical methods

Biographical research methods have become a very useful and popular tool for social scientists. They are rooted in autobiographical eyewitness statements and personal narratives. Although they raise questions of reliability, subjectivity and representativeness, they are valuable quantitative measures of social events. Essentially they are personal accounts and are used by researchers to analyse the spoken and written words of individuals who have experienced specific activities or events. They allow researchers to investigate specific memories. Some researchers have been concerned about the quality and originality of the data and have sought to undertake sampling procedures and interview methods to balance any perceived areas of bias. Some of the material is criticised for being somewhat exaggerated, but it can be used to substantiate marginalised activities and can be seen as reflective.

Chamberlayne, P., Bornat, J. and Apitzsch, U., *Biographical Methods and Professional Practice: An International Perspective.* Polity Press, 2004.

Chamberlayne, P., Bornat, J. and Wengraf, T., *The Turn to Biographical Methods and Social Science: Comparative Issues and Examples.* Routledge, 2000.

Wengraf, T., *Qualitative Research Interviewing: Biographic Narrative and Semi-structured Methods.* Sage, 2001.

Blackout date/period

Blackout dates or periods usually coincide with particularly busy periods, such as school holidays and peak travel seasons. Blackout dates or periods are those dates on which specific fares or special offers are not available. It is a time when special lower prices or fares do not apply.

Block

A block of seats on a train or boat or in a cinema or hotel, for example, are those that have been set aside either for group sale or for reservation purposes.

Blocked space

These are reservations made with suppliers by either travel agents or wholesalers. They are reserved in anticipation of the ability to resell, but are often subject to forfeiture of deposit if the sale does not take place.

Blue Badge Guide

The Blue Badge is the highest level of guiding qualification in Britain and is awarded by the Institute of Tourist Guiding. It involves detailed and comprehensive training and rigorous examination and registration procedures.

See also **certified tour professional.**

www.blue-badge-guides.com
www.itg.org.uk

Breakeven analysis and the breakeven point

In order to identify an organisation's breakeven point, it is necessary to consider the relationships between the various costs and sales in an integrated manner. The breakeven point is defined as being the point at which the level of sales is not great enough for the business to make a profit and yet not low enough for the business to make a loss. In other words, earnings from sales are just sufficient for the business to cover its total costs. This occurs when total revenue from sales exactly equals the total cost of production.

Breakeven point occurs when total cost = total revenue

From this it can be assumed that if the total revenue from sales is greater than the total costs, then the organisation concerned makes a profit. Conversely, if the opposite is true, and the total revenue is less than the total costs, then the organisation can make a loss. It is essential that organisations take this very important factor into account. The organisation will find that it is essential to determine how many units of output it must produce and sell before it can reach its breakeven point. The total cost of the unit of production is made up of two factors, the fixed and the variable costs, where:

Total cost = fixed costs + variable costs

And the total revenue is given by the number of products sold, multiplied by the selling price:

Total revenue = price × quantity

The drawing up and labelling of a breakeven chart makes the calculation of the breakeven point easier. The breakeven chart requires a considerable amount of

B

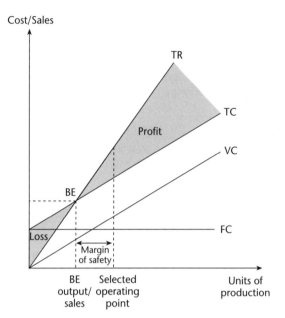

Figure 1 Breakeven chart

labelling in order to be able to identify exactly what the chart is describing about the breakeven point.

As can be seen in Figure 1, the breakeven chart will include:

- Units of production – which are considered to be the most completed product and not, importantly, the components which make up that product.
- Fixed costs (FC) – which are the costs that do not alter in relation to changes in demand or output. They have to be paid regardless of the business's trading level.
- Variable costs (VC) – which change in direct proportion to changes in output, such as raw materials, components, labour and energy. Breakeven charts require the assumption that some costs vary in direct proportion to changes in output. In fact, it is unlikely that any costs are totally variable as raw materials, for example, are likely to cost less per unit if the organisation buys in bulk. In this instance, it cannot be assumed that the cost of raw materials will double if output doubles.
- Total costs (TC) – these are simply the sum of all fixed and variable costs
- Sales and costs – sales are the income generated, i.e. the total revenue (TR), from the selling of the units of production to customers. Costs, on the other hand, are expenses incurred by the organisation in the purchase of raw materials, other fixed costs and variable costs.
- Breakeven point (BE) – this is the point at which sales levels are high enough for the organisation not to make a loss but not high enough for it to make a profit. In other words, this is the point where total sales equal total costs.

- Profit – in terms of the breakeven chart, and the breakeven point, this is achieved when sales exceed total costs.
- Loss – in terms of the breakeven chart, and the breakeven point, this occurs when revenue from sales has not met the total costs.
- Selected operating point – this is the planned production and sales level, which is assumed to be the same as that in given data.
- Margin of safety – this is the amount by which the selected operating point exceeds the breakeven point. This indicates the amount by which sales could fall from the planned level before the organisation ceases to make a profit.

Horngren, C., Sundem, G. and Stratton, W., *Introduction to Management Accounting.* Prentice Hall, 2002.

Breakeven pricing

In a leisure context, producers or providers of **value added** products and services need to assess the profit potential of their offerings. This profit potential is calculated by working out production costs or costs to provide a service. They can then establish an expected selling price based on substitute goods or services and this will help them determine whether a product or service can be produced or supplied for that price.

In many areas breakeven price is referred to as 'per unit cost of production'. This is the price at which the product or service has to be sold in order to cover all associated costs. It is important to note that a breakeven price does not produce a profit for the organisation, but neither does it generate a loss; it simply covers costs. It requires the business to know its variable and fixed costs per unit.

The breakeven price is equal to the variable cost per unit plus the total fixed costs divided by the projected unit sales (breakeven price = variable cost per unit + total fixed costs ÷ projected unit sales).

Taken together, all units of production or services sold at this breakeven price will total the breakeven revenue of the organisation. In other words, this is the amount of income required to cover all variable and fixed costs, unit- or overhead-related, so that the organisation neither makes money nor loses money.

See also **breakeven analysis and the breakeven point.**

Sutherland, J. and Canwell, D., *Essential Business Studies for AQA.* Folens, 2008.

British Academy of Sport

In the late 1990s a feasibility study in the wake of Great Britain's poor performance at the Atlanta Olympic Games revealed that some 45% of British athletes believed that access to scientific support was either poor or very poor. The University of Sheffield and Sheffield Hallam University commissioned a survey as part of a feasibility study for the British Academy of Sport. It was believed that such an academy would be eligible for up to £100 million of Lottery funding. It was originally supported by Conservative Prime Minister John Major, but following the Conservative defeat at the general election in 1997, it was not formally adopted, although many of the facilities suggested were adopted in different guises, and the work undertaken by a variety of different organisations.

B

British Waterways

British Waterways is a public corporation that conserves and preserves a 2,200-mile network of canals and rivers in England, Scotland and Wales. It protects the historic waterways, secures and earns the necessary funding, and encourages investment.

British Waterways maintains the inland waterways so that they are safe and accessible for the 11 million people who visit them every year as well as for the 32,000 boats that are regularly based on them. It works with public sector bodies, private sector partners and those in the voluntary sector and reinvests the income to maintain the canals and rivers.

British Waterways was established by an Act of Parliament in 1962 to look after the majority of inland waterways in England, Scotland and Wales. As well as being governed by the normal accounting, employment, environmental, planning and safety legislation that affects any modern organisation it is specifically governed by many of the original Canal Enabling Acts as well as a number of modern Acts of Parliament.

British Waterways is a public corporation and receives an annual grant. It is sponsored by:

- the Department for the Environment, Food and Rural Affairs;
- the Scottish Government Transport Directorate.

It also works closely with:

- the Department for Economic Development and Transport (Wales);
- the Inland Waterways Advisory Council (IWAC);
- the Association of Inland Navigation Authorities.

The Waterscape brand was developed by British Waterways as the face of their leisure website and marketing communications.

www.britishwaterways.co.uk
www.waterscape.com

Bulk contract

This term applies to an agreement whereby an agent buys a large block of seats at a discount price, which they will then resell to a third party.

Bulkhead/bulkhead seats

'Bulkhead' refers to the walls of a ship or an aircraft that divide the vessel into sections or compartments. The bulkhead seats on an aircraft are those immediately behind the bulkhead, so therefore have limited legroom.

Bumping

This term relates to the practice, most commonly of some airlines, of denying seats to passengers, despite the fact that they have a ticket. This practice most often occurs when the airline has overbooked their seat allocation.

Bureau of Outdoor Recreation (US)

See **Heritage Conservation and Recreation Service.**

Bureaucracy

A bureaucracy is a form of **organisational structure** which has highly routine tasks carried out by its workforce, who are specialised in their area of work. These organisations tend to be grouped into functional departments, with centralised authority and very narrow spans of control. All decision-making follows the chain of command and all activities within the organisation are strictly controlled by rules and regulations.

See also **organisational structure.**

Business class

This class of travel, particularly common on **long haul** flights, is marketed most commonly as being the class between first class and economy class. It is designed to appeal to the business traveller and carries some additional amenities or 'perks' over and above those offered to the economy class traveller, although the benefits vary from airline to airline.

See also **economy class, first class, club class.**

B

Cadw: Welsh Historic Monuments

Cadw is a Welsh government body with the mission to protect, conserve, and to promote the built heritage of Wales. It is the Welsh equivalent of English Heritage and Historic Scotland and is now part of the Welsh Assembly Government.

Most of Wales's great castles, and other monuments such as bishop's palaces, historic houses, and ruined abbeys, are now in Cadw's care. Cadw does not own them, but is responsible for their upkeep and for making them accessible to the public. Cadw is also responsible for listing and ensuring the preservation of historic buildings and archaeological sites.

The organisation was created in 1984; its headquarters are in Nantgarw, just north of Cardiff. Since the creation in 1998 of the National Assembly for Wales, Cadw has been part of the devolved government of Wales, the Welsh Assembly Government.

See also **English Heritage** *and* **Historic Scotland.**

Call brand

This is a general business and marketing term, but specifically applied to leisure in the sense that it is a specific brand-named product that is requested by a customer, usually in a service situation. The customer will ask for a branded product (e.g. Coca-Cola rather than a cola). The latter is a more generic and, perhaps, less expensive house brand.

Cancellation clause/penalty

A cancellation clause in leisure terms is found in a contract between the buyer and the seller. It is a provision within that contract that allows for one of the parties to cancel the contract, provided they make a penalty payment. It will also mention the conditions under which either party can withdraw from the contract. In the vast majority of cases the cancellation clause is never explicitly discussed when a contract is drawn up between a customer and a supplier of products or services, and is usually non-negotiable, as it is a standard part of a business's contract, or terms of business.

Similarly, a cancellation penalty is the amount of money that needs to be paid by one of the signatories of the contract if the contract needs to be cancelled, or one of the signatories to the contract wishes to cancel it.

Capacity dumping

'Capacity dumping' is a term used to describe an action usually undertaken by an airline in which it substantially increases its capacity beyond expected demand. The airline chooses to take this action in order to deter or prevent a competitor from expanding its own share of a network. Typically, an airline will increase the number of seats available on a specific route, in response to a competitor's capacity expansion on that route. By adding substantial capacity to the route the airline is then able to offer fares at, or below, the rate of the competitor. This process continues with probably both airlines registering losses on that route. Ultimately, one of the airlines, and usually the newcomer, drops out of the route as they no longer have the financial resources and strength to sustain the losses on that route. Technically, capacity dumping is an anti-competitive strategy, aimed to prevent or deter competitors from expanding onto the airline's existing routes. In various countries injunctions or orders can be made against an airline that is proved to have used its market power in conjunction with manipulating capacity and fares to unlawfully damage a competitor or deter competition.

Carrier

The term 'carrier' is a generic one that refers to the actual owner of a transportation service which is carrying either passengers or freight on behalf of a third party. Many tour operators, for example, will not have their own transportation systems, but will subcontract the transportation aspect of the package to a third party. The third party in this case is the carrier. An airline, coach company or other transportation company can be their own carrier, but in many cases the transportation is subcontracted out.

Carrying capacity

In relation to leisure and tourism there are two distinct and very different interpretations of the term 'carrying capacity'. The most common one refers to the maximum ability of a transportation network or method to transport or convey a number of individuals and associated luggage or personal belongings. In this respect it can also refer to the maximum number of individuals a destination can accommodate.

This leads on to the broader, but equally relevant leisure concern of maximum carrying capacity, as it relates to the number of individuals, trips or tours that can be reasonably catered for without compromising the ecology or the supporting infrastructure of a particular area. In any given area, resort or region there is a maximum or desirable level of individuals that can be supported within given natural resource limits. This is usually defined as a level that does not degrade the natural, social, cultural and economic environment for either the present or future generations. In normal situations the carrying capacity for any area is not fixed and can be altered by improved technology. The carrying capacity can be altered and improved, but usually if there is a local population increase then the carrying capacity is reduced. Equally, once an environment is allowed to degrade, the actual carrying capacity is diminished, as it has left the environment in a position where it is no longer able to support the number of individuals it was capable of supporting in the past. Fewer individuals can live in the area on a sustainable basis.

In certain areas, however, complex logistical support can allow individuals to live beyond the environment's carrying capacity for limited periods of time. A prime example would be many of the Maldives Islands, in which leisure activities and hotels exist in environments that are incapable of sustaining that level of activity without regular resupply, replenishment and careful eco-management.

Hardin, G., 'Cultural Carrying Capacity: a Biological Approach to Human Problems', *Bioscience*, 36 (1986), pp. 599–606.

Hardin, G., *Living Within Limits: Ecology, Economics and Population Taboos*. Oxford University Press, 1993.

Carry-on

Strictly this is a travel and tourism-related term, which refers to personal belongings that are carried onboard an aircraft, essentially as hand luggage, by the passenger. The personal belongings are not checked in at the airport and are not, therefore, carried in the hold of the aircraft.

Cash budget

A cash budget is simply a budget which seeks to estimate, or forecast, a business's receipts and expenditures over a specific period of time.

Cash flow

'Cash flow' is a term used to describe the net funds which have flowed through an organisation over a period of time. Traditionally, cash flow is usually defined as earnings. The identification of when those earnings were received and when payments had to be made defines the parameters of cash flow. Cash flow is often complicated by the actual value of the cash received in a given period. Cash flow does not take into account expenses which may have been incurred by the organisation prior to the period the cash flow covers, yet during this period the organisation is benefiting from those costs in the past. Equally, the reverse is true; payments may now be due over the cash flow period on equipment or stock from which the organisation has already profited and that has been noted on a previous cash flow.

Cash flow also has a difficulty in dealing with outstanding debts and money owed by creditors. These do not appear on the cash flow as neither has been paid, yet they are important considerations, as they may have a negative or positive effect on the available working capital of the organisation. The available funds which are calculated and identified within the cash flow have enormous implications for the business, particularly as the available working capital determines the organisation's immediate ability to pay subsequent debts and to make necessary investments.

Graham, Alistair, *Cash Flow Forecasting and Liquidity*. Amacom, 2000.

Casual labour

The employment of casual labour, or casual employees, is seen as a viable alternative by many employers to provide a degree of flexibility, particularly when demand may not be easy to predict. Casual labour is usually taken on a once-off job basis, or the individuals are placed on standby by the employer to come in occasionally and carry out work as and when required.

The term 'casual labour' also suggests an employment situation where employees are given low pay, little or no training, no job security, no sick or holiday pay and can be discarded as and when the business sees fit. Casual labour has attracted the unfortunate nickname of 'flexploitation', which refers to situations where minimum wage payments are made, often to individuals who are desperate for work and are prepared to ignore any associated dangers with the work they are asked to undertake.

Philips, Gordon and Whiteside, Noel, *Casual Labour: The Unemployment Question in the Port Transport Industry, 1880–1970*. Oxford University Press, 1985.

Casual leisure

Casual leisure is something that provides immediate intrinsic rewards. The leisure activity is pleasurable and short-lived, hedonistic and undertaken for pure enjoyment. Usually, there is no particular training needed in order to engage in it as an activity. It is usually closely associated with **deviant leisure**. Among the types of casual leisure are:

- Play
- Relaxation
- Passive entertainment
- Active entertainment (games of chance and party games, etc.)
- Sociable conversation
- Sensory stimulation (eating and drinking)
- Casual volunteering

In many respects casual leisure is most closely associated with usual and natural activities, mostly trivial, offering no career or development and usually far less substantial than other forms of leisure.

See also **deviant leisure, serious leisure** *and* **project-based leisure**.

Rojek, C., 'Leisure Theory: Retrospect and Prospect', *Society and Leisure*, 20 (1997), pp. 383–400.

Stebbins, R. A., 'Casual Leisure: a Conceptual Statement', *Leisure Studies*, 16:1 (1997), pp. 17–25.

Stebbins, R. A., 'The Costs and Benefits of Hedonism: Some Consequences of Taking Casual Leisure Seriously', *Leisure Studies*, 20:4 (2001), pp. 305–9.

Stebbins, R. A., 'Pleasurable Aerobic Activity: a Type of Casual Leisure with Salubrious Implications', *World Leisure Journal*, 46:4 (2004), pp. 55–8.

Casual research

This is a form of research that does not follow any formal or set procedures, particularly when collecting or recording information. Researchers will contact a range of respondents and are unlikely to use a standardised set of questions with pre-determined response categories. If they were to use a more structured questionnaire, this would defeat the purpose of the research by inhibiting the researchers from taking advantage of the different areas of expertise and experience of each of the respondents.

Some casual research methods will involve contacting selected acquaintances or experts and, therefore, do not use an information collection process that could be considered to be precise or reliable in terms of objectivity or bias. The casual

C

research does not follow formal tests of research because there is no scientific test regarding the nature of the relationship between the researcher and the attitudes and opinions of the target respondents.

Observations and assumptions based on opinions from casual research can be risky. Most methods of research require a more formal process. The most commonly used hybrid of casual–informal research is the focus group, a directed group discussion of between eight and twelve individuals. The individuals are chosen with regard to specific key characteristics, which are determined to be important by the sponsor of the research project. The moderator will ask a series of questions and will probe the participants for responses. Usually the process is recorded and transcribed in order for researchers and clients to gain valuable insights and draw meaning out of the results. In this respect the process is slightly more formal, but could only really be classed as quasi-formal because the size of the sample is small and there is a lack of formal research procedures that is more closely associated with casual research.

Austin, E. and Pinkleton, Bruce, *Strategic Public Relations Management: Planning and Managing Effective Communication Programs*. Lawrence Erlbaum, 2000.

Centralisation

The process of consolidating certain types of activities or decision-making in one place, as opposed to spreading them across corporate divisions or geographical locations. Centralisation is a measure of how concentrated the decision-making processes are within an organisation. The greater the concentration, the more centralised the organisation is considered to be.

Centralised billing

This is a system in which a leisure organisation will generate a single bill or invoice for several individuals. It is particularly applicable for leisure activities such as training, functions, conferences and team-building exercises. The booking is invariably centralised through one channel and consequently the billing system is also centralised through one channel, with all payment and accounting functions generated by a single office.

In practice, this process helps to streamline the bookings, as well as ensuring that any necessary accounting documentation has been collected or collated, checked and then presented for payment. A prime example would be a travel agent sending out a single bill for travel for a group of individuals who have booked at the same time. Equally, in business travel a consolidated central billing system would be used in order to invoice a business as a customer, consolidating all travel costs and associated payments for a number of individuals over a specified time period (usually a month).

Centralised commission

A centralised commission system is a way in which a supplier, such as a hotel chain or restaurant chain, can deal with commission payments to travel agents, tour operators or other organisations from a central office. This alleviates the logistical issue of each of the individual properties within the chain having to manage and then pay their commissions on a one-by-one basis. A centralised commission system has usually been agreed in advance with the recipients of the commission and provides a clearer and more easily checked commission payment process.

Certification

The term 'certification' in a leisure context can refer to a number of specific situations, where minimum standards or qualifications in specified areas are required. They will invariably identify an individual or an organisation as having recognised professional standards or expertise in a given area. For individuals this may involve having certification related to a specific leisure activity, or the availability of individuals who have been trained either in health and safety or in first aid and accident care.

For organisations, certification may be required by potential customers, as recognition of minimum standards that are required by their own codes of practice. These could include adherence to requirements for health and safety, hygiene, minimum wages, staff contracts or provision for the disabled.

Certified tour professional

Certified tour professionals, or in the UK, Blue Badge Guides, are selected, trained and examined by the training provider and examined by the Institute of Tourist Guiding. The training is detailed and comprehensive, the examinations rigorous and registration an achievement.

Originating in London, this badge was awarded by regional Tourist Boards from 1969, so that every guide would have the same background of national core knowledge combined with in-depth local knowledge. This is now the responsibility of the Institute of Tourist Guiding.

As well as acquiring knowledge, Blue Badge Guides are trained in the selection and presentation of material. The Blue Badge is recognised internationally.

Blue Badge Guides have a wide range of languages, specialities and interests, and can guide on foot, in cars, on coaches, on trains and on boats. They are respected by discriminating tour operators and travel agents throughout the world.

www.blue-badge-guides.com

Certified travel counsellor (associate)

A certified travel counsellor, or associate, is an individual who has attained an award of professional competence after the successful completion of a course. It is a term that is used in the US for those who have undertaken studies that have been approved or arranged by the American Institute of Certified Travel Agents (now the Travel Institute). The certified travel counsellor award is also offered by the Canadian Institute of Travel Counsellors.

www.icta.com
www.thetravelinstitute.com

Certified Travel Industry Specialist

The Certified Travel Industry Specialist programme is offered by the American Bus Association. It is a widely respected qualification and is university administered.

www.buses.org/ctis

Chain ratio

Chain ratio is related to forecasting, in which the starting point in the forecasting process is usually designated as either a breakdown or a buildup process. The breakdown process is often referred to as the chain ratio method, in which the forecaster begins with a variable that has a large scope and systematically works down to a sales forecast. It is widely used for consumer product forecasting. The initial variable will tend to be the total population figure for the target market. Through the use of percentages an appropriate link is built to generate the sales forecast. This is compared with the buildup process, in which all potential buyers in a target market are added up to estimate the overall demand.

Channel-based pricing

This is a pricing methodology in which the prices that can be charged for a particular product or service by a leisure organisation are tied to what is the average price charged for those products or services within a clearly defined market. In the late 1990s Delta Airlines were one of the first to use channel-based pricing. They had switched over from a system by which they sold unsold seats through internet specials.

Channel-based pricing is a recognition of the fact that customers are increasingly price sensitive. This is a way in which a business can aim to match the most common or average pricing levels within their immediate channel, setting their prices so that they effectively match those of key competitors.

There are, however, several problems with channel-based pricing:

- It takes no account of the actual costs incurred by the business and neither does it recognise that costs incurred by one business may be different from those of another.
- It does not take into account any economies of scale that can be enjoyed by larger businesses but not by smaller ones.
- It presupposes that levels of profit will be equal across the channel.
- It also assumes that prices will have a degree of stability and that short-term sales and incentives will not be offered to upset the balance.
- It assumes that no businesses within the channel are interested in increasing their market share or turnover.
- It often suggests a degree of collusion between businesses operating in the same channel.

Keltner, B., *From Channel Diversity to Channel Strategy*. National Science Foundation, 1999.

Charter for leisure

This is a World Leisure Charter that was approved by the directors of the World Leisure board in 2000 and is based on an original that was adopted by the International Recreation Association in 1970. The World Leisure Organisation was founded in 1952. It is a worldwide, non-governmental organisation and is concerned with encouraging conditions that allow leisure to serve as a means by which there can be human growth, development and well-being. The organisation is based at the University of Northern Iowa in the US.

Introduction

Consistent with the Universal Declaration of Human Rights (Article 27), all cultures and societies recognise to some extent the right to rest and leisure. Here, because personal freedom and choice are central elements of leisure, individuals can freely choose their activities and experiences, many of them leading to substantial benefits for person and community.

Articles

1 All people have a basic human right to leisure activities that are in harmony with the norms and social values of their compatriots. All governments are obliged to recognise and protect this right of its citizens.

2 Provisions for leisure for the quality of life are as important as those for health and education. Governments should ensure their citizens a variety of accessible leisure and recreational opportunities of the highest quality.

3 The individual is his/her best leisure and recreational resource. Thus, governments should ensure the means for acquiring those skills and understandings necessary to optimise leisure experiences.

4 Individuals can use leisure opportunities for self-fulfilment, developing personal relationships, improving social integration, developing communities and cultural identity as well as promoting international understanding and co-operation and enhancing quality of life.

5 Governments should ensure the future availability of fulfilling leisure experiences by maintaining the quality of their country's physical, social and cultural environment.

6 Governments should ensure the training of professionals to help individuals acquire personal skills, discover and develop their talents and to broaden their range of leisure and recreational opportunities.

7. Citizens must have access to all forms of leisure information about the nature of leisure and its opportunities, using it to enhance their knowledge and inform decisions on local and national policy.

8 Educational institutions must make every effort to teach the nature and importance of leisure and how to integrate this knowledge into personal lifestyle.

www.worldleisure.org

Churning

Churn, or churning, is the percentage of customers who have been won or lost over a period of time. An organisation may have attracted 20% new customers, but at the same time lost 15% of its existing customers. In this way a business may have an ever changing customer base. Organisations will spend considerable time, effort and money on trying to reduce the churn rate. It is often described as the time that elapses from when a customer ceases purchasing from a business to the time at which they start buying products and services once again.

The concept is very closely related to that of **customer retention**.

Circle itinerary

A circle itinerary is usually a set of leisure activities, or excursions, which begin and end at the same geographical point, usually a city or a specific location. In travel a circle itinerary would start in a particular city and include three or more specific flights that take the individual to two or more different cities. Circle itineraries usually permit at least two stopovers and are typically priced as a series of one-way flights. There are usually restrictions on circle itineraries by airlines. Individuals cannot begin their travel from the furthest geographical point of their trip and the further geographical point is not usually the place that the individual can stay for the longest.

Civil Aviation Authority

The title Civil Aviation Authority (CAA) actually refers to the national body that governs civil aviation in a particular country. This is under a ruling of the United Nations' organisation, the International Civil Aviation Organisation (ICAO). Countries as diverse as Albania, Brazil, Guatemala, Macedonia, Qatar and Great Britain all have their own Civil Aviation Authorities.

In Britain, the Civil Aviation Authority operates as an independent, specialist aviation regulator. It is involved in economic regulation, air space policy, safety regulation and consumer protection. The British Civil Aviation Authority is considered a leader in the world. The Air Travel Organisers' Licensing (ATOL) is a part of the Civil Aviation Authority in Britain. It protects travellers from losing their money or being stranded abroad.

In September 2008 the XL Leisure Group folded, leaving 80,000 British customers overseas. It was ATOL and the CAA that organised their repatriation. They were also actively involved in trying to secure refunds for 200,000 individuals who had forward bookings with the company.

The CAA, in conjunction with the British Secretary of State for Transport, carries out periodic investigations into air passenger experiences at Britain's airports. These are designed so that beneficial improvements can be identified.

See also **ATOL.**

www.caa.co.uk

Client mix

Client mix is also more commonly known as customer mix. It is the specific blend of different types of customer that is categorised using psychographic and demographic criteria. Clearly it is in a business's interest to ensure that they have the broadest possible range of client mix in order to protect themselves from sudden changes in buyer behaviour that they would have been unable to cater for if they were to have focused on relatively narrow customer segmentation targets. Organisations can not only identify specific customer characteristics through customer profiling, but can also identify distinctive customer groups within their broader customer base. The customer mix represents the different and clearly identifiable customer sub-groups or sub-segmentation units, within the broader customer base.

Close out

A close out is a clearance of products or the announcement that a particular service will end at a specified time, usually in order to bring down the inventory to zero, or to give individuals a last opportunity to use that service before it is terminated. In some cases it will involve a particular product or service that has historically not sold very well or has not had a high level of demand.

In other cases 'close out' relates to an organisation that is in the final stages of closure, or perhaps relocation, and, as such, the close out or clearance final sale is part of a liquidation process.

In the leisure industry, however, there are specialist retailers who focus on close out items, buying them from other suppliers and selling them on at a discount. In themselves these close out stores are not in danger of liquidation but merely addressing the close out sale on behalf of a third party.

Close out sales are also associated with seasonal products and activities, such as clearance sales following specific holiday periods (such as the sale of swimwear after the summer season).

Closing question

'Closing question', or 'closing', is a term that is usually applied to selling and is the final stage of the sales process (excluding after-sales service). Closing involves attempting to persuade a customer to make a commitment to buy. Typically this will occur when the salesperson has finished dispelling any buying hurdles or objections.

See also **open question.**

Club class

'Club class' is essentially a term for what is often known as **business class**. It is a premium cabin section on an airline and therefore similar to first class train travel. It is used as a way to differentiate seating and service arrangements, offering customers greater comfort and benefit and suggesting an exclusive travel experience.

See also **first class, business class, economy class.**

Clustering

'Clustering' is usually applied to a number of businesses or organisations that are geographically concentrated. Each of the businesses is somehow interconnecting with another, either as suppliers and customers, or as associated organisations that complement one another's products or services in a specific way. The theory is that by clustering, productivity is increased, allowing each of the individual businesses or institutions to compete on a more effective basis.

Sometimes the term is more clearly defined as an industry, business, competitive, or Porterian cluster. The latter definition relates to the term suggested by Michael Porter (1990). Porter recognised that economic geography, or geographical economics, was a significant factor that determined the success or failure of particular businesses. Clusters can in fact refer to a number of different types of interrelated networks:

- Sectoral clusters – which include a number of businesses that operate together within the same area, such as airlines, tour operators or leisure providers.

C

- Horizontal clusters – these are businesses that share resources, such as knowledge management.
- Vertical clusters – which is another term used to describe a supply chain cluster.

The clusters are usually based on knowledge:

- Techno clusters – in which the clusters have developed according to the need to use specific high technology or knowledge and are usually clustered around universities.
- Historic clusters – although more specifically based on the long-term association that a particular geographical area has with an area of expertise, such as London being a financial centre.
- Factor endowment clusters – which refers to geographical areas that have a comparative advantage, such as Mediterranean tourist resorts, which have an advantage due to the weather and the local environment.

Krugman, P., *Geography and Trade*. Gaston Eyskens Lecture Series, 1991.
Porter, Michael, *Competitive Strategy*. Free Press, 1980.
Porter, Michael, *The Competitive Advantage of Nations*. Free Press, 1990.

Code sharing

This is an agreement whereby airlines permit the use of their computer reservation system (CRS) code in the flight schedule displays of other airlines. It was first introduced into the airline industry in 1990 between Quantas Airways and American Airlines. The code share was part of a cooperative services agreement between the two carriers before the various airline alliances were formed. It refers to a practice where a flight operated by one particular airline is jointly marketed as a flight for one or more other airlines. Code sharing partnerships with other airlines are common nowadays and are a key feature of the major airline alliances.

Under a code sharing agreement, participating airlines can present a common flight number for several reasons, including:

- For connecting flights.
- When flights from both airlines fly the same route.
- It provides a method for carriers who do not operate their own aircraft on a given route to gain exposure in the market through display of their flight numbers.

Under a code sharing agreement, the airline that operates the flight is known as the carrier and the other airlines are known as the marketing or validating carriers.

There are also code sharing agreements between airlines and rail providers. These are known as 'Rail and Fly' systems and involve some integration of both types of transport, for example, finding the fastest connection, allowing exchange between an air ticket and a train ticket, or the air ticket being valid on the train.

Cognitive benefits

Cognitive benefits are aspects of leisure that can improve how the brain processes either the spoken word or other functions, such as understanding, problem solving or decision-making. In a study in 2005 by Stanford University, musical training was shown to lead to improvements in the reading ability of children with dyslexia. It suggested that musical experience can help the brain improve its ability to distinguish between rapidly changing sounds and that this is a key to understanding and using language.

See also **cognitive functioning.**

www.stanford.edu

Cognitive functioning

'Cognition' and 'cognitive functioning' refer to the mental functions and processes, such as comprehension, decision-making, planning and learning, or more broadly the information-processing ability of an individual. There is a strong link between cognitive functioning, social functioning, educational performance and broader areas, such as economic status.

In a study carried out by University College London it was found that participation in cognitively complex, or social leisure activities has an association with adult cognition, which suggests that mental stimulation in leisure has beneficial effects on cognition for most age groups. The study showed that poor cognitive functioning is often a predictor of mortality and that mental stimulation can offer protection against cognitive impairment, such as dementia.

See also **cognitive benefits.**

www.ucl.ac.uk/epidemiology

Commercial recreation

Commercial recreation is a fast growing segment of the leisure industry. It includes amusement parks, water parks, cinemas, golf courses, recreation equipment suppliers, outdoor recreation outfitters and a variety of other businesses. Essentially the commercial recreation industry provides recreation and leisure for profit. There are four different types of commercial recreation, these are:

- the movement of people within the travel or transportation industry;
- the provision of accommodation, food and beverages in the hospitality industry;
- the retailing of products, entertainment or recreational programmes within the commercial recreation industry;
- the support businesses that assist the three main industries.

C

Crossley, John C., Jamieson, Lynn M. and Brayley, Russell E., *Introduction to Commercial Recreation and Tourism: An Entrepreneurial Approach.* Sports Publishing, 2001.
Ellis, Taylor and Norton, Richard L., *Commercial Recreation.* McGraw-Hill, 1998.

Commission

Commission is a remuneration or reward for a salesperson who has managed to sell a particular product or service to a customer. The commission is usually calculated as a percentage of the value of the product or services sold. In many sales-orientated careers only a base salary is paid, with the bulk of the salesperson's income being derived from commission on sales achieved. It is seen as a remuneration-based reward or incentive system. It aims to boost sales by making a direct link between performance and pay.

Commission for rural communities

The Commission for Rural Communities (CRC) is a British-based independent organisation that provides independent advice to the British government, with the intention of ensuring that policies reflect the needs of those who live and work in rural England. CRC has three primary functions:

- As a rural advocate, or voice for rural people, businesses and communities.
- As an expert adviser, giving objective evidence-based advice to government and other bodies.
- As an independent watchdog, monitoring the impact and delivery of policies and how they are affecting the rural community.

Although not solely involved in leisure-related issues, much of CRC's remit does necessarily involve both the availability and provision of leisure facilities, either for the rural communities themselves or for visitors to rural areas in England.

www.ruralcommunities.gov.uk

Commissionable tour

Commissionable tours are designed by tour specialists, operating either in a region or a specific country. The tours are usually available solely through travel agencies, hoteliers and full service tour operators. The tour designers create standardised tours for individuals or groups, which can be purchased by the customer through a travel agency, for example, as a third party. The travel agent will then receive a commission for having sold the tour on behalf of the business that has created the tour. In most cases the cost of the tour is collected by the booking agent, who in turn pays the tour operator minus the commission offered. Commissionable tours are usually available through either retail or wholesale travel agencies. They receive an agreed sales commission from the tour company for every sale made.

Commodity

'Commodity' is a broad term used to describe a product or a service that can be exchanged for payment. In the leisure industry it is often used to describe accommodation or facilities.

Common carrier

'Common carrier' is a term used when referring to different forms of transportation; primarily transportation services that are offered to the public for hire. The term 'common carrier' has a legal background that goes back to the times when stagecoaches were used as the primary transport system in England. The term has been adopted to describe broader public transport providers. A prime example of a definition of a common carrier is provided by the Australian government under the terms of the Carriers and Innkeepers Act (1958):

[A common carrier] exercises the public profession of carrying passengers or the goods of all persons wishing to use its services. To be a common carrier of goods, the carrier must hold itself out, either expressly or by course of conduct, as willing to carry for reward and as a business the goods of all people who send them to be carried, without discrimination, and so long as the carrier has room, at a reasonable price.

O'Connor, W. E., *An Introduction to Airline Economics*. Greenwood Press, 2000.

Communication

The **organisational structure** of the leisure business will determine the channels through which communication is regularly made. Communication channels need to ensure that information flows freely throughout the organisation in order that the right information meets the right person, at the right time. Open communication channels tend to take the following forms:

- Notice boards
- Newsletters
- Minutes of meetings
- Non-confidential internal mail
- Multi-user computer systems
- Email.

Communication channels also have to pass information of a confidential or security-restricted nature and the organisation will restrict access to this information in a variety of ways, including passwords for computer systems.

An organisation will select the most effective method of communication for transmitting information both internally and externally, although taking into consideration such matters as speed, cost, feedback requirements or written documentation needs.

A communication barrier is taken to mean a problem in the communication system or stream which effectively blocks either the communication itself or the understanding of that communication between the relevant parties.

Communication barriers can take a number of different forms, such as:

- Lack of sufficient or effective training of employees.
- Lack of information needed to make a decision.
- Personal relationship problems.
- Faulty or inadequate systems or procedures.

Community leisure

'Community leisure' is a term used to describe sports and leisure facilities that are run by not-for-profit (although not exclusively) organisations in conjunction with local councils or governments. They provide a range of leisure and recreation facilities, from swimming pools to fitness centres and multifunctional venues, which can include racquet sports areas and function rooms. In many cases these community leisure facilities or centres are directly subsidised by local government funding. In Britain over the past decade there has been a trend for many local authorities to externalise their leisure facilities. Some went into partnership with charity groups or community groups, whilst others created social enterprises that are required to reinvest any profits made into improvement of services and facilities. In Britain, for example, these community leisure groups derive their funding from local authorities, public sector partners, the general public, agencies (such as Sport England) and grant makers (such as the Lottery fund).

Community relations

Community relations are programmes that businesses undertake in order to engage the local community. The businesses make a positive contribution in order to bring themselves into partnership with the local community, in exchange for their support. Community relations are also known as 'community involvement' and this is seen by many businesses as being an integral part of their social responsibility, particularly in relation to regeneration. Some larger businesses second skilled employees to provide services to the local community, as well as engaging in training and educational initiatives. Other community relations projects can include sponsorship of sports and arts projects.

Community-based tourism

Community-based tourism is a form of tourism in which often poor, rural and economically marginalised residents are active participants in hosting visitors to their region. They can provide accommodation, services, guide service, introductions to cultures and rituals, and be directly involved in delivery, management and **conservation** issues. The local residents are key stakeholders and the projects inevitably revolve around conservation of the environment, as the tourism provides a financial reason to protect the natural resources of the area. Communities may partner with private sector providers to provide additional expertise, including capital, marketing, the transportation of customers to and from the region and, in many cases, incorporating the community-based project into a broader tour itinerary.

Conservation International was created in 1987 and is one such organisation that is actively involved in promoting community-based tourism holidays (in conjunction with responsibletravel.com). Many of the projects are on a relatively small scale and although demand for these types of tours is growing, booking levels and occupancy levels are low and the community-based projects are still reliant on donors.

www.conservation.org
www.responsibletravel.com

Competitor analysis

Competitor analysis is a process that involves the collection of data, focusing on identifying competitors and what they offer. It also involves looking at the prices of their products and services and comparing customer profiles and numbers. This should reveal competitive advantages and disadvantages. It will also be possible to identify their reactions to newcomers to the market, or any changes in products or services offered and price changes. Competitor analysis has two primary activities: first the data is collected and then it is used to try to predict future competitor behaviour. The marketing specialist Michael Porter suggested a framework to analyse competitors:

- Their objectives
- Their assumptions
- Their strategies
- Their capabilities

These four aspects would determine competitor response.

The competitors' objectives may be apparent either in their mission statements or in the direction in which their business is moving. Their organisational structure also provides vital clues. Equally the background of executives, members of the board and other structural factors may give clues. The assumptions upon which they operate will be based on their own beliefs about their competitive position, their past experience, along with regional factors and industry trends. Their resources and capabilities revolve around understanding how the competitor may wish to respond compared with its ability to respond in an effective manner. This factor needs to be evaluated on a regular basis, as the competitive environment is a dynamic one. The competitor's current strategy should be revealed in the annual report and can be backed up by expert opinion from analysts and careful study of the competitor's press releases. A strategy can also be revealed by looking at their capital investments, promotional campaigns, mergers and acquisitions, partnerships, development projects and their pattern of hiring. This allows a response profile to be created, which should improve the ability to predict their behaviour, or even to influence their behaviour.

Porter, Michael, *Competitive Strategy: Techniques for Analysing Industries and Competitors*. Free Press, 1998.

Computerised reservation system

Computerised reservation systems were originally designed to store, retrieve and carry out transactions by airlines. The systems have been broadened in recent years to incorporate travel agents, allowing them to book and sell tickets through a global distribution system. Over the years the technology has become more sophisticated and the global distribution systems now allow travel agents and consumers themselves to book complex packages of flights, hotel rooms, rental cars, car parking, tours and excursions and other services online. It is believed that the first experimental automated booking system was installed as early as 1946 by American Airlines. The majority of the newer global distribution systems are based on a transaction processing facility. The major systems include:

- Amadeus – used by Air France and Lufthansa
- Sabre – used by American Airlines and Singapore Airlines
- Galileo – used by Air Canada and United Airlines
- Worldspan – used by Delta and Northwest Airlines
- Patheo – used by KLM and Lufthansa
- Abacus – used by Cathay Pacific

Confirmed reservation

At its most basic level this is a written statement from a carrier or hotel, for example, that it has received a reservation request from a customer and will honour it. However, even written confirmed reservations may not be guaranteed. Oral confirmations are usually difficult to uphold.

Conjunction ticket

A conjunction ticket is a ticket that is issued to a customer in relation to another ticket, which together constitute a single contract of carriage.

Conservation

Conservation is concerned with the preservation of cultural property, specifically to protect that heritage for the benefit of future generations. Clearly leisure and tourism can have a detrimental impact on cultural heritage. Conservation is now a broader research area, particularly in relation to the net impact of tourism on certian areas and the development of sustainable tourism initiatives. Table 1 outlines the key areas in which research relates to conservation.

Table 1 Conservation research

Conservation activity	Explanation
Examination	This involves the investigation of the structure, materials and condition of elements of cultural property, including the identification of the causes and extent of any deterioration.
Documentation	The recording of data that is broadly derived from conservation activities.
Treatment	The alteration of cultural property with the purpose of prolonging its existence.
Stabilisation	A treatment option that aims to maintain the integrity of the cultural property, as well as minimising any future deterioration.
Restoration	An alternative treatment route, aiming to return the cultural property to either an assumed or a known state. This may include adding materials that were not originally associated with that cultural property.
Preventative care	Attempts to mitigate any deterioration or damage by carrying out an environmental audit, ensuring that any handling or maintenance procedures are carried out, enhancing storage, carrying out assessments to ensure that emergency procedures are in place and duplicating some objects for display.
Protection of cultural property	Ensuring that collections, specimens, structures and sites are protected from human interference and, if possible, from environmental threats.
Preservation of cultural property	Steps that aim to minimise the deterioration of cultural property either by limiting access, or by providing facilities that aim to shield the cultural property from chemical or physical deterioration and damage.

Consolidator/consolidation

In the leisure and tourism field a consolidator is usually a business that negotiates bulk contracts with airlines or other transportation providers, or in other cases accommodation, and then sells on those services or spaces to customers at a discounted rate.

Consolidation is when a business aims to reduce the number of suppliers that it deals with, with the intention of making cost savings. These cost savings are usually achieved by increasing the value of the transactions with single businesses, in order to qualify for higher discounts.

'Consolidation' can also refer to situations where two or more businesses providing broadly similar products or services to a common customer market decide to enter into a formal merger or relationship with one another. This is done in order to reduce costs. Any duplicated functions of the newly merged businesses can be eliminated, driving costs down, and at the same time the combined purchasing power of the newly merged organisation means it can renegotiate contracts with suppliers, in order to receive discounted products and services.

Consortium

The word 'consortium' refers generally to a group of companies that have entered into a voluntary relationship. They would do this in order to share their resources and thereby gain an advantage over the competition. In the leisure and tourism industry a 'consortium' usually means a group of suppliers. They offer incentives to a travel agency or other transport provider, such as higher commission rates, in exchange for the provider using them as their preferred suppliers.

Consumerism

In the 1970s, 'consumerism' was taken to mean marketing and advertising which was specifically designed to create customers, in other words to make the product or service offerings as approachable and pertinent to the customer as possible. It is probable that consumerism can actually be traced back to the early 1960s when President Kennedy proposed that consumers should be accorded their rights in law.

Since that time, the term has taken on a radically different meaning in that it is more closely associated with the rights of consumers. Consumerism can now be defined as illustrating to businesses in general that the customer is no longer to be considered as an individual who can be manipulated by marketing and that their responses to advertising and other marketing activities is no longer as predictable as it may once have appeared. Consumers now flex their muscles and demand products and services that more closely match the claims made in marketing communications; they are supported by many non-governmental organisations or consumer groups coupled with local and national government bodies responsible for the advancement of consumer protection.

The two alternative definitions can be seen as being almost opposite in their meaning and it is the latter definition that tends to be applied to the term.

Aaker, David A. (ed.), *Consumerism: Search for the Consumer Interest*. Free Press, 1982.

Continuing professional development (CPD)

Continuing professional development is taken to be an ongoing learning process, which aims to increase skills, knowledge and understanding. It is usually associated with members of professional associations and aims to encourage learning through a broad range of activities in order to develop a better skills and knowledge base to improve performance and practice. Many of the programmes are therefore employment related. In many respects it is similar to **lifelong learning**, which aims to enable individuals to fulfil their personal and professional potential, as well as meeting the present and future needs of customers, clients and the organisation to which they belong.

Continuity theory

With regard to leisure, Atchley (1971) suggested that as individuals become older they will have a smoother transition into retirement if they continue to pursue uninterrupted their leisure activities throughout their lives and into retirement.

Atchley, R. C., *Social Forces in Later Life*. Wadsworth, 1971.
Atchley, R. C., 'Continuity Theory and the Evolution of Activity in Later Adulthood', in J. R. Kelly (ed.), *Activity and Aging: Staying Involved in Later Life*. Sage, 1993, pp. 5–16.

Convenience sampling

'Convenience sample' is a term related to market research. In its simplest form it is a process by which a researcher will literally stop any individual who is prepared to answer questions, without any regard to their demographic or lifestyle profile. It is obviously one of the easiest forms of market research to carry out, but it is potentially the most dangerous in terms of drawing conclusions from it. The data will have an inbuilt bias and, although it may be convenient, it will almost certainly not be representative of the broader population or target group. It is also sometimes referred to as 'opportunity sampling' and can by extension lead to snowball sampling, in which a selected individual suggests several other potential respondents who in their view have similar characteristics to themselves.

Convention and visitors bureau

In essence these are the US equivalents of the **Tourist Information Centre (TIC)**. They provide official points of contact for visitors to a particular city or region. In the US they tend to be funded in part by member organisations, such as local businesses and attractions, and also receive funding from the city, county or state. In the US they are also partly funded by Transient Occupancy Tax on hotel rooms (such as in California).

Corporate travel

In the US alone, domestic business travel is worth US$300 billion per year. A conservative estimate of the global business travel expenditure is US$650 billion. Business travel is typically the second or third most controllable expenditure on a business's balance sheet. Increasingly businesses are using third party organisations to provide solutions to their corporate travel needs, including the booking of flights, rail tickets, hotels, insurance, car parking, venues and events.

Costing

There are numerous ways in which a business can establish the true costs of its products and services. One of the common ways is to use activity-based costing, which is a system that assigns costs to products and services based on the activities that are required in order to deliver them to customers.

Alternatively a business may use standard costing, in which fixed costs over a given period of time are allocated to each product or service unit provided. This does, however, mean that the method distorts the resulting unit cost, as there is often a difference between actual costs and standard costs due to variations in volume, costs of material and costs of labour.

Costs must inevitably include:

- Direct costs – which are those that can be directly attributable to a particular activity or product.
- Indirect costs – which are those costs that are not directly attributable to a particular activity or product but are nevertheless incurred by the business, such as administration. These are often referred to as overheads.
- Taken together, direct and indirect costs are equal to *total costs*.

Some businesses may use marginal costing, which incorporates additional variable costs that are incurred by the business as a result of extra or new activities. Marginal costing is useful for short-term decision-making.

Costing can be a complex process, as can the calculation of variable costs. However, costing is an important tool to aid and assist decision-making and is vital for a business to determine whether providing particular services or products is actually profitable.

Cost-plus pricing

Cost-plus pricing methodology is one of the most common forms of pricing policy, it is also one of the more straightforward forms. The pricing methodology simply involves adding a predetermined percentage or gross figure to the costs of production or purchase, thereby creating a price point for the product or the service.

This basic form of pricing does not individually take into account current market conditions and is in many cases considered to be too prescriptive in its structure for standard use. Despite this, many base prices are calculated on this cost-plus assumption.

Countryside Agency (CA)

The Countryside Agency operated between 1999 and 2006. Prior to 1999, parts of it were known as the Countryside Commission. The agency was government-funded and primarily a promotional body in England. In October 2006 it was succeeded by Natural England. During its time, the Countryside Agency was responsible for designating National Parks and Areas of Outstanding Natural Beauty, and defining Heritage Coasts.

See also **Natural England.**

Countyside Council for Wales (CCW)

The Countryside Council for Wales (CCW) is the British government agency responsible for nature conservation in Wales. CCW was previously part of two separate bodies, the Nature Conservancy Council, and the Countryside Commission until 1991. The organisation also provides information on land access, grants, wildlife protection, protected sites, landscape and agriculture.

www.ccw.gov.uk

Coupon

'Coupon' is a broad term used to describe tickets or documents that can be exchanged for a discount when purchasing a product or service. They are often issued by the business or organisation running a specific promotion. Others appear in the print media and increasingly on the internet and via mobile phones. Internet coupons are particularly effective and there are a number of coupon-orientated websites, which allow users to search for cut-price, discount or free entry into a wide variety of attractions and leisure facilities.

Coupon broker

Many promotional incentives for customers, such as frequent flyer discounts and awards, are technically non-transferable, in as much as they cannot be used, sold or presented by a third party. Nonetheless there is a booming trade in the buying and reselling of these promotional awards, often in contravention of the rules of the airline or other leisure and tourism-based organisation that runs the incentive programme. In 2007, in a complex fraud, executives in the US-based International Outsourcing Services clearing house faced criminal and civil charges over a multi-million-dollar coupon business. Law suits were brought against them by twenty-three manufacturers.

Crew to passenger ratio

This is a term that is usually associated with either airlines or cruise ships and describes how many crew members serve a specific number of passengers. On a premium cruise line the ratio is usually 2:1 and on a luxury line it may be 1.5:1. On the reverse of this, budget services will have considerably higher crew to passenger ratios, reflecting the fact that the airline or cruise line has cut staffing costs.

Cross-border ticketing

In 2002, British Airways launched a crackdown on cross-border ticketing, which was commonly used by many British travel agents. In effect it was a form of creative ticketing. A prime example of cross-border ticketing that would be used in **business class** would be to book a Paris to London, London to New York, New York to London, London to Paris itinerary, as this would provide the customer with a cheaper price than a straightforward London to New York, New York to London return. The agent would remove the first Paris to London coupon before sending the ticket to the customer and the customer would not use the last coupon; the London to Paris one. Technically it was not an illegal practice but would have contravened an airline's terms of carriage and service. In the US since the mid-1990s it has essentially been deemed illegal. The legitimacy of cross-border ticketing may well be settled in the future by the European Commission.

Cultural capital

'Cultural capital' refers to the role that particular cultural tastes, knowledge and abilities play in relation to the creation of class formations in society. It has tended to be an influential area of investigation in sociology, where investigations into the middle classes and how they distinguish themselves from the working class have predominated. To some extent cultural capital and its role in the organisation of class differences can help inform and mitigate the effects of social exclusion. Much of the work was originally carried out by Pierre Bourdieu in a large-scale survey carried out in France. He found:

> All cultural practices (museum visits, concert going, reading, etc.) and preferences in literature, painting and music, are closely linked to educational level (measured by qualifications or length of schooling) and secondarily to social origin.

The differences, he believed, were attributable to unequal distribution of three different kinds of capital:

- Economic – derived from an individual's position in the labour market.
- Cultural – which are largely transmitted by the family.
- Academic – acquired through education.

The framework is seen to designate the types of cultural and leisure activities of one group compared with those of another. Each group or class has its own *habitus*, which means the manner in which they use symbolic goods in different contexts. Bourdieu went on to suggest that: 'The very meaning and value of a cultural object varies according to the system of objects in which it is placed.' In the leisure context, objects can include sports, film, food and clothing.

Wynne (1998) carried out specific research into the lifestyles of the new middle class. He interviewed individuals in exclusive residential developments with their own social and sporting facilities. He discovered two groups:

- Former working class – these had got to their position in life by sheer effort and used social facilities mainly for drinking.
- Educated professionals – their occupational advancement was based on education and they tended to use the sports facilities.

Bourdieu, P., *Distinction: A Social Critique of the Judgement of Taste*. Routledge & Kegan Paul, 1984.
Wynne, D., *Leisure, Lifestyle and a New Middle Class: A Case Study*. Routledge, 1998.

Cultural heritage

'Cultural heritage' is a broad term that is used to describe both the tangible and the intangible attributes and artefacts that have been inherited from past generations. On the tangible side this would include buildings, monuments and artefacts. On the intangible side this would include language and culture.

Cultural heritage can also be extended into natural heritage, which is inevitably a key part of the overall culture and includes flora and fauna, which are becoming an increasingly important part of a country's tourist industry.

UNESCO defines cultural heritage as:

Not limited to material manifestations, such as monuments and objects that have been preserved over time. This notion also encompasses living expressions and the traditions that countless groups and communities worldwide have inherited from their ancestors and transmit to their descendants, in most cases orally.

See also **cultural tourism, UNESCO.**

www.unesco.org

Cultural tourism

There is no hard and fast definition of cultural tourism, although according to the State of Missouri Cultural Tourism Development Plan (1998):

Cultural tourism is travel that is motivated entirely, or in part, by artistic, heritage or historical offerings. America's cultural resources offer domestic and international travelers the opportunity to experience what is uniquely American: our regional differences and ethnic character, our history and our most contemporary expression. It is a mosaic of places, traditions, celebrations, and experiences that portrays America and its people and reflects the diversity and character of the United States.

Many preservationists, however, would prefer to use heritage tourism as a description, whilst museums and art galleries tend to prefer cultural tourism as a broad description. Hence, increasingly, many organisations are using the combined term 'cultural heritage tourism', which brings together a wide range of leisure and tourism organisations and aspects incorporating the arts, museums, preservation, heritage areas, humanities and ethnic groups.

Edgell, D., *Managing Sustainable Tourism: A Legacy for the Future.* Haworth Press, 2006.

Culture

Tylor (1874) defined culture as:

That complex hole which includes knowledge, belief, art, morals, law, custom and other capabilities and habits acquired by man as a member of society.

There is a close association between culture and leisure. According to Pieper (1952), leisure was the basis of culture and leisure provided the 'affirmation of a man's true nature'. He argued that through the free time that people have, the building blocks of culture are assembled.

Kelly (1987) suggested that culture was 'the stuff out of which all leisure experiences are made'.

Kelly, J., *Freedom To Be.* Macmillan, 1987.
Pieper, J., *Leisure: The Basis of Culture.* Pantheon, 1952.
Tylor, E. B., *Primitive Culture.* Estes & Lauriat, 1874.

Customer base

See **client mix.**

Customer loyalty

Customer loyalty seeks to define the degree to which customers will remain unpersuaded by other advertisers or other businesses' products and services and continue purchasing from the same business. Given the high costs of attracting new customers to a brand, businesses are prepared to invest heavily in customer loyalty programmes aimed at ensuring that they do not switch brands.

Clearly, customer loyalty is very much related to the overall position of the brands and the business in the market and can be the foundation of an ability to generate profits. Low customer loyalty is generally accepted to be a measure of a brand's inability to sustain, nurture and satisfy customers.

Hill, Nigel and Alexander, Jim, *Handbook of Customer Satisfaction and Loyalty Measurement.* Gower, 2000.

Customer Relationship Management (CRM)

Customer Relationship Management is based on the assumption that there is a relationship between the business or the brand and the customer. This is a relationship that needs to be managed both through the individual buying stages and in the longer term. CRM is very much related to fostering **customer loyalty** and, in the longer term, **customer retention**.

CRM can be used in call centre support and direct marketing operations, software systems assist in the support of customer service representatives and give customers alternative means by which they can communicate with the business (such as mail, email, telephone etc.). Some sophisticated CRM software programs have email response systems which process incoming emails and determine whether they warrant a personal response or an automated response. Recent figures indicate that systems such as this can handle around 50% of the requests from customers (typically requests for additional information, passwords and responses to emails sent by marketing).

Other CRM software systems incorporate the facility for customer representatives to take part in live chat rooms or co-browsing, offering the business a less formal environment in which to make contact with customers. CRM software can also queue customers on the basis of their profiles, by requesting that the customer logs in to the website; it is then possible to pass the customer on to individuals in the customer service team who may be better suited to dealing with customers who share similar profiles. CRM software also provides the facility to maintain and update a database of information about each customer (in other words, a case history).

Customer retention

'Customer retention' is a marketing term used to describe activities designed to ensure that customers remain customers and are not lost to the competition. Customer retention can measure the degree to which the business loses its customers and suggest reasons why they have been lost. Remedial activities are then put in place to stem this trend, and in the longer term, activities and policies are created in order to prevent similar losses. Data is collected regarding lapsed customers through customer-retention-focused market research, which seeks to identify reasons why customers are no longer purchasing from the business.

Murphy, John, *The Lifebelt: The Definitive Guide to Managing Customer Retention.* John Wiley & Sons, 2001.

Customer-activated ticketing

Customer-activated ticketing is a system by which a service provider can allow customers to purchase tickets using a credit or debit card. In effect it is a vending machine. A customer may have already reserved tickets either for an airline or for a cinema or theatre performance and presents their payment card by inserting it in the vending machine. It is then verified by the software and the tickets are automatically printed.

Customised itinerary

A customised itinerary is a service usually offered by smaller tour operators, allowing customers to specify their own departure dates, route, number of nights' stay and other specific requirements. These are differentiated from standardised itineraries used by tour operators, catering for the mass market. Customised itineraries allow multi-destination, tailor-made packages and usually incorporate personal contacts at each destination and self-drive options.

C

Day rate

'Day rate' is a term most closely associated with hotels and venues. It is the fee charged by the venue for a stay of limited duration, typically during stated daylight hours. This allows the venue to accept a separate booking for the evening. Alternatively, 'day rate' can refer to the fee charged for the use of that venue for a full 24-hour period.

Day tour

A day tour has two distinct meanings. The first refers to a round trip undertaken by a customer or passenger that will be completed on the same day. It is also used to describe a series of one-day excursions from a single location. The day tours are designed so that the customer can visit a number of different locations, each based on one-day trips, without having to change hotels in order to experience these different locales.

Deposit/deposit policy

A deposit is a proportion of the full fee payable for a service or for a product that is required in advance of that product or service being delivered or taken up by the customer. In essence the deposit ensures a partial guarantee that the product or service will be reserved for that customer by the business.

Deposit policies differ from organisation to organisation and the deposits may or may not be refundable under certain cancellation policies. Usually, an administration fee is required, which is taken out of the deposit before it is refunded. For flights and hotel bookings where deposits have been made there is a sliding scale of deposit refunds, dependent upon the timing of the cancellation. The closer to the time at which the service will be used, the higher the proportion of the deposit retained by the company.

Depreciation

In the leisure industry, 'depreciation' is used to describe a fall in the value of a country's currency. The currency relative to other currencies, or to a weighted average of other currencies, falls on the exchange market.

Depreciation is also a paper-based accountancy exercise which seeks to take account of the fact that the value of fixed assets gradually decreases over time and that those attendant losses should be written off against the expense accounts of the organisation.

Deregulation

In the thirty years preceding 2000, deregulation was a major driver in changes to open up markets and to remove what were seen as unnecessary restrictions on trade and business practices. The process of deregulation was roundly criticised by many, as it was accused of allowing anti-competitive practices, removing protections for workers and consumers, and directly causing ecological damage. In some countries where leisure activities were provided by publicly funded organisations, or transportation systems were overtly subsidised or run by local authorities or governments, deregulation saw a process known as 'contracting out'. This was a process of either full or partial privatisation in which contractors were brought in to run services, rather than the service remaining under the control of local government and staffed by local government employees.

Deregulation is linked to the writings of individuals such as Milton Friedman and Friedrich von Hayek. It has been a process that has taken place in countries as diverse as Australia, Canada, Japan and Russia, in addition to the US and Britain.

Descriptive research

'Descriptive research' is a term used to describe research projects that neither manipulate variables nor suggest causal relationships, but simply describe events. Descriptive research looks at the who, what, when, where and how of a particular situation, but does not look at the cause of that situation. Descriptive research tends to be used when the requirement is to provide a factual and accurate, systematic description. Descriptive research does allow a researcher to examine the frequency of an event, which can allow statistical calculations to be made. Descriptive research is, therefore, used to describe the current status of an event or phenomenon in relation to the situational variables. Descriptive research tends to have a series of stages, these are:

- an identification or statement of the problem;
- an identification of the information available, and the selection and development of data gathering processes;
- an identification of target and sample size, and the design of information collection procedures;
- the collection procedure;
- an analysis, generalisation and prediction.

Friedman, Milton, *Free to Choose*. Harcourt Brace Jovanovich, 1980.
Friedman, Milton, *The Tyranny of the Status Quo*. Harcourt Brace Jovanovich, 1984.
Hayek, Friedrich, *Law, Legislation and Liberty, Volume II: The Mirage of Social Justice*. Routledge, 1976.
Hayek, Friedrich, *Law, Legislation and Liberty, Volume III: Political Order of a Free People*. Routledge, 1979.

D

Destination management/destination management companies

'Destination management' is a term used for those businesses that specialise in the organisation and logistics of meetings and events in a specific location. Destination management companies base their business on their ability to have complete knowledge of the destination, its venues, and all associated planning resources.

If the client is organising a destination event, or corporate meeting, or planning a one-off event, they may enlist the help of a destination management company to sift through the many possibilities and options available.

The destination or event planning companies specialise in the organisation and logistics of destination events by locating and sourcing the perfect venues, suppliers, transportation, and travel needs to meet the client's requirements. They are experienced in organising events, conventions, trade shows, or conferences.

Besides organising special events, corporate meetings and corporate events, destination management companies can also undertake event procurement and purchasing, event entertainment, catering and corporate dinners, hotel reservations and hotel selections, and provide travel coordination and management, arrange transportation to and from the airport, as well as securing guides and hostesses. They can coordinate motor coaches for transportation, VIP transfers, and limousine and car rentals, and create and specifically designed itineraries.

Destination Management Organisation (DMO)

A DMO is usually the strategic arm of a particular destination's delivery plan. It aims to bring together the expertise and the resources of organisations and businesses in the public and private sector. The purpose is to streamline and improve services, based on better market research, quality delivery of service and improved economies of scale. Effectively these are partnerships, which bring together all of the agencies and stakeholders in tourism. They become the lead body, with a broad remit, all related to tourism promotion.

Destination Management Partnership

See **Destination Management Organisation (DMO).**

Destination marketing/destination marketing organisation

The term 'destination marketing' is used to describe a type of marketing which solely markets tourist destinations.

Destination marketing organisations undertake this type of marketing in order to promote their city, county, area or country. Destination marketing is carried out to increase tourism to that destination, as well as to improve the general public image of the destination.

Some of the purposes of destination marketing, in addition to increasing tourism into the area, include:

- To improve the image of an area in the hope that this will encourage industrialists to relocate their factories and offices to the area.
- To provide jobs for local residents.
- To increase the range of facilities that are available for the local community.
- To give local residents more pride in their local area, which can happen when people see that tourists want to visit their region.
- To provide a rationale and funding for improvements to the local environment.
- To try to make the destination politically more acceptable.

D

Devaluation

Devaluation is a decrease in the value of one currency in relation to another. Devaluation usually occurs as a result of action by the government of the country involved. When a currency is devalued, it buys less in foreign markets. Sometimes devaluation can also be caused by another country's currency rising in value as compared with the currency value of another country.

Deviant leisure

The term 'deviant leisure' looks at leisure practices that involve illegal behaviours. They are activities that operate around legal parameters. They can involve taking banned drugs, trespass, computer hacking, joyriding, and push the boundaries of individual freedom in a leisure context.

Rojek (2005) identified three main types of deviant or abnormal leisure:

- Invasive – these are leisure pursuits, usually related to a dependency on alcohol or drugs, that progressively impinge upon all other aspects of an individual's existence. They may begin as social activities but they may have a tendency to encourage the individual to retreat from social networks in order to avoid a world that is considered to be too complex.
- Mephitic – derived from the term 'mephisis', meaning a foul smell, this is a form of leisure that leads to either self-harm or the harm of others. In many cases it involves violent engagement with others, a degree of dehumanisation and involvement with gangs or networks.
- Wild – typified as being sporadic and opportunistic, such as causing disturbances, public drunkenness, or trespass. There is a narrow margin between this form of leisure and pure criminal activity.

See also **invasive leisure.**

Rojek, C., *Leisure Theory: Principles and Practice.* Palgrave Macmillan, 2005.

Direct billing

Direct billing can relate to a system in which a business's travel agency bills its employees for their business travel. The employee must then submit an expense account and be reimbursed by the business.

Alternatively direct billing can also relate to the practice of some hotels or hotel chains of allowing individuals or businesses that have established credit with the hotel to sign for charges and be billed at their office locations. This means that the individual need not pay the amount instantly, but that their organisation is billed. This provides financial convenience for the business and for the individual. The organisation can pay, for example, on a monthly basis to clear its account.

Direct marketing

According to the Institute of Direct Marketing, direct marketing is described as being: 'The planned recording, analysis and tracking of individual customers' responses and transactions for the purpose of developing and prolonging mutually profitable customer relationships.' Direct marketing seeks to be a far more targeted method of approaching customers. Having analysed and tracked customers' previous buying patterns, the direct marketing activities aim to profit from more directly applicable offers.

Tapp, Alan, *Principles of Direct and Database Marketing*. Financial Times, Prentice Hall, 1998.

Direct spending

'Direct spending' is a term most closely associated with the tourism industry, although it is a broader term that can be applied to any spending that goes directly into a local economy, rather than being spent through a tour operator or event organiser. Direct spending is a key driver as far as local economies are concerned, as it brings the **multiplier effect** into operation. The multiplier effect means that tourist or visitor spending goes into local businesses and organisations, who in turn can pay local employees and make additional investments in their own facilities. This in turn generates spending, which other businesses further from the leisure and tourism industry can benefit from. They in turn pass a portion of this on to other employees and businesses.

Disclaimer

A disclaimer is a statement with the intention of limiting the rights and obligations and specifically the legal and financial responsibility for monetary loss or injury. These usually relate to advice given or products or services sold by a leisure and tourism organisation. A prime example would be a travel agent issuing a disclaimer absolving it from claims for injuries or losses that a customer may incur as a result of using a third party service, such as a charter company cancelling a flight, or an accident occurring during a paid-for excursion.

Disengagement theory

According to Cumming and Henry (1961), ageing is seen as the process of an individual's withdrawal from society by a voluntary reduction in the level of leisure activities. At the same time, it marks a pattern of reduction in the interaction of that society with the individual.

For an alternative view, see also **continuity theory.**

Cumming, E. and Henry, W., *Growing Old: The Process of Disengagement*. Basic Books, 1961.

D

Disneyfication

Also known as Disneyisation and McDisneyisation, this term describes the transformation of something, usually society at large, to resemble the Walt Disney Company's theme parks. The terms are generally used in a negative way, and they imply that everything is offered in the same way, without individualisation or modification, to the broadest possible market.

The terms can also be used more broadly to describe the processes of stripping a real place or event of its original character and repackaging it in a more sanitised format. Any negative references are removed, and the real facts are diluted, with the intention of making the subject more pleasant and easy to understand. In the case of countries or areas, Disneyfication typically means replacing what has grown organically over time with an idealised and tourist-friendly veneer, which is reminiscent of many of the Disney theme parks.

Bryman (2004) saw Disneyisation as complementary to McDonaldisation, outlining four trends that he identified as:

- Theming
- Dedifferentiation of consumption
- Merchandising
- Emotional labour

'Theming' relates to previously disparate elements that are combined into a cohesive and coordinated image or presence, in many cases an integrated fun motif. 'Dedifferentiation of consumption' refers to situations where consumption from potentially different business areas becomes fully integrated, such as theme parks selling merchandise and food and drinks in addition to providing rides. 'Merchandising' is typified by products that promote copyrighted images and logos of a broad range, from theme park characters to sports teams and increasingly children's television programmes, that are designed around the toys. The 'emotional labour' relates to the way in which service provision is delivered, typified by cheerful friendliness. This is designed to divert customers from the fact that they are being sold products and services in an artificially constructed environment.

Bryman, Alan E., *The Disneyization of Society*. Sage Publications, 2004.

Domestic tourism

Domestic tourism relates to the activity of people visiting destinations within their own country's boundaries. In other words, it relates to visitors from the UK who visit another part of the UK. The UK domestic tourism market is significant. According to Tourism Trade, UK residents in 2007 are estimated to have taken 123 million trips lasting for one night or more within the UK. These trips involved a total of 394 million nights away from home, resulting in an average tourism trip length of 3.2 nights. Tourism expenditure on these domestic trips was £21 billion, representing an average spending of £172 per trip and £54 per night away from home. In 2007, the average UK resident:

- Took 2.1 tourism trips of one night or more away from home within the UK.
- Stayed away for 6.6 nights in total on tourism trips in the UK.
- Spent £353 in total on domestic tourism trips.

Also according to Tourism Trade:

- UK residents made 77 million holiday trips in the UK in 2007, representing 278 million nights and almost £14 billion in spending.
- Own homes and friends' or relatives' homes are widely used for holidays, accounting for over two in five trips (42%). They are more often used for short holidays of 1–3 nights (43%) than for long holidays of 4 nights or more (39%).
- The commercial accommodation sector covers three in five holiday trips (59%), with its share being higher for long trips (64%) than for short trips (56%). The pattern is very different between the serviced accommodation sector (principally hotels) and self-catering (mainly cottages and caravans).

- Serviced rented accommodation covers one-third of holiday trips (33%) but tends to be used more for short trips (38%) than for long trips (23%). In contrast, self-catering, which also covers 25% of holiday trips, is more often used on long holidays (40%) than on short holidays (16%).
- The car is the dominant mode of transport used for the longest part of the journey to the destination (77%). Public transport is used for 17% of holiday trips.
- Firm bookings were made before going for just over half of holiday trips (51%) and even more so on longer holidays (58%). This reflects the widespread use of friends' and relatives' homes and of private cars where advance booking is not relevant.
- Holiday trips are taken to a wide range of locations – in large cities and towns (30% of all trips), small towns (24%), at the seaside (28%) and in the countryside/villages (accounting for 22%).
- Large cities and towns are more popular for short trips where they are clearly the leading type of location (36% of all short holiday trips). In contrast, the seaside is more popular for long holiday trips (39% of all long holidays).

Domestic tourism also includes business and work tourism and the following was relevant to the 2007 business and work tourism, according to Tourism Trade:

- UK residents made 18.7 million business and work trips in the United Kingdom in 2007. This represents 45 million bed nights and £4.5 billion expenditure.
- Commercial accommodation is used on six in every seven business trips (85%), mainly in hotels/motels/guesthouses (71%). However, it is worth noting that one in ten of business and work trips involve staying in own or friends' and relatives' homes (10%).
- The car is the main form of transport used for the journey to the destination (64% of trips). Public transport is used in a quarter of business and work trips (26%) – especially train (18%) and plane (7%).
- Business and work trips tend to be short, with nearly half involving only one night away from home (47%).
- Almost half (47%) of trips are taken by those in the professional and managerial (AB) socio-economic group, over twice the share of the UK adult population (20%).

www.tourismtrade.org.uk

D

Downsizing

This term relates to a corporate or organisational restructuring, which is aimed at making the organisation smaller, more efficient, and more profitable by selling various product lines and/or business units. 'Downsizing' refers to an organisation's need to streamline its activities, perhaps involving the closure of certain operations, along with the associated loss of employees engaged in those areas. Vital in the concept of downsizing is the quality, as opposed to the quantity, of employees.

The downsizing process needs planning as the implications are that some employees will be offered voluntary redundancy. Inevitably those who opt to take this method of dismissal will be those who are valued by the organisation because they have the qualifications, skills and expertise to potentially make them more attractive to competing organisations. Within the process of planning for downsizing, the management would have to consider:

- The legal implications with regard to redundancy.
- The implications to the organisation of losing key members of staff to competitors.
- How they will communicate their intention to downsize.
- What alternatives are available to them apart from redundancy, e.g. retraining or redeployment of employees.

Fear of downsizing can be stressful for employees and the organisation needs to ensure that it is communicating with them through the appropriate and effective channels. Certainly consultation with trade union or employee representatives is essential, as is the provision of an employee assistance programme (EAP).

Drop-off charge

This is an additional fee that may be charged when a rental car, or other rental vehicle, is dropped off at a location other than the one from which it was rented. The drop-off charge is usually a set amount.

In October 2008 it was announced that drivers dropping off passengers at Birmingham International Airport will have to pay a drop-off fee. A new Rapid Drop-Off area will cost motorists £1 for the first 20 minutes and £3 for every 15 minutes after that length of time.

Dumbwaiter

This is a small, hand-operated lift system used to transport food and dishes from one level to another, for instance between the kitchen and dining room. Dumbwaiters can be found in restaurants, hospitals, hotels and laundry businesses. They have a number of benefits for the employees and the business:

- Goods can be transported quickly between floors.
- They are inexpensive and reliable.
- They can be customised for employees of different heights.
- They can carry up to 150kg of produce.

Dump store

In a tourist attraction or theme park, a dump store is a shop. It is commonly located at the exit of a ride or of the attraction, meaning that all visitors have to pass through it when they are leaving.

Ecology

Ecology is the study of the environment and the interaction of its various elements, including the flora, fauna, and climate of a region or location. The leisure industry has a significant ecological footprint, as it is known. Often environmentally sensitive areas include:

- energy efficiency
- environmental impact
- pollution control

In America, the US Environmental Protection Agency introduced new regulations (September 2008) that target pollution levels. The new regulations could result in a 25% reduction of smog-forming emissions and carbon monoxide from the nation's motor vehicle sector. Small gasoline engines that power pleasure boats and other recreational watercraft will now be required to reduce their emissions by 35%, beginning in 2010. Lawnmowers and other garden equipment are required to meet the same emissions reduction by 2011.

Begon, M., Townsend, C. and Harper, J., *Ecology: From Individuals to Ecosystems*. Wiley, 2005.

Chapman, J. L. and Reiss, M. J., *Ecology: Principles and Applications*. Cambridge University Press, 1998.

Economic growth

Economic growth is an indicator of an economy's health, in other words, the rate at which national income is growing. Economic growth is measured by the annual percentage rate of change in a nation's gross domestic product (GDP). GDP is the economy's total income from output, or the market value of all a country's goods and services produced within an economic area during a certain period. GDP is the preferred way of measuring economic growth.

Other measures of economic growth include gross national product (GNP). GNP measures the total output of a country's citizens, regardless of job or where they are living and working.

Economic impact assessment

An economic impact assessment (EIA) is used to investigate the economic value of a particular project at a national, regional or local level. It aims to quantify the economic value to the economy. It also aims to identify the characteristics of the supply chain and assess future growth potential. It will usually involve five phases:

- data gathering

- consultation with major stakeholders
- economic modelling (usually input/output models)
- economic assessment to test the impact model
- results and reporting

Economic impact studies

An economic impact study is carried out in order to identify the economic contribution an organisation is making to the community in which it operates. Financial information is used in conjunction with what are known as 'multipliers'. Multipliers work on the basis that when one of a business's employees spends their salary on, for example, petrol, then that money is paying the salary of the petrol station staff, which, in turn, will pay for their weekly shopping, mortgage, etc. These multipliers will vary from region to region. It is assumed that the same pound will be spent again and again within the same community.

The reasons for carrying out an economic impact study are many and will vary from organisation to organisation and from region to region, but such a study can:

- create an awareness of and an interest in the organisation's role in the community;
- provide positive relationships, including media relations;
- identify local partners and supporters;
- identify the organisation's involvement in the local economy and in the community as a whole;
- allow the organisation to advertise itself locally by first identifying its contribution to the community.

Each organisation will benefit directly from such public exposure. The following benefits of an economic impact study are the most common:

- They break down potential barriers to community leaders.
- They raise employees' level of pride in the organisation.
- They increase awareness and interest in what the organisation does.
- They establish an opportunity to maintain a positive image of the organisation in the community and among the local media.

Economy

A country or region's economy is its network of producers, distributors, and consumers of goods and services in a local, regional, or national community.

Economy class

This is the least expensive and usually most numerous class of travel or amenities offered by a transport provider. It is considered to be the basic level of airline service and is usually allocated the largest seating area on an aircraft. It is often referred to as 'coach class', or 'second class'. It is a term that is usually only applied to conventional airline flights. Low cost flights do not have classes as such.

See also **first class, business class, club class.**

Ecotourism

Ecotourism is a style of travel in which an emphasis is placed on unspoiled, natural destinations and on disturbing the environment as little as possible. The International Ecotourism Society (TIES) defines ecotourism as: 'Responsible travel to natural areas that conserves the environment and improves the well-being of local people'.

The main principles of ecotourism are:

- To minimise the impact of tourism.
- To build environmental and cultural awareness and respect.
- To provide positive experiences for both visitors and hosts.
- To provide direct financial benefits for conservation.
- To provide financial benefits and empowerment for local people.
- To raise sensitivity to host countries' political, environmental, and social climate.

The TIES organisation promotes responsible travel to natural areas in order to conserve the environment and improve the well-being of local people by:

- creating an international network of individuals, institutions and the tourism industry;
- educating tourists and tourism professionals;
- influencing the tourism industry, public institutions and donors to integrate the principles of ecotourism into their operations and policies.

Honey, M. (ed.), *Ecotourism and Certification: Setting Standards in Practice.* Island Press, 2002.
Nigam, S. C., *Ecotourism and Sustainable Development.* Rajat Publications, 2008.

www.ecotourism.org

Education as leisure

It may appear from casual investigation that education and leisure are mutually exclusive. Education, being associated with learning, does not immediately imply any sense of freedom and relaxation, whereas leisure tends to be more directly associated with freedom and pleasure. However, this is to assume that all education is formal. According to Page and Thomas (1977): '[Education is a] social process in which one achieves social competence and individual growth, carried in a selected controlled setting which can be institutionalized as a school or college.'

In fact it is, perhaps, the negative definitions of education, implying that it is formal, which are part of the problem of associating education with leisure. According to Barrow and Milburn (1990): 'It is not a name of any particular activity or process. It is a name applied generically to a number of different activities and processes.'

According to Parker (1979) there are two distinct links between education and leisure:

- The extent to which education allows an individual to prepare for a full and satisfying leisure life.

E

- The fact that education and learning activities are inherently enjoyable and thus contain leisure elements.

Roberts (1983) made an even clearer link between leisure and learning:

> Leisure is not precisely bounded. It is more akin to learning and schooling. The beginning and end of a school day may be punctuated with a bell. By contrast, learning is ubiquitous, like work and play. Any sharp definition which clearly separated leisure from the rest of life would distort its own subject matter.

Barrow, R. and Milburn, G., *A Critical Dictionary of Educational Concepts*. Teachers' College Press, 1990.

Page, T. G. and Thomas, J. B., *International Dictionary of Education*. Kogan Page, 1977.

Parker, S., *The Sociology of Leisure*. George Allen & Unwin, 1979.

Roberts K., *Youth and Leisure*. George Allen & Unwin, 1983.

Effects analysis

Part of a broader issue of failure mode and effects analysis (FMEA), this is a procedure that analyses potential failures within systems by classifying them by severity, or how they will have a broader impact on the system itself. Systems can be studied in order to identify the ways in which processes can be modified in order to increase reliability and reduce failures to a minimum.

Sutherland, J. and Canwell, D., *Key Concepts in Operations Management*. Palgrave Macmillan, 2004.

Elapsed flying time

The term 'elapsed flying time' refers to the actual time an aircraft spends in the air, as opposed to the time the aircraft has spent taxiing to and from the gate and during any scheduled stopovers.

Electronic reservation service provider (ERSP)

This term refers to an online service (such as Expedia, Orbitz, and Travelocity) that provides airline and/or cruise line travel reservation services. The provider may also issue either electronic or paper tickets. The ERSP provides corporations and consumers with booking capabilities and travel suppliers' inventory, rates, and information via the internet, intranet or online service. The provider has to be accredited as a travel agent by IATA, the global airline association, or an airline carrier before they can issue tickets.

See also **IATA (International Air Transport Association).**

Electronic ticketing

An electronic ticket (or e-ticket) is used to represent the purchase of a seat on a passenger airline, usually through the airline's website or by telephone. The e-ticket became mandatory for International Air Transport Association members in June 2008. Airlines frequently charge an additional fee for issuing paper tickets.

E-tickets are also available for certain entertainment venues, as well as for road, urban or rail transport. The e-ticket is a digital record in the issuing

E

company's computer and customers print out their own copy, which contains a reservation number.

To check in with an e-ticket, the passenger presents the confirmation or reservation code. Sometimes this is not necessary, as the reservation is confirmed on the basis of the passenger's identity, which may be proved by a passport or the presentation of the credit card with which the ticket was purchased.

Embodiment

Embodiment acknowledges the fact that anyone engaged in leisure is always and already embodied and will always age and die. Leisure is seen as a way of enjoying fleeting qualities, such as pleasure and satisfaction, but beneath this the individual is vulnerable and leisure in itself is not self-sustaining. The body, regardless of leisure activities, even though they may be physical and life-enhancing ones, will not postpone its decline.

Emplacement

This is the position that an individual occupies in relation to abundance and scarcity. Abundance and scarcity cover not only the economic but also cultural and honorific resources. It recognises that there are inequalities. The environment is external, stable and independent of the individual, but the emplacement approach contends that leisure is conditioned by individual action and how leisure institutions are organised. They require individuals to consume leisure resources in particular ways and exhibit legitimate behaviour. However, more hazardous leisure activities provide an opportunity for self-actualisation, rather than for simply engaging in leisure activities within very structured parameters.

Empowerment

Leisure can be seen as a way in which individuals are given opportunities to empower themselves and develop resources, in order to help them cope in a more effective manner with any challenges or constraints in their lives. Leisure helps provide individuals with coping strategies, such as mood enhancement, companionship and palliative coping. It can assist individuals in acquiring a positive mood, particularly if they are suffering from emotional disturbance.

Antonovsky, A., *Unravelling the Mystery of Health: How People Manage Stress and Stay Well.* Jossey-Bass, 1987.

E

Endangered species

An endangered species is a population that is at risk of becoming extinct because it is either few in numbers, or threatened by a changing environmental situation or an increase in predators. An endangered species is usually a taxonomic species (this is the orderly classification of plants and animals according to their presumed natural relationships), but they could also be endangered for another evolutionary reason.

The World Conservation Union (IUCN) has calculated the proportion of endangered species as 40% of all species. This was based on the sample of species that they evaluated during 2006. Many countries have laws to protect these species, for example, forbidding hunting, restricting land development or creating reserves. Only a few of the species at risk of extinction become listed and gain this legal protection. Many become extinct, or potentially will become extinct, without gaining public notice.

When assessing the conservation status of a species it is not simply the number remaining, but the overall increase or decrease in the population over time, its breeding success rates, and any known threats, that are taken into account.

See also **Wildlife Fund for Nature (WWF).**

www.iucn.org

English Heritage

Also known as the Historic Buildings and Monuments Commission for England, English Heritage is the government's statutory adviser on the historic environment and is an Executive Non-departmental Public Body sponsored by the Department for Culture, Media and Sport (DCMS). Their powers and responsibilities were set out in the National Heritage Act (1983) and the organisation reports to Parliament through the Secretary of State for Culture, Media and Sport. In addition, English Heritage also works with DEFRA (the Department for the Environment, Food and Rural Affairs) and CLG (Communities and Local Government). CLG sets policy on local government, housing, urban regeneration, planning, and fire and rescue. They are also responsible for all race equality and community cohesion-related issues in England.

The organisation's funding comes from the government, as well as from revenue earned from the historic properties and their other services. English Heritage is overseen by a Chairman and a board of up to 16 Commissioners who are selected by the government and advised by 13 expert advisory committees and panels.

English Heritage works with central government departments, local authorities, voluntary bodies and the private sector to:

- conserve and enhance the historic environment;
- broaden public access to the heritage;
- increase people's understanding of the past.

They do this by:

- acting as a national and international champion for the heritage;
- giving grants for the conservation of historic buildings, monuments and landscapes;
- maintaining registers of England's most significant historic buildings, monuments and landscapes;
- advising on the preservation of the historic environment;
- encouraging broader public involvement with the heritage;
- promoting education and research;
- caring for over 400 historic properties on behalf of the nation;
- maintaining the National Monuments Record as the public archive of the heritage;
- generating income for the benefit of the historic environment.

www.communities.gov.uk
www.englishheritage.org.uk

Environmental impact assessment

As the term implies, this is an investigation into the possible impacts, both positive and negative, that a particular project proposal may have on the natural environment. Throughout the world there are at the very least guidelines, if not laws and regulations, which govern and control the impact of projects on the natural environment. Some are mandatory, whilst others are discretionary. In the US, for example, there are relatively strict codes based on the National Environmental Policy Act (1970). Across Europe a 1985 directive by the EU (later amended in 1997 and 2003) requires a full description of the project and a clear identification of any significant impacts it may have on the environment. The International Association for Impact Assessment defines the process as involving: 'Identifying, predicting, evaluating and mitigating the biophysical, social, and other relevant effects of development proposals prior to major decisions being taken and commitments made.'

> Glasson, J., Therivel, R. and Chadwick, A., *Introduction to Environmental Impact Assessment*. Routledge, 2005.
>
> www.iaia.org

Environmental scanning

Environmental scanning involves a series of data gathering exercises to provide information for analysis. This information may be about events, unexpected changes, trends and drives that influence customers in the leisure industry. The changes may be economic, such as the credit crunch of 2008, or one-off, such as the Foot and Mouth Disease outbreaks.

Environmental scanning involves three main activities:

- Gathering information – this could be internal (e.g. resources) and external (e.g. demographic trends) to the organisation and be carried out either formally or informally.
- Analysing and interpreting the information – unwanted information has to be filtered out and the useful information is prioritised.
- Applying the information to decision-making – environmental scanning is used in strategic planning and in the decision-making process.

Environmentally sound

The term 'environmentally sound' tends to be applied to technologies and activities that have the potential to significantly reduce harm to, or even enhance, the environment. Broadly they aim to protect the environment and be less polluting. The term also implies the reduced use of resources (or using them in a sustainable manner), the recycling of more wastes and products and the handling of residual wastes in a more environmentally acceptable manner.

There has always been a complex relationship between leisure development, the environment and the use of technology. Leisure does not escape the demand to be more frugal in its use of limited global natural resources. As such, leisure, it is argued, needs to compensate for or mitigate any environmental problems or issues that it may create.

E

Errors and omissions insurance

See **Public Liability Insurance.**

Essentialism

Essentialism is a naturalistic form of explanation in that it tries to explain motivation, location and context in terms of ethnocentric categories. It is a doctrine that human difference is the expression of deep-rooted characteristics that cannot be modified in any significant manner. In other words, a man is essentially different from a woman and, regardless of co-involvement in leisure activity, their approach and their perceptions will always be different.

Ethical tourism

Also sometimes known as ecotourism, ethical tourism has evolved as a term used when travelling to, or developing tourism in, a destination where ethical issues are the key driver. Such ethical issues would include social injustice, human rights, animal welfare, or the environment. Ethical tourism encourages the consumer and industry to avoid participation in activities that contribute to or support negative ethical issues.

There has been an increased demand for ethical tourism, linked with a general trend towards responsible consumerism. This means that the industry is attempting to ensure that tourism does not have a negative impact on the environment, by using hotels that pursue good environmental practices such as conserving water and minimising waste. They try to ensure that local people benefit financially from tourism, not just through direct employment, but also through providing supplies. They also encourage tour operators to use locally-owned hotels and transport companies, and employ local guides.

Encouraging customers to choose a bed and breakfast option, or even half-board, would benefit local restaurants, bars and taxi owners. If the all-inclusive option is chosen it is possible that the local community would not in fact benefit from the visit; it would be foreign companies that control the hotels that would benefit.

Fennell, D. A., *Tourism Ethics*. Channel View Publications, 2006.
Jenkins, T., *Ethical Tourism: Who Benefits?* Hodder Arnold, 2002.

E

Ethnography

Ethnography is the study of human social phenomena and communities through fieldwork. It is a branch of anthropology, which focuses on the study of human societies. Ethnography uses fieldwork and the ethnographer lives among the population being studied, often working with knowledgeable or well placed individuals. After the fieldwork, the ethnographer will write up their experience. Rather than looking at a small set of variables and a large number of subjects the ethnographer attempts to obtain a detailed understanding of the circumstances of the few being studied. Ethnography can be undertaken in any race or culture throughout the world.

Hammersley, M. and Atkinson, P., *Ethnography: Principles in Practice*. Routledge, 2007.

E-ticketing

See **Electronic ticketing**.

Exchange rate

An exchange rate is the price of a particular currency as expressed in terms of another currency. In other words, the number of units of one particular currency required to exchange for a unit of another currency. Exchange rates are affected by investor expectations, interest rates, confidence in the currency, the state of a country's balance of payments and many other factors.

Frankel, Jeffrey A., Sarno, Lucio and Taylor, Mark P., *The Economics of Exchange Rates*. Cambridge University Press, 2003.

Exploratory research

Exploratory research is used primarily for the forming of hypotheses. This includes the clarification of concepts or explanations, the gaining of insights or the elimination of impractical suggestions. Normally, exploratory research will begin by viewing existing market information and then move towards investigating individuals' experiences, usually through focus groups. Exploratory research does not need to find representative samples of individuals, as its primary purpose is to gain greater knowledge and insights into issues. Exploratory research does not test hypotheses, but it does develop them into workable suggestions.

E

Familiarisation tour

There are two main types of familiarisation tour:

- Where the trade, i.e. the tour operators or travel agents, familiarise themselves with the region that they are selling. This is the most cost-effective way in which a product can be marketed or promoted.
- Where the media are producing, for example, a newspaper or magazine article or a book or film from their experiences on the visit.

Familiarisation tours are designed with the tour leader in mind. They will be comprehensive and often arranged on specially selected departure dates throughout the year, usually only one date per year per destination, based on off-season travel.

Familiarisation tours, which can also include cruises and safaris, are provided by some organisations to travel agents at substantial discounts and even sometimes free. The reason suppliers do this is so that the travel agents can get first-hand knowledge of the holiday package and will be better able to sell it to their clients.

Feasibility study

Also known as a 'feasibility analysis', a feasibility study analyses and evaluates a proposed project. The study is carried out in order to:

- Find out if the project is technically feasible.
- Find out if the project is financially feasible.
- Find out if the project will be profitable.

Feasibility studies are usually carried out by organisations that are considering projects that involve large sums of money.

Feeder airline

A feeder airline is a local or regional airline or service that operates on a restricted or secondary basis. It brings passengers from smaller airports to major airline hubs. The major hubs are the main departure airports from the region or country. In some countries feeder airlines are known as funnel flights, or commuter airlines. In the US there are over 100 feeder airlines. These operate on routes where airlines with larger jets could not profitably operate. Many feeder airlines have direct agreements with large operators, ensuring that the feeder flights arrive at the main airport hub in sufficient time for the passengers to transfer to the international flight. Feeder airlines are seen as an essential part of the overall **hub and spoke** system.

Feminist perspective

Feminist perspectives of leisure tend to highlight the structural disadvantages that women experience in leisure. The feminist perspective contends that disadvantage in leisure reflects broader social and economic structures that determine gender inequalities. More recent feminist writers have tended to begin focusing on ways in which individuals can resist oppressive societal forces, and have pointed to leisure as an opportunity for individuals to have a greater feeling of choice and more control over their lives than in many other aspects of their existence.

Shaw, S., 'The Gendered Nature of Leisure: Individual and Societal Outcomes of Leisure Practice', *World Leisure and Recreation*, 38:4 (1996), pp. 4–6.
Watson, B., Scraton, S. and Bramham, P., 'Leisure, Lifestyles, Elderly Women and the Inner City', *World Leisure and Recreation*, 38:4 (1996), pp. 11–14.

First class

First class is the most luxurious class of accommodation on a train, passenger ship, aircraft, or other conveyance. It is usually much more expensive than business class and economy class, and offers the best amenities. The first-class section of a passenger aircraft is normally located in the very front of the aircraft. Some benefits of travelling first class on modern cruise ships include larger cabins, priority check-in, priority embarkation and disembarkation, priority dining selection, and even a butler service. When rail travel is used, the first-class service offers access to dedicated sections of the train, nearly always featuring fewer but larger and more comfortable seats. In some cases additional amenities, such as power outlets for mobile phones or laptops, are available, as well as additional onboard services like food, drinks or complimentary newspapers.

See also **business class, economy class, club class.**

Fixed costs

Fixed costs incorporate all costs attached to a manufacturing process which do not change, regardless of the volume of production. Typically, fixed costs can be related to overheads, such as the rent of the premises, lease payments on equipment or other predictable costs which remain static.

Force majeure

The term *force majeure* refers to a clause that is included in a contract to enable one or both parties to be excused from performance of their contractual obligations, or to suspend or delay performance, upon the happening of a specified event or events beyond the party's control. The events listed in a *force majeure* clause will be a matter for negotiation between the parties, but commonly can include:

F

- Acts of God
- War
- Belligerent action
- Hostilities (whether or not war has been declared)
- Terrorist acts
- Acts of any civil or military authority
- Governmental or regulatory decisions

- Refusal of licences
- Riot or civil commotion
- Strike
- Acts of vandalism
- Fire, flood, earthquake, or extreme weather conditions

It is not possible to benefit from a *force majeure* clause if it has not been explicitly provided for in an agreement.

Forecast

There are a number of associated terms related to forecasting, but forecasting itself is an attempt to predict the future of a variable. Businesses will attempt to forecast the demand for their products or services in order to plan both their stock and manufacturing requirements. The accuracy of a forecast very much depends upon the reliability of the data upon which the forecast has been based and, indeed, the length of time into the future the forecast is expected to encompass. Generally a manufacturing organisation will seek to forecast demand slightly in excess of its average manufacturing lead time. The further into the future a forecast is projected, the more chance there is of a significant error, as variables become far less predictable as a result of other, unknown variables having an influence upon them.

Financial forecasting is essential for all businesses. Banks, for example, or any other providers of finance, including investors, would normally require to see a detailed profit and expenditure forecast. Financial forecasts form the core of any business plan and indeed are at the centre of any proposed project. Financial forecasting remains an integral part of planning and control as it allows budgeting, which can be used to compare actual results with budgeted forecasts. Financial forecasting allows a business to highlight areas where costs require immediate attention.

Typically a business would use a profit and loss forecast to show the relationship between income and expenditure, on either a monthly or a quarterly basis. The profit forecast will allow the business to assess their future viability and can be used as an important guide for potential investors. Cash flow forecasts are also of vital importance as they show the business's anticipated flows of payments in and out of the business. This forecast is different from a profit forecast as payments are not always received in the same period as the income which has been accounted for in the profit forecast. Cash flow forecasts should highlight where there may be problems in terms of the availability of cash, and allow the business to make plans should that contingency arise.

There is great debate as to how valuable forecasts into the far future are to a business. The further a forecast is made into a business, the less likely it is to be accurate. Most businesses, therefore, produce a profit and loss forecast for no more than a month or a quarter, and a cash flow forecast for around a year (in some cases this is 2 years).

Franchise

A franchise is a form of business in which the franchisor enters into a business relationship with the franchisee. The franchisor grants the franchisee a licence to use their common trade name, or trademark, in return for a fee, and during the association the franchisor will render assistance to the franchisee. It is essentially a licensing system which affords the franchisor the opportunity to expand, with the capital required to enable that expansion being provided by external sources.

In the US alone, franchising generates some $800 billion per year and employs around 9 million people. Franchisees enjoy considerable benefits, which include:

- The ability to open a franchise business which is already a proven success.
- Provision of full training and continued support from the franchisor.
- The ability to enjoy the benefits of national advertising.
- A guarantee that the franchisor will not sell a similar business to a competitor in the immediate area.

Frequent independent travel

Frequent independent travel (FIT) is a recognised travel market segment and refers to individualised arrangements, which are custom designed travel packages, paid for in advance by the customer. The majority of frequent independent travellers will make initial booking enquiries and carry out research using the internet, and will design their own schedule or itinerary and then approach specialist travel providers, or regional providers, direct, in order to put together a package that will deliver them an experience rather than just a conventional holiday. Around 20% of all FIT business is booked online, and many more that broadly fit into the FIT category will put together hotel and flight components themselves. This is an aspect of solo or small-group travel that is expected to increase in popularity in the coming years.

See also **backpackers.**

Front of house/front office

In hospitality, the term 'front of house' refers to the area of a restaurant or hotel where guests are allowed. The dining room and bar are all in the front of the house.

'Front of house' (abbreviated FOH) is also a theatrical term, referring to the portion of the building that is open to the public. In theatre and live music venues, it typically refers to the auditorium, box office and foyer, as opposed to the stage and backstage areas.

See also **back of house/back office.**

F

Functionalism

Functionalism is a social science that attempted to explain social institutions as being a collective means of fulfilling an individual's biological needs. Functionalism then came to focus on the ways in which social institutions fill social needs, especially social stability. The theory is associated with Émile Durkheim and more recently with Talcott Parsons and was also developed by other sociologists in the twentieth century.

Functionalism focuses on the structure and workings of society, claiming that society is made up of interdependent sections which work together to fulfil the functions necessary for the survival of society as a whole. People are socialised into roles and behaviours which fulfil the needs of society. Functionalists believe that behaviour in society is structural and that rules and regulations help organise relationships between the different members of society. Values provide general guidelines for behaviour in terms of roles and norms. These institutions of society, such as the family, the economy, the educational and political systems, are major aspects of the social structure. Institutions are made up of interconnected roles or inter-related norms. Society is viewed as a system, or a collection of interdependent parts, with a tendency toward equilibrium. There are also functional requirements that must be met if a society is to survive. Phenomena are seen to exist because they serve a function.

Functionalist sociologists say that the different parts of society, e.g. the family, education, religion, law and order, and the media, have to be seen in terms of the contribution they make to the functioning of the whole of society.

Durkheim, Émile, *The Division of Labour in Society*. Free Press, 1997.
Parsons, Talcott, *Talcott Parsons: Economic Sociologist of the 20th Century*. Blackwell, 2006.

Funnel flight

See **feeder airline.**

F

Gap analysis

'Gap analysis' is both a general management and strategy term as well as having its applications in marketing.

Gap analysis attempts to identify what is known as the performance gap. It does this by comparing current objectives, which have been defined in the corporate goals, against forecasts (particularly of sales), which will arise from existing strategies. Businesses often encounter performance gaps when they switch their objectives, or when environmental conditions change, as well as the relative success or failure of competitors.

It is standard practice to illustrate gap analysis in terms of a graph. This measures sales against time. Both the existing strategies and the new strategies are plotted and the difference between the two highlights the performance gap.

Gateway

The term 'gateway' has a number of potential meanings related to leisure:

- It can refer to a hub city, airport or other location that serves as a major starting point or transit point for a number of regional or local destinations.
- It can mean an entry point or facility, usually on the internet, that provides a comprehensive series of links to other more specialised information on leisure facilities and locations.
- It is also applied to a website that provides users with the opportunity to book tickets, sessions or services from a wide variety of leisure providers.

Gazes

This term is used in relation to the analysis of visual culture. It aims to describe the way in which the viewer or the audience gazes or views the people and the images that are depicted or represented.

It arose out of postmodernist theory and is linked to the theories of Michel Foucault and Jacques Lacan, respectively medical and mirror-stage gazes. It is also an aspect of feminist theory in as much as it is used to describe the social power relationships between men and women. It covers:

- How men gaze at women.
- How women gaze at themselves.
- How women gaze at other women.

The approach seeks to understand the effects of these ways of seeing. Cornel West used the term 'normative gaze' to investigate the ways in which Euro-centric individuals view other races, use social constructs, and may not view other races as being equal to European races.

The application of gaze theory supposes that:

- It can inform the researcher about the relationship between the observer and the observed.
- It can give clues about the subjects of the gaze.
- It can suggest issues arising out of the circumstances of the gaze.

According to Catherine Lutz and Jane Collins, it also suggests the power structures at play between the gazer and the subject of the gaze. According to Jonathan Schroeder it also signifies a psychological relationship of power where the gazer is seen to be more powerful than the object of the gaze (this follows the feminist approach to this theory).

Foucault, M., *Discipline and Punishment: The Birth of the Prison*. Pantheon, 1975.

Lacan, Jacques, *Seminar One: Freud's Papers On Technique*. W. W. Norton, 1988.

Lacan, Jacques, *Seminar Eleven: The Four Fundamental Concepts of Psychoanalysis*. W. W. Norton, 1978.

Lutz, Catherine and Collins, Jane, 'The Photograph as an Intersection of Gazes: The Example of National Geographic', in *Visualizing Theory*. Routledge, 1994.

Schroeder, Jonathan E., *Consuming Representation: A Visual Approach to Consumer Research*. Routledge, 1999.

Gender and leisure

According to the British Office of National Statistics, there are clear divisions in leisure preferences between men and women. Based on the latest figures available (2006–7), the key findings were the following:

- Watching television was the most common leisure activity for over eight out of ten men and women (84% and 85% respectively).
- Spending time with family and friends was the second most popular activity for eight out of ten women (82%) compared with more than seven in ten men (75%).
- Women were also more likely to shop in their free time than men, with three-quarters (75%) doing so compared with just over half of men (53%).
- Women were more likely to take part in cultural activities such as reading (73% compared with 56% of men) and arts and crafts (25% compared with 13%).
- Men were more likely to perform physical activities such as DIY (46% compared with 26% of women).
- Men were more likely to be involved in sport and exercise (58% compared with 43% of women).
- Men were also more likely to use the internet (49% and 40% respectively).
- Men were twice as likely as women to play computer games (27% and 12% respectively).
- Men were more likely to have shopped online than women. Nearly six out of ten men in the UK (58%) had purchased over the internet in 2007 compared with just under half of women (48%).
- The most popular internet purchases in the 12 months prior to interview were films, music or DVDs, which a slightly higher proportion of men than women purchased (53% and 49% respectively).

G

- Twice as many men purchased computer software and hardware and electronic equipment online as women.
- Conversely, a higher proportion of women than men used the internet to buy food and groceries (24% of women and 17% of men) and tickets for events (36% compared with 31%).
- The most popular sporting activity (excluding walking), according to 14% of adults aged 16 and over in England who participated in sports, was indoor swimming or diving. This was the most popular sporting activity for women (17%).
- The second most popular category of sporting activity was health, fitness, gym, or conditioning activities (14%). There was very little difference in the proportion of men and women participating in this activity; it was the one most favoured by men, along with outdoor football (both 14%).
- Outdoor football was one of the sporting activities that had the largest difference in level of participation between men and women: 14% of men had participated in the last four weeks compared with 2% of women.
- The other large difference between men and women was participation in snooker, pool or billiards, where just 3% of women participated compared with 12% of men.
- Conversely, women participated in keep-fit, aerobics and dance exercise more than men, 10% compared with 3%.

www.statistics.gov.uk

Geographic segmentation

Geographic segmentation consists of dividing a country into regions, which normally become an individual salesperson's territory. In sales terms, larger businesses may well subdivide these areas and assign salespeople to specific parts of each area, with a regional sales manager to oversee operations, control targets and act as a link between the salespeople and the business.

In international sales and marketing, different countries may be deemed to constitute different market segments. Typically, geographic segmentation will consider cities, counties, regions, states or even nations as having broadly similar characteristics, usually expressed in terms of the prevalent culture of the area.

Global learning

Global learning is a process by which a multinational organisation ensures that skills and knowledge flow freely between the different parts of the business across the world, regardless of national boundaries. Global learning can take the following forms:

- From the home country to an overseas division or subsidiary.
- From an overseas division or subsidiary to another overseas division or subsidiary.
- From an overseas division or subsidiary to the home country.

Globalisation

The term 'globalisation' in a marketing sense relates to the rolling out of products and services across the world. It has been a considerable feature of the develop-

G

ment of world trade that brands can now enjoy similar levels of success, no matter which country they are offered in. Clearly there are regional differences in both the needs and wants of overseas customers, coupled with the requirement to adapt the brand to meet the tastes of those different markets. Nonetheless, global branding has become a major feature in international marketing.

The development of globalisation has taken place as businesses have sought to find a competitive advantage in overseas markets to compensate for the fact that they do not enjoy this advantage in their home market. Customers have been receptive to the globalisation of brands for the following reasons:

- Consumers in the majority of markets have become more sophisticated and are now willing to experiment with non-domestic products and services, as well as demanding products and services that they have consumed whilst abroad.
- This has been enabled by the gradual elimination of trade and travel barriers, coupled with strong political resolve to open most markets to competition.
- The globalisation of brands has been coupled with the internationalisation of both print and broadcast media, which carry advertisements for global brands.
- Given the fact that a domestic market may be saturated, businesses increasingly look for markets in which their products and services can continue to grow.

Keegan, Warren J. and Green, Mark C., *Global Marketing Management* (7th edition). Prentice Hall, 2001.

Globalisation of markets

The term 'globalisation of markets' is in stark contrast to more familiar views of global marketing. The globalisation of markets implies that many international businesses no longer consider individual national markets to be distinct entities. Given the fact that many nations until recently had been closed by virtue of the fact that it had been difficult to trade in that country, now that trade barriers have been removed, these national markets are merging and can be treated in a very similar manner. Concerns regarding transportation, distance to market and even culture are being subsumed as international businesses increasingly treat newly accessible national markets in a similar manner to markets in which they already trade.

Goal

Goals are targets or states which an organisation seeks to achieve over a specified period of time. Goals need to be attainable, but challenging. The management of the process which delivers the achievement of these goals can be a key function of the strategic management process. The criteria or conditions that should be applied to the setting of goals are set out in Table 2.

Clearly the term 'goal' has a specific relevance in sport, in which it is used as an alternative to 'score', or 'scoring'. Prime examples include football, rugby and hockey.

Table 2

Criteria or condition	Goal description
Goals should be stable over time.	Continually changing the goals leads to problems of attainment and possible de-motivation. Predetermined goals should be achieved, then amended.
Goals should be specific and clear.	Ambiguous goals which are clearly spelled out can be judged more effectively in terms of attainment.
Goals should be linked to reality.	Impossible goals, plucked out of the air, require chance or good fortune to secure their attainment. Goals should be linked to the possible and the real state or position of the organisation.
Goals should be overarching.	Goals need to be central to the organisation in the sense that all parts of the business can see their place in the attainment.
Goals should be unique and designed to differentiate	Sharing similar goals with the competition is not an ideal way forward. They should be aimed at attaining some form of competitive advantage over the competition.
Goals should be linked to actions.	The interpretation of the goals at management and employee level should clearly indicate what has to be done in order to attain the goals. In other words, there needs to be a plan to attain the goals, by steps or actions over time.
Goals should require foresight.	Goals should be linked to cause and effect; by striving to attain the goals, the organisation should be able to see where it is likely to be once those goals have been attained. Above all, the organisation needs to be ready for that altered state and be prepared to set new goals from that point.

'Goal' can also be used to describe the attainment of a specified objective, a goal being an element of a larger or broader objective or mission.

Goold, M. and Quinn, J. J., *Strategic Control: Milestones for Long Term Performance.* Hutchinson, 1990.

Gramscianism

Antonio Gramsci (1891–1937) was a founding member of the Italian Communist Party. His theories became particularly important in Britain in the 1970s and were seen as a starting point to analyse cultural politics from a Marxist perspective. He saw the economy as being the main mechanism of change, and a main agent of that change was the industrial working class. He believed that the ruling class had to manage public opinion, answer to criticism, and required the support of other cultural and political groups in order to maintain control. In order to do this they had created agencies and organisations, some of which appeared to be semi-independent or private. Gramsci saw cultural events in a wider political context, in fact as a struggle for control.

Gramsci's theories have been particularly useful in the study of social class and sub-culture, but his underlying theme was that of hegemony. He used this as a term to describe the way in which control is exercised over a group, usually by the nation state or the ruling class. It incorporates cultural and legal dominance, as well as language.

Gramsci saw hegemony as being in continual flux, dynamic and incomplete. There would always be wider struggles for hegemony. British theorists used this approach to explain the rise and fall of different youth cultures and how they threatened existing orders. In order to deal with them and the threat, the state mobilises public opinion against the youth culture and then incorporates the youth culture in a commercial way, bringing it back into the mainstream.

Gramscianism has been applied to film, football, music, holidays, the celebration of Christmas and all forms of entertainment, leisure and pleasure.

See also **youth culture.**

Grapevine

Grapevine communication is an informal method of communication which often allows the passing on of messages to be one of the speediest forms of conveying information. Often considered to be gossip and rumour, grapevine communication can be very unreliable. Snippets of information get passed from one individual, or group of individuals, to another and the message can become extremely distorted. Grapevine communication is not a method to be encouraged by managers, who should attempt to inform employees of the subject of the communication in a more formal way, stating facts rather than part-truths. A high degree of grapevine communication within an organisation, if it is not adequately dealt with by management, can lead to low morale. Although this method of communication is quite natural and prevalent in all organisations, it should be tackled in an appropriate manner so that employees hear the message from the appropriate level and through the appropriate channels.

Green marketing

In many respects green marketing can be considered as an attempt to make a proactive move by businesses before legislation and regulations force the business to adopt new product development, production and marketing strategies. Essentially, green marketing revolves around safety, satisfaction, social acceptability and sustainability, which are more commonly known as the 4 Ss of the green marketing mix (see Table 3).

The green marketing mix begins with the satisfaction of customer needs, whilst ensuring that both the product and the production are safe with regard to the consumers, employees, society and the environment in general. The mix also recognises that the product needs to be socially acceptable, in terms of both its production and the way in which it is marketed and advertised. Finally, the

Table 3

Green Ss	Description
Satisfaction	of the customers' needs.
Safety	in respect of the product, production and other activities of the organisation.
Social	acceptability of the above.
Sustainability	the ability of the organisation to continue to operate as it currently does.

product itself needs to be sustainable. In other words, businesses need to predict any imminent or future legislation and attitudes which may preclude them from producing and marketing their products and services in the way they currently do.

Allied to the green marketing mix are what are known as the internal and external green marketing Ps. The standard 4 Ps of product, promotion, place and price are coupled with the overtly environmentally orientated need to provide information, examine processes, adopt appropriate policies and consider people, both internally and externally. There are also what are known as the external green Ps, which are:

- Paying customers – looking at customers' needs in relation to green products and services, as well as information that they may require.
- Providers to the business, in terms of how green their products and services are.
- Politicians – this concerns the increasing public awareness of green issues and how the political system is gradually, through legislation, having an impact on the conduct of the business.
- Pressure groups – this concerns addressing their main issues and identifying which groups of individuals are involved.
- Problems – this seeks to identify any past, current or future environmental issues that are attached to the business's operations.
- Predictions – this concerns the investigation of scientific research which may identify potential environmental problems in the future.
- Partners – this addresses how green or environmentally aware any other businesses with which the business has an association are. This aspect considers how these partners are perceived and whether there will be any environmental problems arising out of their operations.

Wasik, John F., *Green Marketing and Management: A Global Perspective*. Blackwell, 1996.

Green paper

A green paper is a government report or proposal that is seen as the first step in a possible change in legislation. Effectively it operates as a discussion document that is designed to create debate and initiate consultation. Some green papers are well structured in the sense that they replicate a legal format that can be readily translated into law or regulation. More broadly, however, they are sets of proposals to which interested groups and individuals are invited to contribute their information and views.

Green papers are used across Europe through the European Commission and in countries that have a Commonwealth style of jurisdiction, such as Britain, Australia, Canada and the Republic of Ireland. Once the consultation process has been completed, a **white paper** may be produced, which is the finalised set of proposals that will then be presented to Parliament for discussion and, ultimately, authorisation to become law.

Green travel

Green travel is a method of **ecotourism** whereby people reduce their impact on the environment while travelling. Green travel involves a wide range of options that are centred round the idea of preserving the planet. There are many forms of green travel, including:

- The use of walking, cycling, and public transport instead of car use, when possible.
- The regular use of biodiesel fuels.
- Staying at a hotel that has been scored as a 'green' hotel.
- Booking and travelling with organisations that have been scored as 'green' travel providers.
- Volunteering time to give back something to the community being visited.
- Making a carbon footprint donation. This is to offset the amount of carbon that the visit has produced.

Green travel encourages travellers to think about their impact on both the physical and social environment of the destination.

See also **ecotourism**.

Grey market

In most developing nations the elderly and the retired are becoming an increasingly important aspect of leisure. Collectively they are known as the 'grey market' and their demands and tastes have considerable implications for leisure services, as well as products and services related to tourism. It is no longer the case that retirement necessarily means a lower income, although it does mean a gradual loss of work-based networks, which has often been linked to a decline in leisure activity. Equally there are questions of deteriorating health and infirmity, which have an impact on leisure.

The grey market, however, has considerably more non-allocated time, even though there may be a trend for those in the grey market to remain in some level of part-time employment. It has been calculated that retirement gives men on average 25 hours non-allocated time per week, and 18 hours for women.

Whilst leisure time is dominated by television, radio and newspapers, there are other major areas of leisure consumption. Understandably this means that the grey market is a sizeable and important target for leisure providers. Coupled with this is the fact that through continued involvement in leisure, both for its inherent

G

physical and mental health benefits, as well as in ensuring that these individuals remain within a social network, there are financial benefits to be enjoyed. As with any specific market, there are differences in terms of class, gender, ethnicity, education, religion and marked differences in the generations as they enter the grey market classification. With life expectancy in Britain, for example, now over 78 years, this is twice the average life expectancy of individuals less than 200 years ago. Again, this has broader leisure implications, with people being involved in leisure activities well past their retirement age.

Godbey, G., *Leisure in Your Life: New Perspectives*. Venture, 2007.

Nussbaum, J. and Coupland, J., *Handbook of Communication and Aging Research*. Lawrence Erlbaum, 2004.

Groups and teams

The definition of a group is two or more individuals who come into contact with one another, for example in a work situation, on a regular and continued basis. Within most organisations there are a number of groups who come together for a particular reason. Groups can be either formal in nature, or informal. The informal type of group often come together to support activities, both within and outside the organisation, and cooperate and collaborate with one another in order to carry out certain tasks and fulfil individual job roles.

A formal group is often formed in order to pass on and share some form of information. Very often they assist in the decision-making process and are seen as an official function within the organisation. Formal groups include *quality circles*, which will usually exist for a longer period of time than some of the other formal groups. Most formal groups consist of a variable number of representatives from different areas of the organisation's activities. They are often given responsibility and authority to implement ideas and amend working practices, giving input into the possible impact of expected change.

Many organisations have gradually come to the realisation that teams represent a proven means by which productivity and performance can be assured. Various industry surveys, particularly in the manufacturing sector, seem to suggest that over two-thirds of all organisations actively encourage teams. The actual nature of the team is of prime importance and their creation is of particular relevance to human resources. Essentially there are three different types of team, all of which have a degree of authority, autonomy or **empowerment**.

Empowered teams are usually given the authority to plan and implement improvements. Self-directed teams are virtually autonomous and are mainly responsible for supervisory issues. Cross-functional teams are more complex as they involve various individuals from different departments who are working towards a common end.

Training needs to be provided to teams both before and during their creation in order to assist the members in establishing their relationships with one another and understanding their new responsibilities. It is also essential that teams are given clear instructions and, above all, support from management in order to carry out their tasks. Once a team has been established and a degree of authority delegated to them, management and **human resources** need to step back and allow the team to develop and learn how their new working practices will operate.

G

The team itself, management, and human resources, retain the responsibility of monitoring and motivating the teams and their members. This requires effective communication skills and a feedback system which enables teams to request additional assistance should be it be required.

G

Health and safety

Health and safety is primarily concerned with the well-being of employees. In most large organisations all health and safety issues are coordinated by a particular individual who is concerned with the maintenance of a safe working environment and safe working practices. Businesses are required by law to ensure that their employees' health does not suffer as a result of their work. Various statistics are collected, primarily of fatal injuries, major injuries and other injuries. There is a continued concern that accidents at work are under-reported by employers.

The Health and Safety Commission estimates that at least 80,000 new cases of work-related disease occur each year and that half a million people suffer from continuing damage to health at work. The principal legislation in Britain is the Health and Safety at Work Act (1974), requiring, as far as is practicable, that employers ensure the health, safety and welfare of those who work for them. Britain's national legislation has been modified in recent years to incorporate European Directives on health and safety. The initial framework directive led to the Management of Health and Safety at Work Regulations (1992), which detailed more specific duties for employers, requiring them to carry out risk assessment, and appoint competent individuals to develop preventative measures and to ensure that employees and others have sufficient information.

The Health and Safety Executive is a public agency responsible for the inspection and the enforcement of health and safety legislation. Its powers include the issuing of improvement notices and prohibition notices. The inspectors may initiate criminal proceedings if the regulations are continually flouted.

Health and Safety at Work Act 1974 (UK)

The Health and Safety at Work Act (HASAWA) places a duty on employers to ensure the health, safety and welfare at work of all their employees (as far as is practicable). The Health and Safety Executive and local authorities enforce HASAWA and there are criminal sanctions for breaches or failure to comply.

In addition to this legal responsibility, the employer also has an implied responsibility to take reasonable steps, as far as they are able, to ensure the health and safety of their employees is not put at risk. Employers are required to assess the levels of risk against the costs associated with the elimination of those risks in order to make a judgement as to whether they have taken all reasonable steps. Usually the employer's responsibility is only to his or her own employees and premises; however, the responsibility can be extended in some circumstances.

www.hse.gov.uk

Hedonism

Daniels (1995) in a study of seventeenth-century colonial New England suggested that the puritans were not only intolerant of leisure, but considered it to be hedonistic. Whilst they accepted that leisure was a part of life, they required it to be integral to work, family and community, rather than being enjoyed just for its own sake. To some extent this begins to explain the nature of hedonism and how it applies to leisure. Our understanding of the word 'hedonism' certainly implies degrees of shortsightedness and perhaps subversion. Daniels explained why this might be the case:

> Play suspended the normal rules of life and substituted its own rules, which allowed violence, deception, destructive competition – even outright lying. Play mocked the community and its moral standards. And, most horrifying of all, formal play had its own rituals, which competed with social rituals for loyalty and time. Play had often given license to transgress society's values. Players might decline to accept moral responsibility for what they did because they were, after all, just playing.

This can lead us to suppose that hedonistic leisure is in some way abnormal, perhaps violating normal codes of practice and even inciting individuals to behave in a barbaric way. Nonetheless, hedonistic leisure provides participants with the opportunity of obtaining intrinsic satisfaction, pure unbridled pleasure-seeking. Hedonistic leisure, however, is largely frowned upon, as it ignores any citizenship rights, duties and responsibilities. It may often lack respect towards the self, but more importantly towards others and to the environment. Despite this, hedonism remains a prominent cultural value.

Daniels, B. C., *Puritans at Play: Leisure and Recreation in Colonial New England*. St Martin's Griffin, 1995.

Heritage

Hall (1999) attempted to define the tricky concept of heritage:

> Heritage is bound into the meaning of the nation through a double inscription. What the nation means is essentialized. It appears to have emerged at the very moment of its origin – a moment always lost in the myths, as well as in the mists, of time – and successively embodied as a distilled essence in the various arts and artifacts of the nation for which the heritage provides the archive.

H

Whether this rather convoluted definition actually cuts to the heart of what heritage is, is questionable. Certainly what is and what is not heritage is necessarily imposed either by the state or by vociferous groups. Therefore unravelling what is heritage is a difficult task, but it has not been a difficult problem for those who consider themselves to be in the heritage business. Across the world, heritage is a major export industry. Heritage can incorporate anything that is manmade, from castles, to gardens and stately homes, to exhibits in art galleries. Even artefacts with only a limited link to a historical event or character are now deemed to be heritage and are incorporated into the heritage industry.

The situation is compounded by organisations such as **UNESCO**, who have compiled 679 cultural, 174 natural and 25 mixed properties as being World Heritage Sites and ratified as such by the World Heritage Convention. These include valleys, monasteries, walled cities, belfries, reefs, tombs, canals, fossil cliffs and caves. Some jar alongside what we would expect to find as a heritage site; old palaces, shrines, monuments, ruined cities and great industrial landmarks. UNESCO defines heritage as:

> Our legacy from the past, what we live with today, and what we pass on to future generations. Our cultural and natural heritage are both irreplaceable sources of life and inspiration. What makes the concept of world heritage exceptional is the universal application. World Heritage Sites belong to all the peoples of the world, irrespective of the territory on which they are located. UNESCO seeks to encourage the identification, protection and preservation of cultural and natural heritage around the world considered to be of outstanding value to humanity.

Heritage is an increasingly important aspect of tourism, but heritage itself can be anything that anyone says it may be. Interestingly, it is often those who do not live where the heritage site or artefact is located who consider it to be heritage. According to Ryan (2002), very few native New Zealanders show the remotest interest in Maori cultural sites. Far more overseas visitors than domestic tourists visit them solely for their heritage and cultural history.

Hall, S., 'Unsettling the Heritage: Re-imagining the Post-Nation', *Whose Heritage?* Arts Council of England, 1999.
Ryan, C., 'Tourism and Cultural Proximity: Examples from New Zealand', *Annals of Tourism Research*, 29:4 (2002), pp. 952–71.

www.whc.unesco.org

Heritage Conservation and Recreation Service
This was an agency that was part of the US Department of the Interior, created in 1977. It was absorbed into the National Parks Service in 1981.

See **National Parks Service**.

Hermeneutics
Hermeneutics is a research and study methodology that seeks to look at the theories buried within texts by interpreting those texts. It has been a key part of the study of religious texts for centuries, but it is widely used to interpret and understand social events, by analysing their meanings to participants and their culture. In sociological terms it came to prominence during the 1960s, but is different from other interpretive schools as it emphasises content as well as form. Those that follow the hermeneutic interpretation of information believe that it is only possible to appreciate the meaning of an action by relating it to its context and the world view that was contemporary to the document itself.

H

Hertzberg, Frederick
Frederick Hertzberg developed his two-factor theory, which included his hygiene factor and his motivator factor, during his investigation of accountants and engineers in the USA. This brought about his angle on the theory of leadership, motivation and management. According to Hertzberg, the five major motivating factors are:

- Achievement – employees have a need to feel that something has been accomplished by their labours.
- Recognition – employees have a need to feel that management and others realise that the role they are playing within the organisation is an important and appreciated one.
- The work itself – employees have a need to feel that they have enough freedom to make their own decisions and that their job role meets or reaches their own potentials.
- Advancement – employees have a need to feel that they have a chance of promotion and that their skills and performance warrant such a promotion.
- Responsibility/growth – in achieving promotion and advancement in the organisation the employees continue to have the ability to develop their personal skills and their position in the organisation.

The hygiene factors that Hertzberg identified are features of the workplace, or the organisation itself, that help to make the employees feel good about themselves, and include:

- Wage or salary paid.
- Bonuses/commissions paid.
- Working conditions.
- Quality of supervision.
- The working environment.
- Job security.

The hygiene factors do not motivate employees and they can never reach a stage either of complete satisfaction or of complete dissatisfaction, but remain in a neutral zone.

Hertzberg's motivators are concerned with the work that the employee undertakes and their performance within each task. An employee cannot be motivated if the organisation is not offering them any of the following, and they will remain in the neutral zone:

- Attainment
- Advancement
- Responsibility

Hertzberg, F., *Work and the Nature of Man*. HarperCollins, 1966.
Hertzberg, Frederick, *Motivation to Work*. Transaction Publishers, 1993.

H

Hierarchical structure

A hierarchical organisation structure is best imagined by use of an image of a pyramid. At the top are the major decision-makers, who are few in number, and further down the pyramid the shape of the organisation broadens as more employees become involved at the lower levels. At the base of the pyramid are the majority of the workers.

Power, responsibility and authority are concentrated at the top of the pyramid and decisions flow from the top downwards. An organisation will choose this form of structure when decisions need to be made by those who have expertise and experience, together with the authority to ensure that decisions are implemented.

The most common version of this form of structure is the steep pyramid where there are many different layers of management, possibly within an organisation that operates in several different locations, needing to fulfil different administrative functions. Equally, organisations of a complex nature may choose this structure.

There are some disadvantages for those lower down the hierarchical structure in that if the pyramid is too multilayered and complex, they often find difficulty in understanding how and why decisions are made. Organisations may also find themselves too bureaucratic in nature and the result could be that the decision-making process becomes too complicated and time-consuming because there are too many layers involved.

Hierarchy of needs

Abraham Maslow initially started his theory of the hierarchy of needs with seven basic needs that individuals have. This was ultimately reduced to the five needs shown in the well-known pyramid (Figure 2) associated with Maslow's theory.

Fundamental to Maslow's theory is that employees start at the bottom of the pyramid and only when they have satisfied their basic needs do they begin to move up the pyramid. According to Maslow, once a need has been fulfilled it is no longer a motivation and it is possible that employees get a desire to progress to the next level of the pyramid before their base-level needs have been fulfilled. The levels of Maslow's pyramid are described in Table 4.

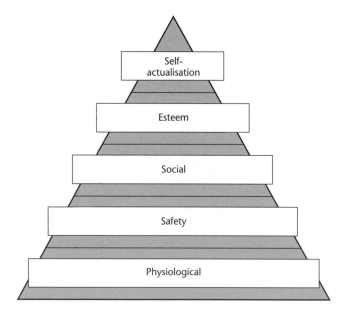

Figure 2   Maslow's hierarchy of human needs

(Abraham Maslow, *Motivation and Personality*, 1954, 1987)

H

Table 4 The levels of Maslow's pyramid

Pyramid Level	Description
Physiological	This basic needs level is seen as the lowest and includes the need for food, water, a roof over our heads and sex.
Safety	According to Maslow the second level only becomes important when the physiological needs have been met. Employees look for a safe and secure working environment from their organisation or employer.
Social	Once the physiological and safety needs have been met, employees then turn their attention to their social needs. This is the time that employees feel the need to make friends, want to feel loved, and want to be accepted by those they work with.
Esteem	This level concerns self-respect. According to Maslow, once employees have fulfilled the first three basic needs, they then have a desire for success. They want to be praised and regarded as being good at what they do.
Self-actualisation	The top level of the pyramid can only be reached once all the other needs have been fulfilled. This level concerns employees' need to realise their full potential and develop their innovative and creative side.

Maslow's theory is popular with management and trainers and it is considered to be an essential learning tool in most programmes of study about motivation. However, it was not initially intended as a management tool by Maslow, but was more about how individuals progress through their personal lives. Certainly it is quite possible that an individual could progress quite satisfactorily through the first two levels of the pyramid without the need to work.

Baker, Betsy and Sandore, Beth, 'Motivation in Turbulent Times: In Search of the Epicurean Work Ethic', *Journal of Library Administration*, 14:4 (1991), pp. 37–50.

Evans, G. Edward, 'Motivation', in *Management Techniques for Librarians* (2nd edn). Academic Press, 1983, pp. 174–98.

Maslow, Abraham, *Motivation and Personality*. HarperCollins, 1987.

Nadler, David A. and Lawler, David E., 'Motivation: A Diagnostic Approach', in *The Management Process: A Selection of Readings for Librarians*, ed. Ruth Person. American Library Association, 1983, pp. 315–26.

Historic Scotland

Historic Scotland was formed in 1991 and is an agency within the Scottish government responsible for safeguarding the nation's historic environment, and promoting its understanding and enjoyment. They deliver policy and advise on the historic environment on behalf of Scottish Ministers, as well as carrying out statutory functions relating to the Ancient Monuments and Archaeological Areas Act 1979, and the Planning (Listed Buildings and Conservation Areas) (Scotland) Act

1997. This act grants the authority to list structures for their architectural or historical significance.

Historic Scotland's staff encompasses a wide range of disciplines and skills to provide the Scottish agency, including:

- Archaeologists and art historians.
- Conservators and craftsmen.
- Custodians and key keepers.

Historic Scotland's main office is in Edinburgh but its staff, properties, monument conservation units and regional offices are also spread across Scotland.

See also **CADW: Welsh Historic Monuments** *and* **English Heritage.**

www.historicscotland.gov.uk

Hobbyist

'Hobbyist' is a broad term used to describe an individual who is involved in some aspect of art, craft or collection outside their regular occupation. It is essentially an individual who pursues an activity in their spare time for pleasure. There are literally hundreds of potential hobbies or interests. Many of them are supported by voluntary societies, clubs and associations. Whilst many of the hobbies are run by enthusiasts themselves, most of them are served by commercial profit-seeking businesses. Hobbies provide either the opportunity for individual preoccupation with the subject in hand, or social opportunities in the form of hobby groups. Hobbyists make use of many public and private sector facilities, in addition to making direct purchases from businesses. They will routinely use meeting rooms in public and private buildings and some may even be supported by local government funding. Whilst some pastimes can thrive without any form of public support, such as dining and drinking, other hobbies, in the arts and sports, do require forms of public support. While some hobbies may strike individuals as being trivial, the key determining factor for individuals' involvement in a leisure activity is an aspect of compulsion and entertainment. Hobbies are considered to be calming and therapeutic, but for some there is a fine line between a hobby and an obsession.

Hold time

Also known as 'holding time', this is the period of time for which a hotel room is kept reserved before it is released to general availability. The hold time period is commonly up to 4 pm or 6 pm, although times vary from hotel to hotel. If arrival is likely to be after the hold time the customer may be asked to guarantee the room reservation with a major credit card. If the customer does not arrive at the hotel to check in and has not cancelled the reservation, they will commonly be billed for the first night.

Hub and spoke

This is an aircraft deployment method. The carrier designates one or more strategically located cities as hubs, through which many scheduled flights pass with passengers and cargo. The passengers and cargo are then taken to their final

H

destinations by smaller aircraft. The smaller aircraft may belong to the same carrier or to smaller, feeder airlines. This set-up forms part of a **code sharing** agreement.

See also **feeder airline** *and* **code sharing.**

Human relations

Broadly speaking, the human relations strand of management theory is based on the individual and sentiment, rather than the individual as an economic unit and notions of efficiency. The human relations school, which developed during the 1930s, arose out of a desire to provide alternative explanations to those proposed by scientific management. The key differences are:

- Scientific management aimed to adjust the employees' actions in order to undertake a particular defined set of tasks.
- Human relations aimed to adjust the tasks to the skills and expertise of the employees.

Both schools were concerned with improvements in efficiency and productivity. The human relations school in turn has given rise to other areas of approach, including:

- Group dynamics
- Industrial relations
- Organisational humanism
- Individualism
- Systemic interdependence

At present, the human relations school has several different sub-disciplines, which include:

- Mutual accountability
- Self-managed teams
- Flexible working and organisations

Human resources

The role of management in the deployment and effectiveness of human resources within an organisation is a vast concern, which has been much written about. Human resource management, as such, can be differentiated from personnel management in the sense that the latter has more to do with the practical aspects of recruitment, appraisal, training and other key issues. Human resource management itself is more strategic and is concerned with the overall deployment of the human resources which are available to the business.

Typically there are four main areas in which human resource management is concerned, these are:

- The aggregate size of the organisation's labour force.
- The training spend on the workforce in order to achieve targets, such as quality or production output.
- Relations with trade unions and other employee-based organisations.

H

- Human asset counting, which analyses the costs and financial benefits of different forms of personnel policy.

The broader approach to human resource management involves a number of concerns, which include the following:

- The implications of the management of change to encourage flexible attitudes to the acceptance of new work practices.
- Making a major input into the organisational development.
- Being prescriptive and initiating new activities as opposed to being responsive to employment law, which is the preserve of personnel management.
- Determining employee relationships by the establishment of a culture which is conducive to cooperation and commitment.
- Taking a long-term view to integrate the human resources of the organisation into a coherent whole.
- The need to emphasise the need for direct communication.
- Developing **organisational culture**.
- Encouraging employee participation in work groups.
- Enhancing employees' capabilities in the longer term and not focusing purely on their current duties and responsibilities.

Bernardin, H. J. and Russell, J., *Human Resource Management: An Experiential Approach.* McGraw-Hill, 1993.

Stroh, C. K. and Caliguiri, P. M., 'Strategic Human Resources: A New Source of Competitive Advantage in the Global Arena', *International Journal of Human Resource Management*, 9:1 (1998), pp. 1–17.

Hybrid segmentation

'Hybrid segmentation' is both a market research and a general marketing term which describes a segmentation process that combines one or two segmentation variables to arrive at another form of segmentation. Standard segmentation relies on the identification of specific characteristics of a target market, perhaps relying on demographic information as its primary segmentation methodology. The expansion of the segmentation methodology to include factors such as lifestyle or other features, will provide the business with an alternative way of segmenting their markets. This additional approach may not have been a standard system used by the business in the past and it may reveal other information about their target audiences that they were not aware of until this point. Hybrid segmentation has therefore provided them with additional market data and a more focused view of the characteristics of their targets.

H

Hyper-reality

The term 'hyper-reality' relates to an individual's inability to distinguish between what is real and what is not. Hyper-reality can be described as enhanced reality, where people become more engaged with the hyper-real world than with the real world. This state is a postmodern theory and is considered to be a result of the modern age.

Celebrities who have every aspect of their lives taken care of are considered to live in a hyper-real world because they lose the ability to interact with people on a normal level. Watching soap operas can also, it is claimed, cause hyper-reality because the viewer adopts someone else's version of reality and loses the reality of, for example, normal social situations. Media images, the internet, computer games and virtual worlds are also making people believe that they can be rock stars or celebrities just by acting as if they are. Advertising is also guilty of causing hyper-reality because it attempts to sell the public an image of a lifestyle that they ultimately desire.

Disneyworld is a hyper-real world, according to Umberto Eco and Jean Baudrillard. Umberto Eco believes that Disneyland's Main Street was created to look 'absolutely realistic', taking visitors' imagination to a 'fantastic past'. In *Simulacra and Simulations*, Jean Baudrillard argued that the 'imaginary world' of Disneyland magnetises people inside and has been presented as 'imaginary' to make people believe that all its surroundings are 'real'.

Baudrillard, Jean, *Simulacra and Simulation (The Body, In Theory: Histories of Cultural Materialism)*. University of Michigan Press, 1995.
Eco, Umberto, *Travels In Hyperreality*. Harcourt Brace Jovanovich, 1986.

H

IATA (International Air Transportation Association)

IATA is an international trade body that was created over 60 years ago and as of 2008 represents 93% of scheduled international air traffic, carried out by 230 airlines. It is one of the lead bodies in the airline industry. It seeks to bring pressure on decision-makers and generally increase awareness of aviation benefits. It also aims to simplify airline processes and increase passenger convenience, while at the same time reducing costs and improving efficiency. It aims to ensure that airlines operate in a safe, secure, efficient and economic way under sets of defined rules.

www.iata.org

Illegal leisure

Aldridge, Measham and Parker (1998) carried out a groundbreaking study into the role that drug use plays in British **youth culture**. They were involved in a five-year longitudinal study. Their argument was that drug use was not necessarily rebellious behaviour, or even hedonistic, but that drug taking had been subsumed into a wider, more acceptable leisure activity. They discovered that 50% of British adolescents had tried illegal drugs and that 25% used them on a regular basis. The study looked at how adolescents made decisions about whether or not to try drugs and how some became regular users.

Illegal leisure does not necessarily have to revolve around drugs; it can equally be applied to the over-use of alcohol and other risky leisure activities, including gang membership, violence and what could now be broadly termed 'anti-social behaviour'.

Aldridge, J., Measham, F. and Parker, H., *Illegal Leisure: Normalisation of Adolescent Recreational Drug Use.* Routledge, 1998.

Independent traveller

Independent travellers are individuals who shun packaged and organised tours and holidays, opting instead for a self-constructed, bespoke trip, which benefits from the avoidance of limitation. Independent travellers, however, are on the one hand flexible in terms of their itinerary, modes of transport, accommodation and other considerations, whilst at the same time many will create complex itineraries after considerable research into the area or region in which they intend to travel. Independent travellers tend to focus on areas of the world or regions within a country that are not well served by conventional package tour operators and lack tourism infrastructure. Typically they will purchase flight-only tickets to major hubs and then rely on local or regional transport. Many will book accommodation and other services ahead by making direct contact with the service provider. The independent traveller is an exciting and expanding niche market. The definition is necessarily broad, but usually refers to those over 35 with above average income, and can refer to individuals, couples or small groups. They assiduously avoid mass tourism and holiday package concepts and desire a more individualistic and fluid approach to travel. They have some distinct economic behaviour, such as being primarily interested in heritage, culture, food, architecture, environmental awareness, but above all it is autonomy and freedom that attracts them to this form of travel. The rise of low cost airlines in the US and Europe has begun to see independent travellers driven out of these regions, and opting for more diverse locations. Independent travellers custom-build their own trips, relying on friends, forums, speciality providers and websites such as Lonely Planet and Wikitravel. In effect, independent travellers are either DIY travellers or sometimes referred to as 'free independent travellers', or 'frequent independent travellers'.

See also: **frequent independent traveller** *and* **backpacker**.

www.ivebeenthere.co.uk
www.lonelyplanet.com
www.wikitravel.org

Indigenous people

The term 'indigenous people' is used to describe a distinct ethnic group that inhabits a particular geographical area with which they have a very early histori-cal connection. There have been many attempts to define this term more clearly, but it is usually used in a fairly narrow sense. It refers to individuals who inhab-ited an area before any form of colonisation or annexation. They also tend to be a largely independent group and, perhaps, isolated from the government of the nation state in which their territory is now located. Above all, they tend to retain much of their original cultural, social, organisational and linguistic characteristics, and remain somewhat differentiated from the more dominant cultures in the nation state. Indigenous peoples are also referred to as 'aboriginals', 'natives', or 'autochthonous people' (this means 'sprung from the earth').

For indigenous peoples leisure and tourism is a two-edged sword. On the one hand it is their very difference that attracts tourists and those interested in culture and heritage to experience their ways of life. This naturally leads to economic benefits for the indigenous group. But at the same time it exposes them to broader cultural influences and may require them to make adaptations to their lifestyles in order to take advantage of the financial opportunities.

Johansen, B., *Indigenous Peoples and Environmental Issues: An Encyclopedia*. Greenwood Press, 2003.

Indirect spending

'Indirect spending' is a term closely associated with the **multiplier effect**. Essentially, it is the recycling of money that is spent by tourists in a local economy. It is differentiated from **direct spending**, which moves directly from the tourist into the local economy. Indirect spending is money that is re-spent within the local economy after it has been earned from the tourist. In New York, for example, in a study carried out in the late 1990s, Broadway theatres generated $2.7 billion for the city's economy. Much of this was spent in restaurants, hotels and other services. The money earned by these businesses was re-spent as indirect spending back into the New York economy at a rate of $1.7 billion. This was nearly a 40% increase over similar figures in the early 1990s.

Inflation

Inflation is a general and sustained increase in an economy's pricing levels. It is usually caused by an excess in demand within the economy and may also lead to a devaluation of the country's currency. Inflation is measured in the US by the Consumer Price Index (CPI) and by similar measures in other countries. It can also be measured by inflationary indicators such as the Producer Price Index, which is prepared by the US Bureau of Labor Statistics.

Inflation is typified by a persistent rise in both prices and wages. As wages rise production costs increase, thereby leading to a further rise in prices. In effect, if it is not controlled, then the economy can find itself in an inflationary spiral in which the rate of inflation increases at such a speed that it becomes almost impossible to control without significant restrictions on the supply of money and a major devaluation of the currency.

Inflation can be caused by a wide variety of different situations, such as a rapid increase in the money supply. This was a suggestion made by the US economist Milton Friedman. Monetarists such as Friedman believe that inflation can be controlled entirely by a strong grip on the money supply. Other approaches, such as that of John Maynard Keynes, suggest that a rigid incomes policy would maintain low inflation and low unemployment.

Countries such as the US and the UK have experienced a broad range of inflation from virtually zero to in excess of 23%. It is generally considered, however, reasonable and controllable to expect an annual inflation rate of between 2% and 3%.

Informal organisation

Informal organisations tend to occur amongst employees at the same or different hierarchical levels of a business. These informal groups may develop as a result of background, ethnicity, personal affinities or even hobbies.

Informal organisations have the following implications for a business:

- Management needs to understand the contribution these informal groups make to the business.
- Informal organisations can contribute to the stability of the business.

The characteristics of informal organisations have both positive and negative connotations; the positive ones include:

- Support between employees – individuals are no longer 'strangers'.
- They help employees carry out their work through verbal and informal support mechanisms.
- Enhancement of communications – when problems arise, situations can be dealt with 'unofficially'.

The negative characteristics are:

- Informal organisations may divert employees.
- Informal organisations may work against the management.
- Informal organisations may resist change, by silent dissent.

Informal power

Whilst managers and supervisors have clear formal power to assert their authority over subordinates, others are given informal power to operate and direct on behalf of those with formal authority. Informal power tends to occur in situations where an individual's job description does not explicitly imply authority or power. Usually, by virtue of their age, experience or understanding of the processes and tasks required, an individual is granted informal power as a form of *delegation*, to exercise authority over peers.

Infrastructure

The term 'infrastructure' refers to all of the key technical structures that support a society, city or region. Therefore they incorporate roads, water, power, communications and other elements. Sometimes they are referred to as public works of civil or municipal infrastructure. Infrastructure can also apply to information technology, along with social and political networks. Clearly infrastructure has a major influence on many aspects of leisure and tourism and some, such as emergency services or systems that are in place to deal with sudden damage or disruption, can be considered to be critical elements of infrastructure. Infrastructure tends to be very interdependent. It is usually high cost and in most cases its true value is difficult to determine.

Infrastructure can also apply to specific organisations and generally refers to the internal framework of that organisation, in other words, its management, supervision, resources and the general way it is organised.

There is considerable interest in the management, maintenance and development of infrastructure projects. The World Bank Infrastructure for Development Program specifically provides funds for emergency assistance and for infrastructure improvements. There are also research organisations, such as the Next Generation Infrastructures Foundation, which is a consortium of institutions, major businesses and government bodies.

www.nginfra.nl
www.worldbank.org

Innovation

The innovation-adoption model can be applied both to consumers and to businesses. In consideration of its application to consumers, the innovation-adoption model charts the process of gradual acceptance of a new product. The key stages are awareness, interest, evaluation, trial and adoption for consumers.

The innovation-adoption process in relation to businesses was developed by Rogers and it details the five stages of the innovation process, together with the associated activities at each of these stages:

1 Agenda setting
2 Matching

These two stages involve information gathering and planning, which all lead up to the decision-making stages:

3 Redefining and restructuring – this is when the innovation is modified and changes are made to the organisational structure to cope with the innovation.
4 Clarifying – a clearer definition of the relationship between the innovation and the organisation is established. This is to ensure that the innovation is a good fit and can be used on a regular basis.
5 Routinising – the innovation is fully incorporated into the standard routines of the business, but no longer has a separate identity as an innovation and is part of the organisation's overall processes.

Rogers, Everett M., *Diffusion of Innovation*. Free Press, 1995.

Institute for Sport, Parks and Leisure (ISPAL)

ISPAL was created in January 2007 with the merging of the Institute of Leisure and Amenity Management and the National Association of Sports Development. ISPAL is a membership body that represents sports, parks and leisure industry professionals. They are closely involved in the provision of continuing professional development, they hold four main conferences and events each year, provide information to their membership and seek to influence government policy in areas affecting their members.

See also **continuing professional development (CPD).**

www.ispal.org.uk

Intangible asset

An intangible asset is also known as an invisible asset. It is an asset which does not have a physical presence. In other words, intangible assets include goodwill, brand names, patents, trademarks, copyrights and franchises. Clearly intangible assets are the opposite of tangible assets.

Interestingly, intangible assets can be more, or less, intangible. Since brand names, trademarks or patents, for example, have, to some extent, a presence in the sense that they can be clearly identified as being an asset; other intangible assets are rather more ethereal. Goodwill is probably one of the most intangible assets as it has no supporting documentation and is of variable commercial value. Goodwill, for example, can be a very valuable intangible asset in the sense that it can offer a business, or a potential purchaser of a business, the opportunity to capitalise on future profits based on the work and relationships which have already been established and constitute the goodwill.

There is, however, a slight distinction between some forms of intangible assets. Goodwill could be described as either an intangible or an invisible asset, whereas insurance policies, for example, are invariably referred to as invisible rather than intangible assets.

Donaldson, T. H., *The Treatment of Intangibles: Banker's View*. Macmillan, 1992.

Integrated Marketing Communication (IMC)

Integrated marketing communications represent a holistic view towards marketing. IMC incorporates the planning, development, execution, evaluation and coordination of all marketing communications by a business. There is an inference that it ensures non-duplication of effort coupled with a standardised image. Businesses which have adopted IMC tend to show the following characteristics:

- A clearer awareness of where the target audience receives its information, through having assessed their media viewing, reading and listening habits and preferences.
- An understanding of the audiences' current knowledge and an understanding that this level of knowledge will have an impact on their response.
- The use of a mixture of different promotional tools, each of which has specific objectives, but which collectively aim to work in conjunction with one another.
- A view that a consistent message needs to be relayed throughout all of its advertising, sales promotion, public relations and personal selling activities.
- Awareness that in order to achieve the maximum impact on the market, there is a need to produce a continuous flow of information to the target audiences, which is timed to the best effect.

The greatest problem with attempting to initiate IMC is that a business's internal organisation may not yet be sufficiently developed or flexible in order to plan and coordinate effectively. An IMC programme can be evaluated on a number of different levels, but specifically relating it to advertising, personal selling, sales promotion and public relations, the following determinants can be considered:

- In relation to advertising, a series of well timed and related campaigns need to reinforce sales promotion and personal selling.
- The personal selling effort needs to be closely coordinated with the advertising programme. In other words, the sales department needs to be aware of the media schedule and when advertisements will appear.
- Sales promotion materials, such as at the point of sale, need to be prepared in advance and coordinated with the advertising and personal sales efforts. If necessary, products need to be pushed through the distribution channel by offering incentives along that channel.
- Public relations work not only needs to coincide with the other three activities, but it also needs to emphasise themes being drawn out in the advertisements.

Pickton, David and Broderick, Amanda (eds), *Integrated Marketing Communications*. Prentice Hall, 2001.

Inter-line agreement

This is a voluntary commercial agreement between two or more airlines. It is also known as 'inter-line ticketing'. The agreement allows passengers to travel on itineraries that require multiple airlines.

See also **inter-line connection**.

Inter-line connection

An inter-line connection is made possible by an **inter-line agreement**. In effect it allows passengers to change aircraft and also airline. In some cases the inter-line agreement and inter-line connection are even more flexible and the airlines may in fact allow one another to handle each other's baggage and to accept one another's tickets. An inter-line connection is also known as an 'off-line connection'.

International agreements

International agreements are broad classifications of legally binding arrangements between different nations. Typically, these international agreements will include accords, annexes and conventions, memoranda of understanding, protocols and treaties. They may also include declarations, pacts and statutes. Most of these terms are synonyms of one another and they have very little differentiation. A treaty, for example, as defined by the Vienna Convention on the Law on Treaties, states that it is 'an international agreement concluded between states in written form and governed by international law, whether embodied in a single instrument or in two or more related instruments and whatever its particular designation'.

Since many nations will sign several dozen, if not more, international agreements each year, some will be treaties while others will simply codify existing arrangements between the two nations. Protocols can be stand-alone arrangements, but are usually supplementary agreements or amendments. Annexes are usually subsidiary agreements to already established relationships. Accords are usually non-binding agreements; whilst memoranda of understanding are very detailed and take into account the practices and requirements of both governments.

International marketing

'International marketing' is a rather collective term used to describe global marketing activities undertaken by certain businesses. International or multinational businesses will have identified target markets in a variety of different countries across the world. International marketing is designed to impose some kind of coordination between these disparate activities. It is not always appropriate to run either simultaneous, or indeed similar, advertising and marketing campaigns in different markets. Given the fact that each market has its own peculiarities, seasonal fluctuations and specific customer needs and wants, the imposition of a standardised marketing system, incorporating identical advertising, is not always appropriate. Nonetheless, international marketing can offer a business the opportunity to compare like-with-like in different overseas markets. It may be possible, for example, to compare response rates against costs, running similar advertisements or sales promotions in different countries. The purpose of coordination and planning is to establish the correct mix of activities for each overseas market and to learn lessons from similar markets when first entering a new overseas market.

Doole, Isobel, *International Marketing Strategy: Analysis, Development and Implementation*. Thomson Learning, 2001.

Interpellation

In terms of leisure, interpellation is the process by which a subject comes into being. In this sense the subject can be an individual or a behaviour, in other words it is the process by which an individual or a group begin to adopt a particular way in which they carry out a leisure activity, adopt a social attitude or even begin wearing particular clothes. Clearly, interpellation is not necessarily an individual process; it can be affected by the media, or by other individuals, particularly if the subject itself has some kind of emotional or persuasive appeal. It may mean, for example, that an individual begins identifying with a specific sub-culture.

The original term 'interpellation' was suggested by Louis Althusser (1918–90). Althusser was an Algerian-born French Marxist. He originally referenced it to police shouting 'Hey you!' in a street, and the fact that someone who had made the association between guilt and subjectivity would turn around, believing the police were hailing them.

Althusser, L. 'Ideology and Ideological State Apparatuses' (1970), *Lenin and Philosophy and Other Essays.* Monthly Review Press, 2001.

Invasive leisure

There are two distinct and radically different interpretations of the term 'invasive leisure'. On the one hand it refers to situations where individuals who are in full-time demanding employment can suffer from invasive leisure symptoms. Leisure, or free time, is not experienced by these individuals as a source of validation or self-worth, but more that of isolation. If an individual is exhibiting invasive leisure patterns then that individual's public face may be one that is sociable and harmonious, but inwardly they believe that their work and their required mode of behaviour is inauthentic and worthless. They turn to drugs or alcohol to try and offset these oppressive feelings. This in turn leads them to disengagement and in extreme cases they may feel worthless and, according to Rojek (2000), they may become psychologically damaged by this split life.

'Invasive leisure' can also be applied to modes of leisure that directly impact on the lives of others in a negative way. In this respect the two aspects of invasive leisure can be brought together. An individual who over-consumes alcohol or drugs may exhibit both inward and outward invasive leisure characteristics.

Rojek, C., *Leisure Theory.* Macmillan, 2000.

Investment strategy

Business investment strategy can be typified as having three primary exponents, namely exploration, exploitation and expansion. Investment strategy, be it internal or external, can involve strategic alliances, partnerships, acquisitions or mergers. Equally, investment strategy can move a business vertically, horizontally or laterally in terms of its involvement in a specific market or markets. Investment strategy is not for the risk averse, as typically higher risk investments often offer longer-term advantages, assuming that the investment is a sound one. Clearly, any form of investment strategy requires the diversion of resources from the core business area to a new, or allied, area of operation. Investment strategy therefore requires a sound technical capability, a tacit knowledge of the market and, above all, an understanding of the rapidly changing markets themselves.

Business investment does not require having to secure ownership of all of a partner's or subsidiary's assets. It can involve a cooperative arrangement which seeks to enhance both businesses' competitive position. Businesses will seek horizontal mergers and acquisitions in the hope that they will capture a larger proportion of the market. They may also create new entities in order to reduce costs through synergy effects.

Businesses will look for the optimum business investment which will not only minimise their transactional costs, but will enhance their strategic objectives.

> Bouchet, Michael Henry, Clark, Ephraim and Groslambert, Bertrand, *Country Risk Assessment: A Guide to Global Investment Strategy.* John Wiley & Sons, 2003.

Investors in People (IIP) (UK)

Investors in People, as a standard of good practice in the training and development of employees, was developed during 1990 by the National Training Task Force (in partnership with organisations such as the Confederation of British Industry (CBI), the Trades Union Congress (TUC) and the Institute of Personnel and Development (IPD) as well as the Employment Department).

The standard aims to provide a national framework for the improvement of business performance and competitiveness by developing people to achieve these objectives. The IIP standards are based on four key issues or principles:

- Commitment to invest in people to achieve business goals.
- Planning how skills, individuals and teams are to be developed to achieve these goals.
- Taking action to develop and use necessary skills in a well defined and continuing programme directly tied to business objectives.
- Evaluating outcomes of training and development for individuals' progress towards goals, the value achieved and future needs.

www.iipuk.co.uk

Itinerary

In the leisure and tourism field an itinerary can actually incorporate any number of different types of information. In effect it is a proposed route or schedule over a period of time. It can incorporate travel arrangements in the form of dates, times and destinations, including estimated arrival and departure times. It can also list confirmed activities, entertainment, accommodation and other services, along with pricing. Travel itineraries, or schedules, can be prepared either by a travel agent or tour operator, or by the client. At its most basic an itinerary is a path or a travel plan and at its most complex it can be a travel guidebook. Basic itineraries are often provided by tour operators or by leisure activity providers. Other itineraries can be self-constructed by independent travellers, using either conventional means or proprietary itinerary planners.

I

Joint venture

A joint venture implies a long-term agreement by two or more business entities to cooperate and jointly control a separate business entity. Typically, a joint venture would involve a manufacturer and, perhaps, a distributor, in developing a new business venture which affords both parties the potential for profit and a more secure share of the market. A contractual arrangement, setting out the terms of the joint venture, forms the basis of the association between the two separate founding businesses.

The term 'joint venture' is also applicable to international business deals which see collaboration between organisations that are based in two different countries. They will contribute to the new business enterprise, in which in one way or another ownership and control are shared.

Joint ventures may be characterised as being either populated or unpopulated. A populated joint venture is a legally independent business, with its own management and staff. An unpopulated joint venture is one which is typified by the concept of a shell company, in which the partner companies temporarily loan their management and staff to the joint venture.

Vermeulen, Erik, *The Evolution of Legal Business Forms in Europe and the United States: Venture Capital, Joint Venture and Partnership Structures.* Kluwer Law International, 2003.

Judgement sample

A judgement sample is associated with market or social research. A judgement sample is a non-probability or purposive sample, where the researcher selects respondents on the basis that they appear to conform to the specific criteria of the population that needs to be sampled. The researcher may in fact be incorrect and whilst the individual may exhibit some of those characteristics they may not, however, be part of that particular target. This can lead to sampling errors and bias.

Junk mail

'Junk mail' is often used as an alternative way of describing materials sent as part of a direct mail shot. Professional direct marketing organisations, which have systematic processes in place and more precisely target recipients of direct mail, do not, strictly speaking, send out junk mail. The generally accepted definition of the term refers to unsolicited mail, which may or may not, depending on your stance, include all direct mail. Junk mail is generally typified by sales literature or product offerings, which are received by mail without any prompting or request made by the recipient. Often unsolicited mail bears no relevance to the recipient and in this case, as it is invariably consigned directly to the bin, it can be considered as junk.

Plusch, Jackie, *Junk Mail Solutions.* Clutter Cutter, 2001.

J

Key factors for success (KFS)

There are, of course, many interpretations of key factors for success, or KFS. The KFS of different businesses radically differ in accordance with their primary business plans and objectives. In effect, KFS relates to the essential elements of a business's plan which determine whether or not that plan will be followed through and achieved.

For a retail operation, for example, at least seven key factors for success could be identified, these would include:

- The selling of products or services at a sufficient gross margin to sustain profitability.
- The offering to customers of a convincing and compelling range of products and services.
- Ensuring that customer acquisition costs are in line with average sales
- Providing customers with a user-friendly environment.
- Attracting significant visitor traffic and managing a high conversion rate.
- Providing and managing cost effective and efficient product fulfilment.
- Providing significant and quality customer support before, during and after purchase.

Key performance indicators

'Key performance indicator' (KPI) refers to a system which seeks to develop both organisational and individual skill levels within a business. Typically, the KPI system of development includes the five processes shown in Figure 3.

A more detailed look at the 5 steps is addressed in Table 5.

Smith, Jeff, *The KPI Book: The Ultimate Guide to Understanding the Key Performance Indicators of your Business.* Insight Training and Development, 2001.

Knowledge management

Knowledge management can be seen as one of the key factors of organisational development. Knowledge management recognises that information and ability are among the most valuable assets an organisation possesses. In the past, organisations have not been able to quantify or recognise this aspect as being one of their prime assets, as it is intangible. Knowledge is not just information or data, it needs to have a meaning and a purpose, and in **human resources** this means the ability to apply and use information. In other words, knowledge management is all about people and the process of being able to use information. There is no compelling definition of the term 'knowledge management' and it has been vari-

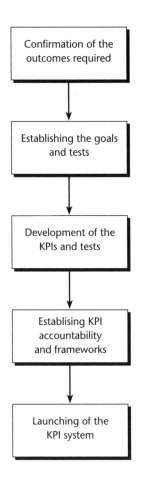

Figure 3   Key performance indicators

ously described as intellectual capital or property, amongst a variety of other different attempts to explain its purpose and worth.

The key concern for human resources is the retaining of individuals who are able to impart knowledge as an essential function of their relationship with the business. This knowledge management is a complex process, but includes questions as to how to share this knowledge, how to find it, how to use it and how to convert it or transfer it from one individual to another.

Davenport, Thomas H. and Prusak, Laurence, *Working Knowledge: How Organizations Manage What They Know*. Harvard Business School Press, 2000.

von Krogh, Georg, Ichijo, Kazua and Nonaka, Ikujiro, *Enabling Knowledge Creation*. Oxford University Press, 2000.

K

Table 5 Key performance indicators

Step	Detail
Confirmation of the outcomes required	The KPIs are based on what the business hopes to achieve, typically customer service improvements, improvement of stakeholder relations, or the reduction of operating costs.
Establishing the goals and tests	Each KPI will need a specific goal; the test refers to whether the accomplishment of the goal will achieve the outcome required.
Development of KPIs and tests	What are the drivers of the outcomes? How will the performance and move towards performance be measured? How will the KPIs need to be amended to fit in with the existing management information systems?
Establishing KPI accountability and frameworks	Who will ultimately be accountable for each of the KPIs? Some of the KPIs will be achieved by cooperation, but who will monitor this?
Launching of the KPI system	'Goals down, plans up' is a term which is associated with the development of key performance indicators (KPI) and change management. When launching KPIs there are four usual stages: • Goals down, plans up – which requires the KPIs to be cascaded down to the operational teams. The KPIs are the goals and the teams develop their relevant KPIs through the plans they develop to achieve these goals. • Individual performance plans – which require management and team leaders to create their own KPIs from the organisational plan. • Documentation development – all KPIs are logged and a process for updating the next planning cycle is organised. • Training – both 'hard' and 'soft' skills are developed in terms of group training, and individual skills training for technical and functional skills (hard skills) and behavioural performance (soft skills) are included.

Knowledge-based pay systems

Knowledge-based pay systems reward employees on the basis of their knowledge and skills. In effect, there are three different ways of assessing and rewarding the overall knowledge or skills levels of employees, these are:

- Horizontal skills – which reflect the variety of tasks the employee is capable of performing.
- Vertical skills – which reflect the management tasks the employee currently undertakes or may be capable of performing.
- Depth skills – which reflect the overall quality and productivity results displayed by the employee.

Lawler III, Edward E., *Rewarding Excellence: Pay Strategies for the New Economy.* Jossey Bass Wiley, 2000.

Layover

'Layover' is a term associated with travel, specifically long-distance travel. It refers to situations where passengers need to take a break between vehicles, usually on a multivehicle trip, which could incorporate buses, planes, trains or trams. Layovers can involve passengers spending time at a terminal or at a transport hub after they have left one mode of transport and are waiting to board the next transport on their journey. These are particularly common when travellers are making intercity trips and especially if international travel is involved. In the travel and tourism industry the term 'layover' is also used for providing a break both for the mode of transport, so it can be checked, serviced, cleaned and refuelled, while also allowing a crew change or for the crew to have a rest period.

Lead-time

There are a number of definitions related to lead-time. The term 'lead-time' refers to the length of time that an organisation takes to produce a product or a component. The 'planned lead-time' is a time parameter which is used in a planning and control system to determine the start date for an order.

The planned lead-time for a manufacturing order is the sum of the planned lead-times for all of the necessary activities in the assembly of that order. For a single operational step, this typically includes:

- The queue time before the production process begins.
- The setup time for the machine for production.
- The run time to process the order.
- The post-production waiting time for the product to continue to the next stage.

From a customer perspective, the promised customer lead-time is the length of time they can expect to wait for the product, and refers to the planned difference between order placement and order receipt.

All lead-times have random variables: means, modes, medians, standard deviations, minimums, maximums, etc. Therefore, it is important that organisations are clear about when to use the word 'lead-time'.

Leadership strategy

The precise leadership strategy of a business will very much depend on a number of priorities, but it is important to realise that there is a distinct difference between leadership and management. Beginning with the priorities, it is safe to assume that leadership strategy will be based on some, or all, of the following:

- The achievement of optimal performance.
- The acquisition of an overview rather than detail.
- The ability to become involved in detail if necessary.
- Issues including development, continuity and improvement.
- The taking of remedial action.
- Monitoring and evaluating work and those involved in work.
- Ensuring that those with the right skills and capacities are matched to the right jobs.
- Continuous improvement through systems such as **total quality management**.
- Motivation and the promotion of a harmonious workplace.
- General operational management activities.

It is generally thought that leadership requires a number of different and often mutually supporting skills, these are:

- The ability to show measurable results.
- The ability to inspire.
- The actuality or illusion of hard work.
- The receiving and giving of respect.
- The ability to *add value* to the organisation, its processes, products and services.
- A degree of apparent honesty.
- The ability to take and give responsibility, accepting and giving the rewards associated with this responsibility.

It is also believed that any leadership role should effectively represent a specifically named role, in the sense that the organisation and its employees understand the precise nature of that leader's function. These leadership roles can be typified as any of the following:

- A figurehead – who effectively represents the organisation or a part of the organisation to the external environment.
- An ambassador – where the leader acts as an advocate or a problem solver.
- A servant – which is based on the premise that the manager is a servant of the business, its customers, its employees, its products and services.
- A maintenance leader – who attends to problem solving, continuous improvement, procedures and practices, and may handle crises.
- A role model – who sets the standards and attitudes and tries to influence the behaviour of those who work in the organisation.
- A ringmaster – who may adopt several different roles, as outlined above, and may have to shift their emphasis as needs arise.

Pittinger, Richard, *Introduction to Management*. Palgrave Macmillan, 2002.

Leakage

'Leakage' is an economic term that is closely associated with Keynesian models of the circular flow of national income. A leakage is defined as a saving, tax or import which effectively takes money out of the circular flow of income and reduces the money available in the economy. The theory suggests that funds circulate around the income being earned and spent, but if funds are taken out of that flow, either to pay for imported products, or to provide tax payments to the government, or are simply held in reserve as savings, then that is a leakage and does not benefit the broader economy.

Learning organisation

An exact definition of the term 'learning organisation' is somewhat problematic since there are a number of different categories and the emergence of the idea of the 'learning organisation' is closely associated with notions such as 'the learning society'. A learning organisation is best defined as one that recognises that traditional education systems are no longer able to respond to the demands made upon them. Instead, society looks toward the idea that learning is at the heart of change. The two essential facts being that there is an increased proportion of free time, and the rapidity of change.

The main recognised categories of learning organisations are:

- The knowing organisations – which tend to be businesses in static or mature markets.
- The understanding and thinking organisations – which are prepared to adapt their culture and structure within certain parameters.
- The learning organisations – which accept change as being both necessary and desirable, and are ultimately the businesses which drive their competitors to mimic them.

Clearly, a human resource department which operates in a learning organisation, of whatever type, has to be far more adaptable and flexible, as well as effective and efficient, in driving changes within the organisation. It has been recognised that there are two stages of evolution of a learning organisation, of which **human resources** are an integral part. The first is known as a single-loop or adaptive learning organisation, where new techniques and ideas are assimilated. The second type of learning organisation is also known as a double-loop or generative learning organisation. In this case the business continually evaluates its goals and objectives, as well as organisational culture, to suit any emerging external opportunities. Both forms of learning organisation offer considerable challenges to human resources, who have to quickly learn that they are in an ever-shifting and adaptive organisation.

Chawla, Sarita, *Learning Organizations: Developing Cultures for Tomorrow's Workplace.* Productivity Press, 1995.

Kline, Peter and Saunders, Bernhard, *Ten Steps to a Learning Organisation.* Great Ocean Publishers, 1998.

Left-wing politics

This refers to supporters of broadly social progressive or socialist views and it can also incorporate more radical reforms. It originally is a term that was used during the French Revolution, simply to describe those who sat on the left of the French parliament, and were opposed to the monarch and were more radical. The term is now more broadly used to describe any political party or movement that can be associated with modern liberalism in the US, or social liberals, social democrats, socialists, anarchists or communists.

See also **right-wing politics.**

Leisure

At its most basic level leisure is a voluntary behaviour. It involves choice, freedom and voluntarism. The desire for leisure is nowadays considered to be an essential part of human nature and a desirable activity.

Leisure is also a historical product. There may have been a time when leisure did not exist, as life revolved around obtaining food, securing shelter, staying alive and producing children. As leisure has developed into a distinct cultural set of activities, whole new rituals and institutions have been created. Over time, leisure has developed and changed, often in radical ways. Perhaps the most common thread is the fact that leisure is always identified as being separate and contrasting with work. Without this distinction the term 'leisure' is too vague. Also, work and leisure have been valued in different ways, but this does not mean to say that there are blurred areas between work and leisure.

When humanity ceased to become hunter gatherers there were opportunities to begin to recognise non-work situations, times of freedom, where individuals could choose to involve themselves in an activity that was not directly related to their work.

Writers such as de Grazia (1962) were firmly of the opinion that the Greeks actually discovered leisure. They made a distinction between 'work' and 'not work' and realised that non-work time was essential for individuals to realise their humanity.

Leisure provides individuals with the opportunity to converse, involve themselves in free activities, create art, play sports and make music. According to Durkheim it was leisure, not work, that held societies together. Toynbee (1955) took a different stance:

> [Even though] the progress of civilization during the short period of 5,000 years can be seen to have been the work of this leisured minority the individual creators of civilization have been only a minority of the [leisured] minority. A majority of the privileged minority have probably been drones, always and everywhere.

Leisure may in fact have very dark roots. Patterson (1991) suggested that early leisure revolved around blood sports, execution, torture and intrigue. It also encompassed over-indulgence, idleness and overt and exploitative control over others. In many periods, leisure has often been described as a loss or a passing of time, or indeed simple idleness. It was not really until the Industrial Revolution that many individuals in the developing countries had any free time in which they could develop leisure interests. The Industrial Revolution fundamentally changed many structures and as it transformed families and societies, what had been twelve-hour days, six days per week, were gradually reduced to five-and-a-half-hour days. Equally, laws that ensured that workers were given holidays had an impact on the development of leisure pursuits. Whatever changes were affecting the lower classes, the upper classes still found themselves with sufficient time to pursue particular leisure activities or obsessions, including holidays, sports and other more sedentary pastimes. For many, leisure was still a luxury that could only be afforded by the few. Money could not be spent on leisure in a frivolous way. Recreation, or leisure, tended to revolve around clubs and social activities.

In a modern context, however, leisure has a far broader and all-encompassing set of connotations. It can refer to any type or range of activities or, for that matter, non-activities that are undertaken, enjoyed or endured during times that are not directly associated with work. Leisure is inextricably linked to life options and life satisfaction. It is an individual choice and pursuit. Life satisfaction can come from relatively harmless and solitary activities, or it can come from more intrusive or frowned upon activities, such as taking drugs, over-drinking, or hunting animals.

De Grazia, V., 'Leisure and Citizenship: Historical Perspectives', in *Leisure and New Citizenship*, Actas VIII, Congreso ELRA, Bilbao, 1962.

Durkheim, E., *The Division of Labour in Society*. Free Press, 1964.

Patterson, O., *Freedom in the Making of Western Culture*. Basic Books, 1991.

Roberts, Ken, *The Leisure Industries*. Palgrave Macmillan, 2004.

Rojek, C., *Leisure Theory: Principles and Practice*. Palgrave Macmillan, 2005.

Rojek, C., Shaw, S. and Veal, A., *A Handbook of Leisure Studies*. Palgrave Macmillan, 2006.

Toynbee, A., 'Man at Work in God's World in the Light of History', *Vital Speeches of the Day*, 22 (15 November 1955), pp. 87–95.

Leisure, complementary

In this classification of leisure, the activity is carried out because others expect the individual to take part. Individuals will feel obligations to participate. This leisure has social meaning and there is little freedom of choice.

Leisure, coordinated

The major purpose of these classes of leisure is for people to be with others and share social interaction. The leisure is valued because of the relationships involved among participants. There is a high degree of freedom to choose and social meaning.

Leisure, recuperative

These are classes of leisure where the primary purpose is to rest, recover and unwind. This leisure may provide opportunity for compensation for the constraints of life conditions and responsibilities. Normally, the leisure is chosen for intrinsic reasons and has low freedom of choice.

L

Leisure, unconditional

This is classified as leisure that is not influenced by work. It involves intrinsic satisfaction and the activity is chosen for its own sake. The individual has a high sense of freedom to choose what to do. These forms of leisure have characteristics of excitement, opportunity for personal expression and creativity, and are emotionally fulfilling.

Leisure Marketing

Peter Drucker (1969) defined marketing as follows:

Not only much broader than selling, it is not a specialized activity at all. It encompasses the entire business. It is the whole business seen from the point of view of its final result that is from the customer's point of view. Concerns and responsibilities for marketing must therefore permeate all areas of the enterprise.

Perhaps more than any other range of services offered by businesses and organisations, leisure, and thus the marketing of leisure, needs to be entirely customer focused. As such, an individual or an organisation must incorporate the 'customer first' attitude in every aspect of their operations. It necessarily means that leisure industries need to be customer satisfiers and not goods or service producers. It may be necessarily more complex to consider the marketing of many aspects of leisure that are essentially service-based, rather than more conventional mass-market marketing, which is involved in selling consumer products. However, it would be naive to suggest that even niche leisure services should not be afforded the same attention in terms of marketing as cans of baked beans. Perhaps the focus is far more sophisticated; the target market will be more informed and the ultimate choices of the customer will determine the success or failure of the leisure product or service. Equally, leisure services are by definition and nature intangible. They cannot be seen or touched, so it is often difficult for leisure organisations to get across a particular idea that consumers can hold in their minds with any degree of clarity.

It is perhaps true to say that in very few instances do individuals really know what they want even when they say they do. This suggests that potential participants in leisure activities are susceptible and vulnerable to persuasive forms of promotion. Although participants differ in terms of their disposable income, available time, desire to be involved in social activities and a host of other demographic and psychographic characteristics, all are potential targets for leisure marketing.

Leisure in particular has seen that certain forms of activity fade into and out of popularity. Customers are not static and neither are they unquestioning. They are dynamic and invariably erratic, perhaps even more so in their use of free time and their attachment to leisure activities. This makes the process of leisure marketing all the more challenging. Leisure services cannot possibly satisfy everyone all the time. All that can be hoped is that whether public or private, leisure organisations should try to satisfy as many of those people as possible.

In order to sell leisure, the benefits need to be stressed. Some leisure activities undoubtedly come with a ready list of benefits, whether they be related to the health of the body or mind, a skill, or a social activity. Leisure marketing needs to tap into any degree of motivation that an individual may have to involve themselves in an activity. Packard (1965) wrote:

> The use of mass psychoanalysis to guide campaigns of persuasion has become the basis of a multimillion dollar industry. Professional persuaders have seized upon it in their groping for more effective ways to sell us their wares – whether products, ideas, attitudes, candidates, goals or states of mind.

Cheskin (1967) supported this view:

> Motivation research is the type of research that seeks to learn what motivates people

in making choices. It employs techniques designed to reach the unconscious or subconscious mind because preferences generally are determined by factors of which the individual is not conscious.

Cheskin, L., *The Secrets of Marketing Success*. Trident Press, 1967.
Drucker, P. F., *The Age of Discontinuity*. Harper & Row, 1969.
Horner, S. and Swarbrooke, J., *Leisure Marketing: A Global Perspective*. Butterworth Heinemann, 2004.
Morgan, M., *Marketing for Leisure and Tourism*. Pearson, 1996.
Packard, V., *The Hidden Persuaders*. Penguin, 1965.

Leisure studies

It is generally held that leisure studies does not have clearly defined boundaries and that over time the focus of leisure studies is on different topics and concepts. For some, leisure studies may incorporate physical activities, sports and tourism. Others may feel that it is more at home with media studies and social sciences, or even history and economics. Broadly, leisure studies looks at the experience of leisure and how it operates as a human activity. It can involve subjects as diverse as eating and body piercing, or visiting heritage sites and playing electronic computer games.

For some, leisure studies is more akin to the broader and equally ill defined cultural studies. Understandably there are ongoing academic disputes regarding areas of research and interest that impinge upon other areas of study, including the media, sociology, tourism, and recreation in the sports sense. Many students of leisure studies will discover that their own college or university has a distinct definition of what the institution considers to be leisure studies. It is often shaped by the personal interests of those running or teaching the programmes. Equally, the scope and extent may be shaped by commercial considerations, in order to attract students or to meet specific vocational requirements. Undoubtedly, leisure studies have a place within the broader social science family, including media studies, cultural studies, and sociology and sports studies. There are also aspects of psychology, business management and economics.

The key issue with leisure studies, as with many other dynamic areas of investigation, is that they are constantly changing, diversifying and changing focus. One thing that can almost certainly be said about leisure studies is that it is an expanding area of research. It is becoming embedded in government policy through negative reactions either to aspects such as the perceived undesirability of particular forms of **youth culture** or to leisure activities that impinge on the freedoms or peace of mind of others. Leisure has a currency in terms of moulding individuals to be in a position to interact in social situations, or to accept layers of cultural expectation. It is also significant in the study of the post-work period of an individual's lifecycle, where notwithstanding economic restrictions, individuals find themselves with more free time to devote to leisure activities, be they active or sedentary. Leisure studies is therefore a broad area of study; it is almost impossible to set parameters. It encompasses what we would automatically expect to find in terms of commercial leisure, but it also incorporates issues such as drugs, drink, anti-social behaviour and, above all, the development of tastes and trends in leisure participation and activity.

L

Roberts, Ken, *The Leisure Industries*. Palgrave Macmillan, 2004.
Rojek, C., *Leisure Theory: Principles and Practice*. Palgrave Macmillan, 2005.
Rojek, C., Shaw, S. and Veal, A., *A Handbook of Leisure Studies*. Palgrave Macmillan, 2006.

Leisure theory

Leisure theory seeks to explain the relationships among constructs based on empirical evidence. They should also be testable through further research. One criticism that is often levelled at theory is that it fails to address the practice of leisure, in other words, the devising and providing of programmes, products and services for those who require or demand leisure services. There is therefore a major difference between leisure theory and leisure practice. Leisure practice focuses on the knowledge, skills and abilities to provide services.

For those who suggest that there is a gulf between theory and practice, perhaps a more valuable approach is to consider a broader definition of theory. Many practitioners have their own tried and tested theories of delivering leisure services, but by theoretical standards they lack the scientific or academic rigour that could class them as a theory.

Leisure theory tries to ascertain the social influences that have a direct impact on the individual or the group in their experience of leisure. This assists us in understanding the meaning and value of leisure and, more broadly, socio-economic issues. These scientific theories strive to be value free. Sylvester (1995) wrote:

> It seems that modern reason, which insists on segregating facts and values, is disembodied, having no mind to tell researchers what should be done with what they know. Restricted by an epistemology that has been inhospitable, if not hostile, toward values, rational enquiry that limits itself to empirical science is too narrow for the morally relevant needs and interests of human beings.

Sylvester is arguing for a theory of reason that is rational and relevant, that can be empirical, interpretive and clinical, all at the same time.

Roberts, Ken, *The Leisure Industries*. Palgrave Macmillan, 2004.
Rojek, C., *Leisure Theory: Principles and Practice*. Palgrave Macmillan, 2005.
Rojek, C., Shaw, S. and Veal, A., *A Handbook of Leisure Studies*. Palgrave Macmillan, 2006.
Sylvester, C., 'Relevance and Rationality in Leisure Studies: a Plea for Good Reason', *Leisure Sciences*, 17 (1995), pp. 125–31.

L

Leisure travel

Leisure travel implies a degree of discretion, as it is dependent upon discretionary time, income and family life stage. Leisure travel, in terms of discretionary time, is time that is available away from work and from other obligations. 'Discretionary income' refers to funds that an individual has to spend as they please. This marks a difference between business travel and leisure travel, where the latter is discretionary whilst the former may be mandatory.

Life chances

The term 'life chances' can probably be attributed to the sociologist Max Weber (1864–1920). In using it he was referring to the specific material, cultural and political advantages or disadvantages that an individual may experience as a result of being a member of a particular class. In leisure terms, the key determinant related to life chances would certainly be issues such as income (economic divisions), cultural status or cultural differences, geographical location, race, occupation, gender and even accommodation. It presupposes that life chances are entirely dependent upon the availability of opportunity within an essentially capitalist society. In this, the inference is that an individual's life chances are entirely self-driven and that there is no societal safety net to ensure that minimum life chances are offered even to those whose economic resources are limited, or for whom other factors inhibit life chances.

Life course developmental perspective

This perspective takes the approach that an individual's leisure behaviour changes over time as the individual ages. The behaviour and preferences are linked to changes in tastes, disposition and political attitudes.

Essentially, this is a biological perspective, assuming that leisure behaviour has a direct link to the 'psycho-biological–maturational process' (Rapaport and Rapaport 1975). It is commonly held that there are three key phases in life course development, or stages of the lifecycle that have a direct impact on the way in which an individual approaches the concept of leisure and openly becomes involved in an activity or continues to take part in that activity, as can be seen in Table 6.

A life course perspective aims to offer a clear set of relationships between leisure practice, choice and age. However, there is considerable variation when elements such as religion, sub-culture, class, ethnicity and gender are brought into the equation. There is also the question of generations. Mannheim (1952) identified three elements in the formation of a generation:

- Location – the life chances of individuals in respect of their social values, beliefs, power and wealth.
- Actuality – how individuals orientate towards one another and whether there is a sense of collectivity and common destiny.
- Unity – whether there is a common approach or attitude toward particular socio-cultural conditions.

This seems to suggest an explanation as to why successive waves of youth subcultures are periodically replaced by new sub-cultures, as the individuals within the older sub-cultures enter new life stages. Many will abandon their sub-culture roots whilst only a handful will continue to hold the same views as they did in their youth. Thus, as individuals slide out of their sub-culture into a more mainstream view, their attitudes, life chances and leisure activities inevitably change.

Beck, U., *Risk Society*. Sage Publishing, 1992.

Hollands, R., *Friday Night, Saturday Night*. University of Newcastle, 1995.

Mannheim, K., 'The Problem of Generations', *Essays on the Sociology of Knowledge*. Routledge & Kegan Paul (1952), pp. 276–322.

L

Table 6 Phases in life course development

Life Stage	Explanation
Youth	Few social responsibilities, limited funds and dependent on families. Something of an experimental period, focusing on individualisation and beginning to adopt leisure activities, which will see them into adulthood. Hollands (1995) contended that the youth stage extends to the early thirties, reflecting the fact that both emotional and financial dependence on the family still continues. According to Roberts (1999) and Beck (1992), this is a period of risk and uncertainty.
Middle Age	Financial constraints inhibit leisure, as do new family commitments. Leisure tends to be home centred and is difficult to coordinate in terms of continued social activities. Leisure activities diversify toward the end of this period, dependent upon whether the individual still has a parental responsibility or not. There are considerable gender differences in take-up of leisure, dependent on household and work commitments. Those in higher paid work have more intensive and expensive periods of leisure activity.
Old Age	There is generally a decline in leisure involvement, particularly outside of the home. However, many leisure patterns have been cemented into the life of the individual. Where leisure activity tails off it is largely due to lower income and the loss of work-based social networks. There is more non-allocated time, however, and a new focus is on personal health management.

Rapaport, R. and Rapaport, R., *Leisure and the Family Lifecycle*. Routledge & Kegan Paul, 1975.

Roberts, K., *Leisure in Contemporary Society*. CABI Publishing, 1999.

Life satisfaction

Thirty years ago there were many researchers and students of what we now understand to be leisure studies who believed that a more appropriate term would be 'life satisfaction studies'. There are three key reasons why this is too narrow a description of the subject matter:

- Although the study focuses on how individuals allocate their own time and space and have a commitment to particular activities that give them an intrinsic interest, there are enormous inequalities, despite the fact that there has been a growth in leisure time and space, particularly in developed countries. Much of this has been born out of the fact that many low-paid and labour-intensive jobs are now carried out in developing countries.
- Inequality, even within developed countries, is still marked. There are huge health, generational, gender and ethnic inequalities, which shape life options and chances.
- Many leisure activities that involve a degree of free choice are actually opposed by society in general. Activities that are likely to satisfy individuals,

from drinking and smoking to other activities that are seen as being in some way non-beneficial to the individual or to society at large, are condemned.

Giddens, A., *Modernity and Self Identity*. Polity Press, 1991.

Giddens, A., *Runaway World: How Globalization is Reshaping our Lives*. Profile Books, 2002.

Lifelong learning

This is a very broad term and there is considerable debate about its precise meaning. As the phrase implies, the inference is that learning can take place not just in a traditional educational environment, but throughout life, at work and in different situations. As such, it would include, but not exclusively:

- Continuing education.
- Work-based learning (on-the-job training).
- Adult education.
- Personal learning environments (self-directed or online).
- Home schooling.

Lifelong learning has specific resonance, as it reflects the availability of technological means by which to deliver learning programmes and also reflects the fact that there have been major changes in the style of delivery and the needs of those in search of learning opportunities.

See also **continuing professional development (CPD).**

Field, John, *Lifelong Learning and the New Educational Order*. Trentham Books, 2006.

Lifestyle

Lifestyle or psychographic segmentation is a market research method which suggests that individuals have characteristics that are reflected in the products and services they buy. There are a wide variety of different lifestyle segmentation methodologies seeking to incorporate individuals' views and approaches to life which suggest the products and services that they may purchase. A typical example of lifestyle segmentation is the set of categories listed in Table 7.

Lifestyle research

Lifestyle research, or psychographic research, attempts to explain individuals' buying behaviour by analysing their attitudes, activities and opinions. Groups are categorised according to similarly held views and desires, which provide the researcher with clues as to how they will respond to particular products and services.

See also **lifestyle.**

Load factor

Load factor, or passenger load factor, is a measure of the amount of an airline's passenger carrying capacity that is being used. It is often presented as the number of passenger kilometres or miles that have been flown, as a percentage of seat kilometres or miles available. In effect it is a measure of capacity utilisation.

L

Table 7 Lifestyle segmentation

Category	Description
Mainstreamers	This is the largest group of individuals as they are said to account for around 40% of the population. They have a tendency to purchase branded products as opposed to supermarket or own-label brands.
Reformers	This is a smaller group, but a significant one in terms of demanding changes in the products and services offered. As they are largely responsible for the purchases of supermarket brands and environmentally friendly items, they have driven many markets into providing substitute or replacement brands to accommodate their needs.
Aspirers	Aspirers are typified as being younger consumers who are ambitious and wish to be the first to own new designs or the latest version of a product or service.
Succeeders	These are individuals who consider products on the basis of them fitting into their general view of the world. They do not seek brands which are status symbols, but require reliability and usefulness.

More broadly, 'load factor' can also be applied to any form of leisure facility. The facility would calculate the maximum possible capacity and then compare it with the actual use of that facility, to work out the usage percentage. In effect, this is an efficiency measure, but it does not incorporate any other factors, such as pricing or profitability.

Long haul

'Long haul' is a travel-based term and generally refers to extended travel time, usually on an aircraft. There are numerous definitions as to the precise point at which a short haul flight becomes a long haul flight, but usually this is taken to mean a flight in excess of four to five hours.

Look-to-book ratio

Look-to-book is a conversion rate, which can be applied across the whole of the travel, tourism and leisure industries. Essentially, it is a key ratio that illustrates the percentage of individuals who actually make a firm booking as a result of seeing or reading a brochure, pamphlet, poster or website and any other type of advertisement. On websites, for example, the look-to-book ratio is the number of transactions that were actually generated from the searches for products or services on that website. The lower the look-to-book ratio, then, the higher the success rate is considered to be. Package holidays tend to have the highest look-to-book ratio, as they are high-value items. Customers are likely to look at multiple sources. Flight-only tends to have a lower look-to-book ratio.

Loyalty programmes

Loyalty programmes have become an integral part of marketing and are characterised as being differentiated treatment towards existing customers, or those who purchase from the business on a regular basis. Loyalty programmes have become increasingly popular over the last few years, and aim to build a lasting relationship between consumers and the business. There is, however, considerable confusion over the definition and measurement of loyalty, and indeed the value of loyalty programmes. From an attitudinal perspective, loyalty programmes aim to establish an attachment to a business, brand, product or service. Behaviourally, loyal behaviour is typified by repeat purchases and recommendation. At the centre of all loyalty programmes is the desire to reduce the churn rate (see **churning**). But, underpinning this, regardless of any incentives offered, the business needs to assure the consumer that they are receiving a level of service far superior to that of the competitors. Unfortunately for businesses who had pioneered customer loyalty programmes, the concept has become more of an expectation than an additional incentive. Most businesses competing in the same market will offer, on the face of it, very similar customer loyalty programmes. The businesses are trapped into continuing to provide the customer loyalty programme on the basis that although its continuation does not yield any advantage, it offers considerable disadvantages if it is terminated.

There have been various attempts to frame a model of effective loyalty programmes. In essence, most recognise three key aspects or propositions, which are:

1 The level of competition in most markets and a business's need to collect, collate and analyse their customers' data to create customer profiles has led to the development of customer loyalty programmes.
2 The effectiveness of a customer loyalty programme is dependent upon the structure of the market.
3 The use, validity and application of information derived from customer loyalty programmes have to provide tangible results and policies. This is typified by businesses being able to differentiate their products, and aspects of the programme, and to show flexibility in order to cater for customers' differing preferences.

L

Macro-environment

The term 'macro-environment' refers to all of the external activities or influences which may affect the operations of a business or organisation. Some do not have a direct impact, but may influence how the business operates over a period of time. In the vast majority of cases organisations have little or no possibility of affecting these macro-environmental factors. Typically the macro-environment would include society in general, politics, economics, socio-political change, technology or socio-cultural changes and trends.

Most businesses develop a means by which they can assess, or analyse, the macro-environment and identify strategic issues which may have an impact upon their operations. Typically this would include:

- An identification of the principal phenomena that will have an impact on the organisation.
- A determination of the trends of each of those phenomena.
- Classification of the phenomena in terms of opportunities or threats.
- An evaluation of the phenomena in terms of their importance as opportunities or threats.

Once the opportunities and threats have been prioritised, the organisation can then identify the strategic impacts upon the business.

Management, approaches to

Management gurus are individuals who, for a limited period of time, galvanise management thinking and are the darlings of the lecture circuit. Management gurus do not, necessarily, offer a complete solution to management thinking, but attempts are always made to apply their theories, or in some cases their business practices (such as those of Branson, Prahalad and Gates), to a more holistic approach.

It is difficult to be precise regarding the general thrust of particular management theorists in terms of their adherence to specific management schools. Some theories can be attributed to a scientific approach, whilst others adopt a bureaucratic or administrative stance.

Whilst management gurus come and go, their promotion, exposure and study is variable, but one such attempt to categorise and quantify their impact is made by www.thinkers50.com. The website ranks the top fifty living management gurus; hence many of the management gurus from the past, such as F. W. Taylor and Elton Mayo, and recently deceased gurus such as Igor Ansoff, are not included. The latest list available covers 2003:

1 Peter Drucker – born in Austria, worked as a journalist in London and then moved to the US. His first book, *Concept of the Corporation* (1946), was a major study of General Motors. He has written 29 books, notably, *The Practice of Management* (1954) and *Management: Tasks, Responsibilities, Practices* (1973). His latest contributions include *Management Challenges for the 21st Century* (1999) and *Peter Drucker on the Profession of Management* (1998).

2 Michael Porter – born in 1947, he became Harvard's youngest professor. His Five Forces theory remains a solid part of all undergraduate and graduate business courses. Porter's main books include *Competitive Strategy: Techniques for Analyzing Industries and Competitors* (1980); *Competitive Advantage* (1985); *The Competitive Advantage of Nations* (1990); and *Can Japan Compete?* (2000).

3 Tom Peters – born in 1942 and is considered to be the first of the modern gurus, primarily through his two books *In Search of Excellence* (1982) and *Liberation Management* (1992). Critics claim that his theories are simply rhetoric, because as a businessman Peters has failed to make his mark.

4 Gary Hamel – born in 1954, is the co-author (with C. K. Prahalad) of *Competing for the Future* (1996) and *Leading the Revolution* (2000). He is a visiting professor at Harvard Business School and London Business School and runs a multidisciplinary management consultancy.

5 Charles Handy – born 1932; his first book, *Understanding Organizations* (1976), developed the concept of the shamrock organisation. His latest book is *The New Alchemists: How Visionary People Make Something Out of Nothing* (1999).

6 Philip Kotler – born 1931, is the lead writer on the classic marketing textbook *Marketing Management: Analysis, Planning, Implementation, and Control* (eleven editions). In his latest book *Marketing Moves: A New Approach to Profits, Growth & Renewal* (2002), he explores 'holistic marketing'.

7 Henry Mintzberg – his first book was *The Nature of Managerial Work* (1973), which examined the nature of managerial work. Arguably, in later books Mintzberg has set the agenda as far as the study and practice of strategic management is concerned.

8 Jack Welch – born 1935, is the former CEO and chairman of General Electric and was instrumental in making the business the second most profitable in the world. Now a consultant.

9 Rosabeth Moss Kanter – a Harvard Business School professor with a sociology background. Kanter takes a more humanistic view of business than many other gurus. Latest books include *Common Interest, Common Good: Creating Value through Business and Social Sector Partnerships* (1999) and *E-volve!* (2001).

10 Jim Collins – perhaps best known for his influential book *Built To Last: Successful Habits of Visionary Companies* (1994); his most recent bestseller is *Good To Great: Why Some Companies Make the Leap . . . And Others Don't* (2001).

11 Sumantra Ghoshal – Founding Dean of the new Indian School of Business. Working with Christopher Bartlett, he has written *Managing Across Borders: The Transnational Solution* (1988); *Transnational Management* (1990); *Organization Theory and the Multinational Corporation* (1993); and *The Individualized Corporation* (1997).

12 C. K. Prahalad – born in 1941, writes extensively with Gary Hamel for the Harvard Business Review as well as best-sellers including *Competing for the Future: Breakthrough Strategies for Seizing Control of Your Industry and Creating the Markets of Tomorrow* (1994). Primarily interested in strategic management.

13 Warren Bennis – born 1925, was a protégé of Douglas McGregor, leading to his first major book *The Temporary Society* (1968). In a number of subsequent titles, he has written extensively on the nature of leadership.

14 Peter Senge – born 1947, is best known for his work on the Fifth Discipline (learning). *The Fifth Discipline* (1990) was his first major success; since then he has written *The Fifth Discipline Fieldbook: Strategies and Tools for Building a Learning Organization* (1994), *Schools That Learn* (2000) and *The Dance of Change* (1999).

15 Robert Kaplan and David Norton – this writing team created the Balanced Scorecard; they have extended and applied its use in their latest book *The Strategy-Focused Organization: How Balanced Scorecard Companies Thrive in the New Business Environment* (2000).

16 Stephen Covey – his book *7 Habits of Highly Effective People* (1989) was an international best-seller for over five years. Covey runs a highly successful and influential training company.

17 Edgar H. Schein – born in 1928, another protégé of Douglas McGregor. His initial work culminated in the publication of *Organizational Culture and Leadership* (1985). He returned to the subject of organisational culture in 1999 with *The Corporate Culture Survival Guide: Sense and Nonsense about Corporate Culture*.

18 Chris Argyris – highly influential in the area of the 'learning organisation', his key titles include *Personality and Organization* (1957) and *Organizational Learning* (1978). His latest book is *Management Trap: How Managers Can Know When They're Getting Good Advice and When They're Not* (1999).

19 Kenichi Ohmae – born 1943, is a highly respected Japanese guru. He is a strategic thinker and has written, amongst others, *The Invisible Continent: 4 Strategic Imperatives of the New Economy* (2000) and *The Emergence of the United States of Chunghwa* (2003).

20 Bill Gates – born 1955, Harvard drop-out and arguably the most successful businessman alive. Runs the Microsoft computer software giant.

Other notables in the listing are: Kjell Nordstrom and Jonas Ridderstrale; Clayton Christensen; John Kotter; Nicholas Negroponte; Jim Champy; Andy Grove; Scott Adams; Richard Pascale; Daniel Goleman; Naomi Klein; Chan Kim and Renée Mauborgne; Don Tapscott; Michael Dell; Richard Branson; Edward De Bono; Ricardo Semler; Thomas A. Stewart; Geoffrey Moore; Jeff Bezos; Paul Krugman; Lynda Gratton; Alan Greenspan; Manfred Kets De Vries; Robert Waterman; Watts Wacker; Patrick Dixon; Geert Hofstede; Don Peppers; Stan Davis and Fons Trompenaars.

Clearly, any top fifty or attempt to rank the management gurus only offers a snapshot of the range and scope of the thinkers. The Thinkers 50 ranking adopts a pragmatic approach, grading the management gurus on the following criteria:

- Their originality of ideas.
- The practical use of their ideas.
- Presentation of the ideas.
- Their writing ability.
- Their following, in terms of those applying the ideas in the real world.
- Whether the gurus put their own ideas into practice.
- The international flavour of their ideas.
- How well researched their ideas are.
- The impact their ideas have had on business.

The Thinkers 50 website is www.thinkers50.com

Other links to management guru coverage include:

www.pfdf.org (the Peter Drucker Foundation for Non-profit Management – which has a range of notes and articles).
www.business2.com (covers 30 or so management gurus and rates them by the Star Power and Big Ideas.
www.derekstockley.com.au/guru.html (an Australian-based link and resource site for 50 management gurus).
www.sosig.ac.uk (a useful general search site known as the Social Science Information Gateway).
www.gurusonline.tv/uk/index_uk.asp (a large guru-interview and link site also available in Portuguese and Spanish).

Management information system (MIS)

A management information system, or MIS, is a computer application which is used to record, store and process information which can be used to assist management decision-making. Generally a business will have a single integrated MIS into which data from various functional areas of the business is fed and to which senior management has access.

There are two additional sub-types of MIS which are decision support systems and executive information systems. A decision support system also collects, stores and processes information accessible by management. They contain data on the business's operational activities and allow managers to manipulate and retrieve data using modelling techniques to examine the results of various different courses of action. An executive information system (EIS) provides similar facilities for senior management, combining internal information along with external data. It is used to support strategic decision-making and presents the information in a variety of formats, primarily aimed at enabling the users to identify trends.

Laudon, Kenneth C. and Laudon, Jane P., *Management Information Systems.* Prentice Hall, 2003.

Manifest

'Manifest' is a term that is used to describe a passenger list, either on a commercial flight or on a vessel. It is also used in the broader transport industry as another term for packing list.

Market

'Market' is a generic term which is used to describe a group of potential customers who have similar needs. These potential customers are willing to purchase various products and services in order to satisfy their needs. The term 'market' can be used to describe both consumers and other businesses, either as specific segments or as target audiences, whether they are part of a population in a given country, or more widely spread across the world. The term can equally be applied, therefore, to UK home owners and to airline operators – both are markets; one is focused primarily in a single country, with specific criteria; the other is a more global target, which includes operators, large and small, often located in other countries.

Market demand

The coordination and control of finances is vital. But many businesses' cash flow forecasts and budgets are inaccurate and at times unrealistic. They may have little idea about the likely changes in demand, or whether the prices charged by suppliers or the prices expected by customers are static or volatile.

A change in demand can radically affect cash flow, it can undermine budgets and it can mean the difference between profit and loss. Costs can be notoriously difficult to control at the early stages of a start-up business, or for that matter for even the largest companies as is demonstrated by the collapse of companies such as XL Leisure. Many factors can affect demand, many of which cannot necessarily be anticipated by business, as can be seen in Table 8.

Sutherland, J. and Canwell, D., *Essential Business Studies*. Folens, 2008.

Market follower

A market follower is a business that does not necessarily wish to challenge the **market leader**. They may consider that they have more to lose than they have to gain by tackling the market leader head on. Market leaders, in any case, will bear the highest costs in terms of research and development, as well as advertising and the time it takes to build up demand for a product or service. Market followers wish to avoid these costs and the impact they may have on their profits. Market followers are typified by providing copies, or in many cases improvements, to an original product offered by a market leader. They need to have the capacity to be able to produce new products and services which match the market leader's offerings as soon as is practicable.

Market followers are never likely to overtake the market leader, but they do enjoy high profits because of their lower development costs. Most market followers also replicate the way in which the market leader does business, and position their products in a very similar manner.

Market forecast

A market forecast is a key component of analysing a market. It aims to project future numbers, characteristics and trends in a **target market**. It should show the projected number of potential customers in their segments. It is important to remember that these numbers are only ever estimates and at best an educated

Table 8

Factor	Implications
Price	Price does tend to affect demand, even if it is a change in price of products or services that customers need to consume, such as electricity or gas. The effect of a price increase in these areas simply means that the customer has less to spend elsewhere. Price changes can mean customers switch brands and look for close substitutes. Complementary goods can also be affected by price changes in the main product. If car prices increased there could well be a fall in the demand for petrol and diesel as there might be less cars on the road.
Income	Most small businesses are interested in their share of customers' disposable income. The disposable income is dependent on mortgage or rent payments, council tax, pay rises and whether the customer has been made redundant, is on sick pay or has been injured.
Taste, fashions and customs	Fashion and music are just two examples of volatile markets that change almost weekly. The latest available products and services need to be made available by new businesses and they need to be aware of not overstocking on fashionable products, the demand for which may suddenly disappear.
Population change	The balance and makeup of the population of any area are constantly changing; the age distribution can affect demand, as can the ethnic background, race and culture of an area. Other population characteristics, such as a tourist town needing a wide range of catering facilities and cheap accommodation, also have an effect.
Lifestyle change	One major lifestyle change is the number of women in work, which has changed the patterns of demand, as are the facts that many more people own their own home and that most people now take at least one holiday a year.
Promotion and unique selling points (USP)	It is difficult for new businesses to show that their products or services are different or better than their competitors'. Customers look for products and services that satisfy their needs and a business needs to ensure that it can predict what customers may want, the quantity they will want and when they will want it.
Advertising	Advertising can have an impact on demand, but people are still unlikely to buy things that they do not need. Advertising can be effective in helping to launch a new business, showing customers they have a wider choice.
Law	There are laws that limit the age at which alcohol, cigarettes, car driving and a host of other activities and factors are legal. Equally the ban on smoking in the workplace and in pubs and restaurants has led to a drop in demand, as more people opt for a night in rather than a night out.

M

guess. The figures are based on estimated populations of target users in a given area and then incorporate annual growth rates. A business would look at not only the market size but also the market value. They would try to identify customers who are likely to spend more than others and specifically target them and incorporate them into their forecast. The market forecast should deliver the average purchase per customer and the market value. The average purchase per customer is again an educated guess, but based on experience. Usually the management of the organisation will meet to come up with the estimate. This would ideally be linked to some kind of external source of information. The market value is then simple mathematics. The number of potential customers in the market is multiplied by the average purchase per customer. Each segment can be calculated separately and the forecast is usually calculated over a one- to five-year period. It is then possible to calculate the full market value and provide the business with the forecast. Much of the forecast, however, is subjective and an organisation always needs to try to check the reality of the figures, ideally by comparing sales with those of likely competitors if this information is available.

Macro-economic data should also help to confirm the size of markets compared with other markets that have similar characteristics. The market forecast will allow the organisation to develop its strategic market focus, which means targeting key markets. This will enable the organisation to focus on segmentation and the positioning of the leisure products and services that they offer. Each of the target segments will have inherent differences, keys to success, and may offer the organisation a competitive advantage, but it may expose some weaknesses in what the organisation is capable of achieving.

Market Leader

Market leaders are businesses which have the largest **market share** in a given **market**. Market leaders usually determine prices, promotional strategies and intensities and are also deeply involved in new product development. Market leaders are, in effect, a **benchmark** for all other competitors who may choose to challenge them, avoid them or simply imitate them. In all respects a market leader is recognised as such by its competitors, as being the dominant force in that market.

In most markets market leaders are constantly under pressure from market challengers who seek different strategies to wrestle leadership. Market leaders tend to protect their market share in three main ways (see Table 9).

Being a market leader usually means that the business does enjoy a higher than average return on investment. It has been calculated that businesses with a market share exceeding 40% have an average return on investment of 30%. This is compared with businesses with a market share of less than 10%, who only enjoy a return on investment of around 10%. It is usually the case that the following assumptions can be made regarding a market leader:

Superior quality/new product development = market leader = premium pricing = higher profit

Harari, Oren, *Leapfrogging the Competition: Five Giant Steps to Becoming a Market Leader.* Prima Games, 1999.

Table 9 Protecting market share

Market Leader's Strategy	Description
Expand total demand	A market leader may choose to target new users in allied markets, perhaps by identifying new uses for the product. Another notable tactic is to encourage the rate of usage by existing customers by running sales promotion campaigns.
Protect and defend market share	This tactic, although defensive in its outlook, incorporates the aggressive use of promotion, distribution and new product development in order to ensure that customers remain aware of the fact that the business is the market leader. All other competitors must try to match the strength of the market leader, but usually have little hope of being able to catch up.
Increase market same share	It should be noted that market share and profitability are not the same issues and it may not be the market leader's short-term goal to increase profitability. Market leaders will use new product development, advertising, pricing strategies, distribution incentives, mergers and take-overs, as well as expansion overseas in order to increase their market share.

Market nicher

'Market nicher' is a term which describes a specialist supplier. Niche markets are, by their very definition, comparatively small compared with mass markets. Many niche markets, however, offer the potential for high growth and many are, in themselves, sufficiently large for a number of businesses to be attracted.

A market nicher will usually look for a market which is sufficient in size, with the potential for growth and profitability, but which is not currently receiving very much interest from potential competitors. The market nicher, with its specialist skills and resources, can serve the niche market and defend itself by building up strong customer loyalty.

Market nichers are usually relatively small businesses with limited resources. Alternatively, they may be parts of larger organisations which have been tempted into the market by the prospect of high profits and low competition. This is, in fact, a way in which market challengers can gradually build up sufficient resources in order to make a challenge on a market leader.

Market nichers differentiate their products and services by their level of service, quality, rarity of offering and price. Many successful market nichers are able to develop their niche markets, and their associated products and services, sufficiently to bring them into the mass market. A prime example of this is The Body Shop, which successfully operated as a market nicher for a number of years before entering the mass market, whereupon it encountered, for the first time, a number of **market leaders** and potential challengers.

Sander, Peter and Basye Sander, Jennifer, *Niche and Grow Rich: Practical Ways of Turning your Ideas into a Business*. Entrepreneur Press, 2003.

M

Market orientation

Market orientation is an underlying marketing corporate philosophy. It is based on the creation, dissemination and use of market intelligence derived from market research. Integral to market orientation is the satisfying of customer needs and wants.

A market-orientated business will continually try to improve its position in a given market by carrying our market research. It will also attempt to be better placed to initiate proactive marketing, with the sole intention of meeting customer needs more efficiently than its competitors. There is a strong correlation between market orientation and the performance of a business.

Jaworski, Bernard J. and Kohli, Ajay K., 'Market Orientation: Antecedents and Consequences', *Journal of Marketing*, 57:3 (1993), pp. 53-70.

Kohli, Ajay K. and Jaworski, Bernard J., 'Market Orientation: The Construct, Research Propositions, and Managerial Implications', *Journal of Marketing*, 54:2 (1990), pp. 1–18.

Market segmentation

Market segmentation involves the identification of specific **target markets** for broader based products and services, in order to enable a business to develop a suitable **marketing mix** for each of their target segments.

Market segmentation probably came into existence in the 1950s when product differentiation was a primary marketing strategy. By the 1970s, however, market segmentation had begun to be seen as a means of increasing sales and obtaining a competitive advantage. In recent years more sophisticated techniques are being developed to reach potential buyers in ever-more specific target markets.

Businesses will tend to segment the market for the following reasons:

- To make marketing easier in the sense that segmentation allows the business to address the needs of smaller groups of customers which have the same characteristics.
- To find niches, typically non-served or under-served markets, and be able to target these buyers in a less competitive environment.
- To increase efficiency in being able to directly apply resources towards the best segments, which have been identified by the business.

There are some common rules regarding market segmentation which determine whether the identified segments are significant enough or measurable. These are listed in Table 10.

In effect, there are two ways of segmenting a market. These are known as either *a priori* or *post hoc*. These two approaches are typified in the following manner:

- *A priori* is effectively based on a mixture of intuition, use of secondary data and analysis of existing customer database information. *A priori* segmentation takes place without the benefit of primary market research and may well produce relatively simplistic segmentation, such as male or female, young or old, regional segments, or buyers and non-buyers.

Table 10   Market segmentation rules

Segmentation Criteria	Description
Size	The market itself needs to be large enough to warrant segmentation. Once a market has been segmented, it may be revealed that each of the segments is too small to consider.
Differentiated	There must be measurable differences between the members of the segment and the market in general.
Responsiveness	Having segmented the market, marketing communications need to be developed to address the needs of that segment. If a business cannot develop marketing communications which can contact this segment and have an impact upon it, there is little value in knowing about the segment in the first place.
Reachable	Marketing communications need to be able to get through to the segment in order to be effective. There may well be a single best advertising medium or promotional device which can reach the segment and tell them the business's message.
Interested	Having established what benefits the segment is looking for, the business needs to be assured that this is precisely what the potential customers require and that the product or service matches these needs.
Profitable	A decision needs to be reached as to whether it is cost effective to reach these segments, considering the cost which may be incurred in running multiple marketing programmes alongside one another. Existing products or services may need to be redesigned in order to match the specific needs of the segment.

- *Post hoc* segmentation uses primary market research to classify and describe individuals within the target market, but segments are not defined themselves until after the collection and analysis period. The definition of each segment requires the placing of all members of the target market into specific segments.

There are a number of different types of information which are used extensively in market segmentation. These can be best described by category as in Table 11.

McDonald, Malcolm and Dunbar, Ian, *Market Segmentation*. Macmillan, 1998.
Wedel, Michel and Kamakura, Wagner A., *Market Segmentation: Conceptual and Methodological Foundations*. Kluwer Academic, 1999.

M

Market share

Sales figures do not necessarily indicate how a business is performing relative to its competitors. Changes in sales may simply reflect changes in the market size or changes in economic conditions. The business's performance relative to competitors can be measured by the proportion of the market that the firm is able to

Table 11 Market segmentation

Measured Variable	Description
Classification	Broadly speaking, classification actually encompasses the demographic, geographic, psychographic and behavioural. It requires a system of classifying individuals and placing them into segments by using a mixture of these variables.
Demographic	Demographic features are age, gender, income, ethnicity, marital status, education, occupation, household size, type of residence and length of residence, amongst many other demographically based measures.
Geographic	This broad range of variables includes population density, climate, zip or postcode, city, state or county, region or metropolitan/rural area.
Psychographic	Another broad range of variables, which include attitudes, hobbies, leadership traits, lifestyle, magazines and newspapers read, personality traits, risk aversion and television or radio programmes watched or listened to.
Behavioural	These variables encompass the current ways in which the target market views, buys and responds to products, services and marketing. The category includes brand loyalty, benefits sought, distribution channels used and level of usage.
Descriptor	Descriptor variables actually describe each segment in order to distinguish it from other groups. The descriptors need to be measurable and are usually derived solely from primary research, rather than secondary sources of information. Descriptors will typically explain in shorthand the key characteristics of each segment and the members of that segment, so that these characteristics can more readily be exploited by subtle changes in the marketing mix. A descriptor variable may be featured as aged under 30, single, urban dweller, rented accommodation, medium to high income, etc.

M

capture. This proportion is referred to as the business's market share and is calculated as follows:

Market Share = Business's Sales/Total Market Sales

Sales may be determined on a value basis (sales price multiplied by volume) or on a unit basis (number of units shipped or number of customers served).

While the business's own sales figures are readily available, total market sales are more difficult to determine. Usually, this information is available from trade associations and market research firms.

Market share is often associated with profitability and thus many businesses seek to increase their sales relative to competitors. Businesses may seek to increase their market share in the following ways:

- Economies of scale – higher volume can be instrumental in developing a cost advantage.

- Sales growth in a stagnant industry – when the industry is not growing, the business still can increase its sales by increasing its market share.
- Reputation – market leaders have the power, which they can use to their advantage.
- Increased bargaining power – a larger market share gives an advantage in negotiations with suppliers and channel members.

The market share of a product can be modelled as:

Share of Market = Share of Preference × Share of Voice × Share of Distribution

According to this model, there are three drivers of market share:

- Share of preference – can be increased through product, pricing, and promotional changes.
- Share of voice – the business's proportion of total promotional expenditures in the market. Thus, share of voice can be increased by increasing advertising expenditures.
- Share of distribution – can be increased through more intensive distribution.

From these drivers market share can be increased by changing the variables of the **marketing mix**.

- Product – the product attributes can be changed to provide more value to the customer, for example, by improving product quality.
- Price – if the price elasticity of demand is elastic, a decrease in price will increase sales revenue. This tactic may not succeed if competitors are willing and able to meet any price cuts.
- Distribution – adding new distribution channels or increasing the intensity of distribution in each channel.
- Promotion – increasing advertising expenditures can increase market share, unless competitors respond with similar increases.

Miniter, Richard, *The Myth of Market Share*. Nicholas Brealey, 2002.

Marketing mix

The major marketing management decisions can be classified in one of the following four categories:

- Product
- Price
- Place (distribution)
- Promotion

These variables are known as the 'marketing mix' or the '4 Ps of marketing'. They are the variables that marketing managers can control in order to best satisfy customers in the target market. The marketing mix is portrayed in the diagram in Figure 4.

The business attempts to generate a positive response in the target market by blending these four marketing mix variables in an optimal manner.

- Product – The product is the physical product or service offered to the

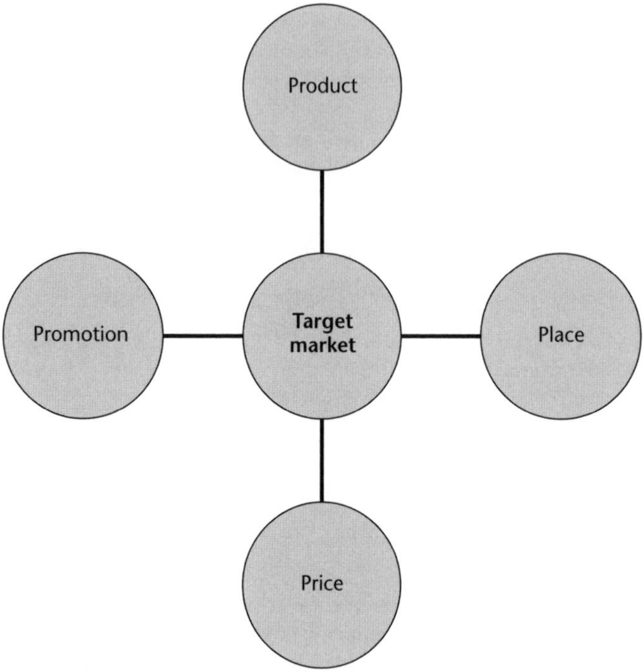

Figure 4 The marketing mix

consumer. In the case of physical products, it also refers to any services or conveniences that are part of the offering. Product decisions include aspects such as function, appearance, packaging, service, warranty, etc.

- Price – Pricing decisions should take into account profit margins and the probable pricing response of competitors. Pricing includes not only the list price, but also discounts, financing, and other options such as leasing.
- Place – Place (or placement) decisions are those associated with channels of distribution that serve as the means for getting the product to the target customers. The distribution system performs transactional, logistical, and facilitating functions. Distribution decisions include market coverage, channel member selection, logistics, and levels of service.
- Promotion – Promotion decisions are those related to communicating and selling to potential consumers. Since these costs can be large in proportion to the product price, a **breakeven analysis** should be performed when making promotion decisions. It is useful to know the value of a customer in order to determine whether additional customers are worth the cost of acquiring them. Promotion decisions involve advertising, public relations, media types, etc.

Table 12 summarises the marketing mix decisions, including a list of some of the aspects of each of the 4Ps.

M

Table 12   Marketing mix decisions

Product	Price	Place	Promotion
Functionality	List price	Channel members	Advertising
Appearance	Discounts	Channel motivation	Personal selling
Quality	Allowances	Market coverage	Public relations
Packaging	Financing	Locations	Message
Brand	Leasing options	Logistics	Media
Warranty		Service levels	Budget
Service/Support			

Marketing plan

A marketing plan is a detailed document which aims to itemise and quantify actions that need to be taken in order to pursue **marketing strategies**. The components of a full marketing plan are:

- Executive/management summary or overview.
- Objectives, including the business's mission statement, stated objectives and product or product group goals.
- Product or market background, detailing the product range, sales summaries and market overview.
- Situation or **SWOT analysis**, showing the performance of current **marketing strategies**, and opportunities and threats, along with necessary analysis.
- Marketing analysis, detailing the marketing environment, trends, customer requirements, segments and competitor analysis.
- Marketing strategies, identifying the core **target markets** or segments, any of the business's advantages, and statements on product and brand positioning strategies.
- Sales forecasts and results, an estimate of the presumed sales figures, incorporating an analysis of the impact of the proposed marketing strategies.
- Marketing programmes, which detail the marketing mixes, tasks and responsibilities.
- Monitoring of performance, which details the controls and examines the evaluation methods.
- Financial implications, detailing the budgets, costs and apportionment, and expected returns on investment.
- Operational considerations, featuring communications and research, development and production needs.
- Appendices, various inclusions, but usually SWOT analysis, background data and market research findings.

The marketing plan has an associated cycle of development:

1 The development or revision of marketing objectives (relative to performance), which reappraises the current marketing objectives.

M

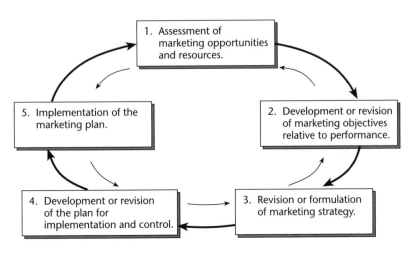

Figure 5 Marketing planning cycle

2 Assessment of marketing opportunities and resources, which assesses existing or possible opportunities and whether financial resources are available to exploit them.

3 Revision/formation of marketing strategy – a revision, amendment or total rewrite of marketing strategies.

4 Development/revision of plan for implementation and control, the creation of control systems or the review or improvement of existing ones to allow effective reports on progress.

5 Implementation of marketing plan.

In this marketing planning cycle it is important to note that this is a continuous process, with the stages being influenced in both a clockwise and an anti-clockwise manner (see Figure 5). For example, the development of a revised plan (4) would lead to the implementation of the plan (5). Conversely, in the implementation stage, issues may arise that require further development or revision.

Canwell, Diane, *Marketing Campaigns*. International Thomson Publishing, 1998.
Westwood, John, *How to write a Marketing Plan*. Kogan Page, 2000.

Marketing research

Marketing research attempts to adopt a scientific approach to building a clear picture of customers, the market and the competition and latterly it has been extended as an investigation into the wider environment in which the business operates.

Marketing research aims, in a systematic manner using reliable and unbiased questions, to discover ideas and intentions, as well as trends, which may affect a business, its markets and its customers. Marketing research processes data, analyses the data and interprets the facts and is employed extensively in marketing management to help plan, evaluate and control marketing strategy and tactics.

Marketing research is often confused with market research, which has a considerably narrower definition. For the most part, market research simply refers to consumer surveys, normally questionnaires, carried out face-to-face or over the telephone. Marketing research, therefore, can be seen as a broader church in terms of information gathering, collation and analysis.

Marketing research must provide information to a business to help them understand their situation more clearly. In other words, it needs to have a real value. The value, of course, is based on a number of different determinants, which include the following:

- The business should be willing and able to act on the information received from marketing research, no matter what its conclusions may be.
- The researchers and the business need to be assured that the information which has been gathered is accurate.
- The business needs to recognise that they would probably be indecisive without the benefit of the marketing research information.
- The business also needs to be clear that whilst accepting the validity of the information gathered, there may be a degree of variation or a margin of error.
- The business can also recognise that accurate and pertinent marketing research can reduce risk.
- The business needs to be cognisant that competitors may well react on the basis of decisions made by the business arising out of their marketing research.
- Marketing research needs to be cost effective, in terms of both money and time. Any marketing research must be up-to-date, otherwise its value is limited, therefore any marketing research programme has to have a definite purpose and deadline.

The majority of marketing research projects are typified by following a clear series of tasks. These are:

1 Define the problem.
2 Determine the research design.
3 Identify data types and sources.
4 Design data-collection forms and questionnaires.
5 Determine sample plan and size.
6 Collect the data.
7 Analyse and interpret the data.
8 Prepare the research report.

Birks, David and Malhotra, Naresh, *Marketing Research: An Applied Approach*. Financial Times, Prentice Hall, 2002.

Marketing strategies

The term 'marketing strategies' refers to specific processes adopted by the marketing function of a business in order to achieve specific goals or objectives.

Marketing strategy also encompasses the deployment of a business's resources in order to develop and maintain the business's market opportunities. At the core, marketing strategies seek to deploy a **marketing mix** in the most effective manner, not only to achieve the business's goals and objectives, but also to satisfy the customers' needs and wants.

> Fill, Chris, *Marketing Communications: Contexts, Strategies and Applications*. Financial Times, Prentice Hall, 2001.

Maslow, Abraham
See **hierarchy of needs.**

Mass marketing
Mass marketing is typified by a product- or production-orientated business which uses shotgun marketing tactics, rather than more precise targeted activities. Mass marketing is, to all intents and purposes, a blanket approach to all forms of marketing. The business does not differentiate between its different customer groups; it has ignored segmentation and does not consider it worthwhile to specifically address each individual market segment.

Mass marketing is best described as a business which chooses to use the same balance of the **marketing mix** in all situations.

> Tedlow, Richard S., *New and Improved: The Story of Mass Marketing in America*. Butterworth-Heinemann, 1990.

McDonaldisation
'McDonaldisation' originally referred to the technological advances in the preserving and storing of foodstuffs and to the growing ownership of automobiles during the 1950s, coupled with the development of US suburbs which transformed the way in which Americans shopped and ate. The larger supermarkets in the US succeeded in overwhelming many smaller and longer established businesses; a trend which has been replicated in many other countries. The emphasis of service had moved from quality to price and efficiency. The key characteristics of McDonaldisation are:

M

- Efficiency – in as much as consumers can obtain what they need very quickly, with very little effort on behalf of the business. The employees can perform their tasks more easily and, above all, quicker, thus serving customers more efficiently. Coupled with this increase in efficiency, the quality aspects reduce, particularly given the fact that technologies which do not require the input of humans perform many of the tasks.
- Control – McDonaldisation radically changed both the way in which employees were treated and expected to behave and the way in which customers were expected to interact with the business. For very much the first time customers queued up at a cash register to collect their food, and cleared tables after they had finished eating.
- Predictability – was important as consumers knew exactly what they were purchasing, as to all intents and purposes, the product was identical no matter which store or outlet the customers visited. This meant that

McDonaldised businesses could more easily sell their business as a **franchise** operation.

- Calculability – there should be a quantifiable objective, such as sales, rather than a subjective goal. As far as a business is concerned this means delivering a high level of product to the customer. It also means that customers can quantify how much of the product they are receiving for the price they are paying. These two aspects are closely linked, as it is the organisation's intention to deliver a large amount of product for a reasonable cost. As far as employees are concerned, they are judged on how fast they deliver the product, rather than the quality of work that they achieve.

McDonaldisation has spread across the globe, not simply in the retailing of hamburgers and related products. The concept now revolves around the idea that the consumer can purchase standardised items at relatively low prices and that the quality of that product does not differ significantly in the various outlets scattered around the world. Given that there is a far great availability of products and services on the global market, McDonaldisation is said to have been an integral part of making these goods available to larger proportions of the population. Consumers, by purchasing standardised products, are able to obtain what they perceive they need without very much delay. Convenience and uniform quality has competed well against other economic alternatives, notably higher priced customised products and services. In settling for standardised products, individuals in different countries around the world can now afford products and services which hitherto they could not afford.

McDonaldisation has been seen to be an ideal solution in providing faster, efficient products and services to a working population which has considerably less free time than in the past. McDonaldised products provide a familiar, stable and safe alternative to taking risks in purchasing unknown products. It has also been a feature of McDonaldisation that consumers can compare competing products more easily.

Ritzer, George, *The McDonaldization of Society.* Pine Forge Press, 1996.

Media

'Media' is a collective term used to describe the intermediary or carrier of an advertising message. The media includes the print media (newspapers and magazines), internet (electronic magazines and publications), radio, TV and outdoor advertising (posters, billboards, etc.).

Media kit

A media kit is most closely associated with public relations. Typically a media kit would include copies of press releases, related information, photographs and, if appropriate or practicable, samples of the products or services. The purpose of a media kit is to provide the media with all the necessary information in order to write editorial copy on a specific event related to a business, such as the launching of a new product or service.

Media plan

A media plan is the schedule or outline of the advertisements and other activities that make up a marketing campaign. A media plan would initially involve analysing the different media in order to assess which of them would be the most appropriate channels for the messages that the business wishes to convey. A media plan allows the business to coordinate their activities in the promotion of their products or services so that they can assess whether the overall campaign is likely to be both consistent and effective.

Barban, Arnold M., *Essentials of Media Planning*. Contemporary Books, 1994.
Scissors, Jack Z. and Barron, Roger B., *Advertising Media Planning*. Contemporary Books, 2002.

Media release

Media releases, or news releases, or press releases, are an integral part of **public relations**. They are written and designed in order to provide the media with an easy to translate, newsworthy story regarding the business or their products and services. Press releases are sent to reporters and editors, in the hope that some editorial space will be assigned to the story. Typically press releases will include quotes, have a personal angle, and may be accompanied by relevant photographs or other illustrative material, in order to reduce the amount of legwork that needs to be done to follow up and present the story in the media.

See also **media kit**.

Northmore, David, *How to Get Publicity for Free: How to Write a Press Release, Contact the Media, Gain Radio and Television Interviews and Organise Press Conferences*. Bloomsbury, 1993.

Media research

Media research is an integral part of a **media plan** as it involves the systematic investigation and assessment of various media options prior to placing orders for advertisement space. Typically a business would look at the media's existing audiences and compare them with their own customer profiles in order to achieve the closest possible match. An assessment would also be made as to the cost effectiveness of each of the different media. A business may choose to use a variety of different techniques, including CPT (cost per thousand) as a comparative measurement.

Jensen, Klaus Baruhn, *Handbook of Media and Communication Research: Qualitative and Quantitative Methodologies*. Routledge, 2002.

Meet and greet

In many aspects of travel, tourism and leisure, meet and greet has become an extremely important facet of customer service. There are many different variations, such as meet and greet airport parking services, or valet or chauffeur parking. This system allows a customer to arrive at a departure terminal and leave their vehicle with a meet and greet parking representative. The customer can then proceed to check-in and on their return a member of the meet and greet team will be there with their car at the terminal where they dropped it off. Although the service adds to the costs for the customer, it is often seen that the advantages outweigh the costs, purely on the basis of convenience.

For other leisure organisations and activities a meet and greet service can often set the organisation apart from many of its competitors. The organisation provides a greeting service by a member of staff who has been trained in customer service provision. They can direct the customer or visitor to the activity point or room within a venue in a professional and efficient manner. In an increasingly competitive market, where there is little differentiation between leisure provision, elements of customer service such as meet and greet can be a key success factor.

Micro-environment

'Micro-environment' refers to a business's external stakeholders which are in direct contact with the organisation. These are the groups which significantly influence the action of the organisation, and may include partners, providers of finance, regulators, government and competitors. Some of the micro-environmental external stakeholders will have a positive effect on the business, such as creating demand or supplying the business with resources. Others, on the other hand, such as regulators or government, for example, may impose constraints on the business which can affect its development. Typically a business will attempt to analyse its micro-environment and may carry out the following steps:

- An identification of the key stakeholders as far as the organisation is concerned.
- An assessment of the influence of each of these key stakeholders.
- A classification of the stakeholders in terms of opportunities or threats (in some cases a stakeholder may be classified as both an opportunity and a threat).
- An evaluation of the importance of each of these opportunities and threats.

On the basis of the opportunities and threats identified, the organisation can now establish its strategic objectives.

See also **macro-environment**.

Micromarketing

Micromarketing is a dependent form of marketing which heavily relies on accurate **market segmentation**. Micromarketing seeks to target specific and often relatively small groups of customers, through purpose-built promotions to that defined group. Typically the target markets may be defined geographically, demographically, behaviourally or psychographically. In this way micromarketing allows a business to concentrate on fulfilling the specific needs, wants and expectations of target groups without risking the message that they wish to convey to them being lost in a more general marketing campaign.

Minimum connecting time

This is a travel-related term, which at its most basic describes the minimum time necessary for a passenger on one flight to change aircraft at a transport hub. The minimum connecting times are often agreed in advance between airlines and airport authorities. They take into account that a passenger will need to retrieve their luggage and to get to the appropriate departure gate after arrival. In many cases this is referred to as 'transfer time' and may need to incorporate security and passport control. Clearly minimum connect time, or transfer time, will be dependent on the airport's facilities and the distance between arrival and departure gates. In many cases the minimum transfer time is around twenty minutes.

Minority marketing

Effectively minority marketing is akin to **micromarketing** or the activities of a **market nicher** in the sense that the business aims its products, services and promotions towards a niche market. Minority marketing is also used as an all-embracing description of marketing that is aimed at specific ethnic or national groups which form a minority in a specific country or region. Clearly there are specific alternatives and requirements of a business wishing to market to these particular groups, which may include advertisements in different languages and a different approach to the process of selling to accord with ethnic or national customs and traditions.

See **niche marketing**.

Halter, Marilyn and Ralston, Susan (eds), *Shopping for Identity: The Marketing of Ethnicity.* Schocken Books, 2000.

Schreiber, Alfred L. and Lenson, Barry, *Multi-cultural Marketing: Selling to the New America: Position your company today for optimal success in the diverse America of tomorrow.* McGraw-Hill Education, 2000.

Mission statement

In many cases indications of a business's fundamental policy will be contained within a mission statement. A mission statement essentially describes, as succinctly as possible, the organisation's business vision. This would include their fundamental values and the essential purpose of the organisation. It will also make allusions as to its future or its pursuit of that future, as mission statements tend to be a statement of where a businesses wishes to be rather than a description of where they are at the current time. In this respect, mission statements, although the fundamental ethos may remain the same, are subject to periodic change. A business may choose to incorporate within its mission statement a vision of how it wishes its employees and systems to respond, react and fulfil the needs of its customers or clients. Businesses will, therefore, seek to match these aspirations by instituting employee development programmes and associated training, in order to fulfil the espoused desires and commitments made in the mission statement.

Talbot, Marianne, *Make Your Mission Statement Work: How to Identify and Promote the Values of your Organisation.* How To Books, 2000.

Multiculturalism

Perhaps the first issue to point out is the fact that there is no broad accepted definition of the term 'multiculturalism'. In fact many believe that the term 'multiculturalism' is largely redundant. All that multiculturalism implies is a diverse range of cultures and identities, and for many this will mean a dual identity. An individual living in a specific nation state will not necessarily have precisely the same culture as others who live within that state. Equally there is no overarching thread that determines what is or what is not a separate culture. Many different cultural beliefs can easily coexist alongside one another without any friction or overt difficulties. For some, however, multiculturalism has the inference that different cultural communities should live their lives in some kind of self-contained manner. But this meaning has been rendered largely obsolete as a pure definition of multiculturalism. All multiculturalism can really mean is that no specific culture represents a perfect set of ways in which to live, and that all can benefit from a critical dialogue with other cultures. This means that all cultures need to be open, interactive and self-critical. A truly multicultural society, therefore, has shared common values but respect for diversity.

In most nation states, successive waves of minority ethnic communities have wrought changes on those states. Some have incorporated fully, virtually adopting the dominant culture, whilst others have found it more difficult as they have found themselves to be socially excluded, or even subjects of racist attacks. Multiculturalism as a process involves a sense of belonging and a sense of being valued.

In terms of leisure and particularly in sport, arts and the media there are perceived inequalities on racial grounds. In many areas of leisure-related activities there is under-representation of minority groups and this is filtered through the availability of funding. Equally, media bias can directly or indirectly affect the involvement of ethnic or racial minorities in particular activities. A prime example in Britain is the comparative absence of any Asian professional football players, whilst there are large numbers of African and Afro-Caribbean footballers playing at the very top of the game. The reverse, however, is true of sports such as cricket. Whether the involvement in particular sports as a prime example is related to indirect or direct discrimination, or whether there are deeper cultural reasons for non-participation, is an area that requires considerable research.

Multiplier and leakage

Multiplier and leakage is an economic phenomenon that is linked to the impact of tourism and thus leisure activities. In the **multiplier effect** a visitor to a particular area will spend money on products and services. A proportion of this money will go to the employees of the leisure facility. Those employees will then spend the money in the local economy in local stores, which also employ individuals, and the money is thus trickled down through the local economy. The more businesses that serve local needs, the better and more contained the multiplier effect will be. However, in many cases a large proportion of the money that is spent by tourists does not reach the local economy. If the facility is owned by a national or a multinational company then a large proportion of the earnings will leave the local area. This is the leakage part. This is particularly serious in tourist resorts around the world that are dominated by **all-inclusive** complexes. The visitor to the complex has already paid, probably in their home country, the full cost of their trip. Since food, drinks and leisure activities are already paid for there is little reason for visitors to spend money in the local economy and therefore there is a minimal

M

multiplier effect. In essence the money that does not reach the local economy is leakage. This is also a feature when customers pay with credit cards or even in extreme cases where a resort effectively has its own money, such as many of the Disney resorts. Gift cards are another main way in which retail outlets and restaurants can stop the flow of money out of their company and into the local economy.

At the 2006 football World Cup the Allianz Arena did not actually allow visitors to spend cash. They purchased cards that they could top up outside the arena entrance. The cards could then be used for all purchases within the arena. The money that they would spend had to be spent inside the arena and therefore local entrepreneurs operating around the arena would not have access to the supporters' money.

Multiplier effect

The financial implications of the multiplier effect serve to illustrate that a considerable injection of cash into the economy is multiplied in its impact as it flows through the economy.

Whilst major government spending or considerable investment in the form of overseas investment (foreign direct investment) represents additional national income equal to its original value, it will stimulate other parts of the economy.

The original investment provides direct wages, the purchase of products, services and raw materials, which in turn creates more employment in the supplying businesses, leading to increased demand elsewhere for products and services. As employees and shareholders earn from the knock-on effects of the original investment, demand will increase, wages will rise and there will be a positive impact on profits. This will eventually filter down to the consumer market.

Arguably, one of the most effective multipliers is investment in the construction industry. These investments tend to have wider multiplier effects on the economy as a whole. Negative multiplier effects can also occur when considerable sums are removed from the economy by a large reduction in government spending, such as the cancellation of a major infrastructure project.

Multi-skilling

The term 'multi-skilling' relates to incorporating a higher level of flexibility into the job roles across an organisation, usually in those activities requiring unskilled to skilled or technical expertise. This flexibility often crosses boundaries which have historically or traditionally been set, and it requires the willingness of employees if it is to succeed. The newly multi-skilled employees would also have to be prepared to work at their newly acquired skills and follow training or retraining programmes in order to do so. Commonly, trained employees will assist with the retraining of those going through the multi-skilling process.

There are some advantages and disadvantages to multi-skilling, including those shown in Table 13.

The introduction of multi-skilling can affect an employee in more than their work situation and may spill over into their domestic life, particularly if their extended role involves irregular work hours. However, employees could find that their job satisfaction is increased due to the fact that they are no longer so strictly supervised or controlled.

Table 13 Advantages and disadvantages of multi-skilling

Advantages	Disadvantages
An organisation can introduce new equipment and working methods quickly.	Labour turnover can increase as employees become more skilled.
The employees improve their overall level of skills and knowledge.	The costs of training and retraining programmes can be high.
All of the organisation's resources are used to their full potential.	Because individuals can move from one group to another, there could be resultant shortages in particular groups. This can affect the way the group performs in the longer term as there is a constant risk that one member of the group or team will be missing.
The employees can contribute more effectively and to their full potential to the meeting of the organisation's objectives.	Managers tend not to be involved in the multi-skilling process and often remain rigid in their views of the tasks they should perform.
	Employees do not always enjoy job satisfaction, particularly if they are not involved in tasks they were initially trained to do.

Museums, Libraries and Archives (MLA)

This is a British development agency that aims to provide strategic leadership in England for museums, galleries, libraries and archives. It is a non-departmental public body, financially supported by the Department for Culture, Media and Sport. It was launched in April 2000 as a strategic body. The MLA's approach is that museums, libraries and archives are the best place to serve communities, as they can deliver local agendas and maximise impact.

www.mla.gov.uk

National conservation strategies

An enormous number of countries have their own national conservation strategies, including Pakistan, Kenya and Botswana. The national conservation strategies aim to reflect the needs and priorities in preserving biological diversity and aim to provide guidance for sustainable development. In Botswana, for example, in the 1980s, after a five-year nationwide consultation process a national conservation strategy was created with objectives to ensure the direct use of renewable resources in a more beneficial and environmentally friendly manner and to sustain such resources for future economic benefit. One of the main activities has been to encourage local inhabitants to diversify from cattle production by the reduction of herd sizes, and to focus more on tourism, wildlife, the harvesting of natural products and other more environmentally sustainable occupations.

The International Union for Conservation of Nature and Natural Resources, *Protected Areas of the World*, 1992.

National Parks Service

The US system of national parks was the first of its kind in the world. It is responsible for caring for 400 natural, cultural and recreational sites across the United States. It includes the Grand Canyon, the Statue of Liberty and the Gettysburg battlefield. It operates on a budget of some $2.3 billion each year, administering 27,000 historic structures, 27,000 cultural and museum buildings plus dams, border lands, bridges, camp grounds, national preserves and reserves and millions of acres of land

www.nps.gov

National Tourism Organisation

The term 'national tourism or tourist organisation' is used to describe the usually government-funded or subsidised tourism governing body of a nation state, such as the Greek National Tourism Organisation (GNTO) or the National Tourism Organisation of Montenegro. Usually the national tourism organizations are either part of the Ministry of Tourism or a Ministry of Culture. They incorporate tourism education and training and tend to have close links with hotel organisations, agro-tourism and other tourism institutions, such as travel agents' associations, tour guides, exhibition and conference organisers, organisations representing owners of rooms and apartments, car rental companies, yacht owners, passenger ship owners, airline representatives and leisure attractions.

www.gnto.gr
www.montenegro.travel

National Trust

The National Trust was founded in Britain in 1895 and it was originally concerned with the impact of development and industrialisation on the nation's buildings, countryside and coastline, which was deemed to be under threat. The National Trust has broadened its remit and is now involved not only in the preservation of buildings, the countryside and coastline, but also in practical conservation. As of 2007/8 it had 3.5 million members and its 300 historic houses and gardens and 49 industrial monuments and mills were hosts to over 50 million visitors.

www.nationaltrust.org.uk

National Trust for Scotland

The National Trust for Scotland was established in 1931 and very much mirrors the work of the National Trust, which is responsible for England, Wales and Northern Ireland. The National Trust for Scotland is responsible for 128 properties and 76,000 hectares of countryside (2008).

www.nts.org.uk

Natural England

Amongst Natural England's key responsibilities are the promotion of access to recreation and of public well-being. It aims to ensure access to the natural environment and promote physical activity. The organisation estimates that visits to the countryside or open spaces in urban areas are already an important source of recreation for around 50% of the population and that 20% of English adults are members of conservation and recreation organisations. In terms of recreation, the organisation has launched an investigation into how different sectors of society can have an equal opportunity to enjoy England's natural heritage (Diversity Review and Action Plan). They have also successfully launched the Walking the Way to Health initiative, which encouraged those who take little exercise to take up walking. The organisation was launched in October 2006, bringing together English Nature, the environmental responsibilities of the Rural Development Service, as well as the Landscape, Access and Recreation Division of the **Countryside Agency**.

www.naturalengland.org.uk

Net fare/net rate

There are three accepted definitions of these terms, all of which broadly relate to travel. It can refer to the wholesale price of a particular fare that is then marked up for sale to the customer. It can also be a fare after **commission**, or the price at which a **consolidator** sells a ticket to a travel agent.

Net wholesale rate

This is a term closely related either to travel tours or to conventions. It is a rate that is slightly lower than the usual wholesale rate. From this base rate the price is then marked up by the resale sellers of a tour, in order to cover their costs, such as promotion and administration.

N

Niche Marketing

Niche marketing involves targeting a specialist area of the market. Traditionally, businesses will target very clearly defined **market segments** which are not currently being directly targeted by larger organisations. The attractiveness of being able to offer tailor-made products to match the needs and wants of these niche markets is typified by the fact that there is little competition and that premium prices can often be levied. Many niche markets remain just that – a specialist area which will not necessarily attract the attention of a larger business. Many other niche markets have been developed to such an extent that inevitably they draw the attention of larger competitors. Similarly, some niche markets have actually been expanded and the products and services to them recognised sufficiently for them to develop into what is, essentially, a **mass market**. Certainly many products and services which were initially aimed at a niche market have now spread successfully into the mass market.

Marketing and selling into niche markets requires a considerably different approach from mass market selling. Given the fact that there are fewer potential customers, there is little room for error in not being able to offer them precisely what it is they demand.

Milder, David N., *Niche Strategies for Downtown Revitalization: A Hands-On Guide to Developing, Strengthening, and Marketing Niches.* Alexander Communications Group, 1998.

Niche strategy

Niche strategy approaches by businesses seek to concentrate their attention on a narrow piece of the total market. Having achieved this, they seek to provide for niche buyers more effectively than their rivals. The key success factors involved in dealing with niche markets are:

- to choose a market niche where buyers can be distinctively identified by their preferences, special requirements or unique needs;
- to then develop unique capabilities to serve those needs of the segment.

There are two ways in which businesses seek to achieve this:

- by achieving lower costs than competitors serving that market niche (low cost strategy);
- by offering something different to the buyers in that market (differentiation strategy).

Niches are attractive to businesses for the following reasons:

- They are big enough to produce a profit and may offer growth potential.
- They are often overlooked by the industry leaders.
- Competitors involved in a more multi-segment approach may consider them too expensive in terms of meeting the buyers' needs.
- Few competitors will be specialising in that niche.
- The business may be able to deploy most of its resources into that niche.
- Once established, superior service can effectively defend that niche from rivals.

No-show

This is a term that can be broadly applied across the leisure, travel and tourism industries. In airline travel it can refer to an individual who has purchased a ticket for a particular flight but failed to appear for the flight despite not having cancelled their booking. It can also apply to any individual who has purchased a ticket for an event or for an activity, but again fails to turn up at the appropriate time, without explanation or contact with the organisers. It can also more broadly apply to those that fail to meet an appointment or to notify a hotel or restaurant when they have made their reservation.

Not-for-profit organisations

Not for profit organizations are often ignored in any analysis of strategic management issues. There are vast numbers of not-for-profit organisations, which include:

- Special interest organisations
- Government entities
- Educational or medical organisations
- Charities
- Religious foundations
- Political groups
- Social groups

Undoubtedly many of these not-for-profit organisations compete openly with profit-based organisations and provide similar products and services. This is particularly the case in the medical and educational field.

Broadly speaking, the revenues obtained by not-for-profit organisations come from two different areas, these are:

- Customers or clients who receive products or services from the organisation.
- Sponsors or fund providers in the form of grants, government agencies and donations.

On the one extreme there are organisations such as private schools or hospitals that derive the bulk of their revenue from their customers or clients. On the other hand there are organisations that derive the bulk of their revenue from sponsors, which is the common case for charities. Between these two radically different forms of not-for-profit organisation, the vast majority of these organisations can be found, as they combine both elements in terms of funding.

The primary differences between not-for-profit organisations and for-profit organisations are:

- Their outputs and results are often intangible and therefore difficult to measure.
- They may not be unduly influenced by their clients or customers.
- Contributors, financially, may well have different priorities from those of the customers or clients that the organisations actually serve.
- Many of the employees are such in name only, as they are volunteers.

N

- These volunteers may be subject to external influences and other commitments, which could affect their commitment to the organisation itself.
- There are more constraints on finances as not-for-profit organisations tend not to have access to credit facilities. They cannot offer shares on the market and therefore have fewer debt options.

In terms of strategic management, there are a number of considerations with regard to not-for-profit organisations, these are:

- Goal conflicts – as they often lack unifying central goals (such as profitability).
- The management and planning has to take into account inputs of resources as they have a direct impact upon what the organisation is able to output.
- There is considerable political infighting in many organisations as the result of either conflicting or ambiguous objectives.
- Many of the organisations are controlled by professionals, who may not have managerial expertise, but are recognised as being experts in their field.
- Many not-for-profit organisations are centralised to ensure that maximum value is achieved from the inputs.

N

Obesity epidemic

This phenomenon can be directly linked to leisure activities, or rather more to the point the lack of leisure activities. Scientists and researchers have suggested that households with low levels of disposable income and where those that are in work require high levels of physical energy are more likely to be involved in home-based leisure activities, or at best in social situations that may revolve around drinking or food consumption.

The National Center for Chronic Disease Prevention and Health Promotion (US) was one of the first to use the term 'obesity epidemic', describing increased problems with weight amongst the US population and linking it to sedentary home-based leisure activities. The obesity epidemic has severe implications for the individual in terms of health, and broader ones for society. Whilst some of the individuals are undoubtedly affected by genetic imbalances, the general consensus of opinion is that the obesity problem in countries such as the US is not genetically based but lifestyle driven. This is linked to the consumption of convenience food, fast food and other products that have high calorific value, and are high in fats and sugars. In addition, the obesity rate has been affected by improved transportation and labour-saving gadgets at home, such as washing machines, lawnmowers and dishwashers. Up to a quarter of all US adults, according to the Behavioral Risk Factor Surveillance System, engage in no physical activity in their leisure time.

www.cdc.gov

Off-line point

This is a travel- and tourism-related term that refers to a destination that has no service from an airline or another carrier.

Off-peak

As the term suggests, these are periods of time in which there is a minimal or reduced demand for services, either at a leisure facility or activity, or on an airline or travel service. The general solution for smoothing out the differences between peak and off-peak times is to reduce prices during periods where historically the organisation or service has experienced low demand. The term may not necessarily simply apply to a period during a specific day, but may also refer to a season at a particular tourist destination or resort. During the off-peak seasons there are, understandably, reduced services or connections to that resort or location. Yet the infrastructure still remains in place to provide for inbound visitors. In order to smooth out the income and other issues, such as seasonal employment, many resorts and destinations actively market their off-peak seasons, focusing on the reverse benefits of less crowded beaches, less overwhelmed infrastructure and the extremes of weather. A prime example is that of the Mediterranean resorts, specifically Spain and the Balearic Islands, who have for many years catered for long-term stay guests during the off-peak season, so that their guests can avoid the extremes of the winter weather in their own countries. This has provided all-year-round employment and maximum use of facilities and accommodation at times when seasonal unemployment would be high and hotels would generally be closed.

Ombudsmen

An ombudsman is either an independent individual or an office which responds to complaints from consumers regarding the service which they are receiving. The ombudsman also initiates proactive investigations, protecting the interests of the consumer. Once the ombudsman has intervened, an attempt is made to determine whether action, under the particular circumstances, is valid. They seek to act as a negotiator between the providers and recipients of a particular service and come to a conclusion about satisfactory redress.

Ombudsmen are considered to be mediators or negotiators, acting independently and being an accessible service.

Open jaw itinerary

An open jaw itinerary is frequently a preferred choice for the **independent traveller**. The customer will fly into one city and fly out of another, allowing them the freedom to tour between the arrival airport and the subsequent departure airport. Many airlines will offer their own versions of open jaw itineraries, allowing the customer to identify flight times that offer significant financial savings. Some travellers also choose an open jaw itinerary with a side trip option, which allows them to take an additional round trip from one of the cities on their itinerary.

Open question

Open questions are closely associated with questionnaires and are designed to receive a relatively long and detailed answer from a respondent. In other words, they produce qualitative data for the researcher. Rather than presenting the respondent with a number of options from which they are expected to choose their most appropriate response, an open question allows the respondent to answer in any way they see fit. This brings its own specific difficulties as far as the researcher is concerned when trying to categorise and to report back from open questions. This is largely due to the fact that there is no restriction on the type or length of answer received. Open questions are designed to gather information in greater depth. It is usual that closed questions would be used at a rate of 3:1 compared with open questions. Open questions are designed for the respondent to give opinions and feelings, and allow them to think and reflect. In effect, they give control of the responses to the respondent. They can be used as follow-on questions. For example, a respondent could be asked which of a number of named destinations they have visited in the past five years. The follow-on open question could be framed as 'Which did you enjoy the most and why?'

Open ticket

An open ticket can apply both to airlines and to other forms of travel, as well as to the use of leisure facilities. It is a ticket type that within certain limitations allows an individual to use the service or the facility at any time. For example, in Ho Chi Minh City an open ticket, costing less than US$30, can be used on air-conditioned private buses at any time without restriction. For airlines the customer does not have to specify their return travel date and time using an open ticket. In theory a customer only has to produce the open ticket and they will be allowed to board the next available flight.

Operations management

Formerly operations management was known as 'production management' and was applied almost exclusively to the manufacturing sector. For many organisations this term is still used as opposed to 'operations management'. However, the management function related to manufacturing has broadened to incorporate many other aspects related to the supply chain. It has therefore become common to use the term 'operations management', to describe activities related both to manufacturing and increasingly to the service sector. At its heart, operations management deals with the design of products and services, the buying of components or services from suppliers, the processing of those products and services and the selling of the finished goods. Across all of these disparate areas of business, operations management can be seen as an overarching discipline which seeks to quantify and organise the whole process. Nonetheless, there is still a considerable emphasis placed on issues directly related to manufacturing, stock control and, to a lesser extent, the management of the distribution systems. A large manufacturing organisation will include aspects of operations management under a wide variety of different, but closely related managerial disciplines. Primarily, human resources, marketing, administration and finance and, of course, the research and development department of an organisation support and are mutually dependent upon the operations division.

Given the wide spread of different job roles and tasks within operations management, it is notoriously difficult to give a perfect definition of what an operations manager would actually do. Certainly they would be responsible for a wide range of different functions, but the functions themselves will often be determined by the nature of the business itself, whether it is a service-based industry or an organisation primarily concerned with manufacturing.

O

Organisational behaviour

The study of organisational behaviour incorporates both an academic and a practical approach. Any such investigation begins with the primary definition of the word 'organisation', or 'organisational'. Clearly it refers to a form of social collectivity, or in the organisational sense, a series of collectivities. The study of organisational behaviour can be a highly specialised area of investigation. Typically, researchers and theorists will tackle many of the different aspects of organisational life, including performance, goal, product or service-related issues and general performance.

The dominant approaches to the study of organisational behaviour tend to revolve around culturalist, institutionalist or utilitarian explanations. Undoubtedly the study of organisational behaviour began with a simple study of organisational structure and functions. This moved further into the field of the behaviour of groups and individuals. The study draws heavily on psychology and sociology, but latter studies have begun to incorporate industrial relations, political science, economics and engineering.

The study of organisational behaviour does derive elements from both the theoretical and the empirical. It attempts to understand how and why organisations develop their ways of regulating their operations and their employees and management. The studies of F. W. Taylor could be considered to be a scientific management approach to organisational behaviour. Much of the structural theory is derived from Max Weber, the group theory from Elton Mayo (Hawthorne Experiments).

Cole, G. A., *Organisational Behaviour*. Thomson Learning, 2000.
Mullins, Laurie, *Management and Organisational Behaviour*. Financial Times, Prentice Hall, 2001.

Organisational culture

There are a number of ways in which an organisation's culture can be classified. The main classifications were suggested by a number of researchers, including Harrison, Handy, Deal and Kennedy, and Quinn and McGrath. As years have passed, so these classifications have become more developed, making it possible only to generally approach them in broad terms.

In 1972 Harrison suggested four main categories of organisational culture – power, role, task and person. Charles Handy reworked Harrison's theory and identified them as described in Table 14.

During the 1980s Deal and Kennedy developed their own set of theories about organisational culture and the way in which it affected how management made decisions and formed their strategies. Their conclusions are shown in Table 15.

Quinn and McGrath also identified four different organisational cultures, as shown in Table 16. It should be remembered that no one organisation fits neatly into any one of the categories mentioned and the majority are too complex to be categorised generally. The classifications should be regarded only as a reference point for comparison of extremes.

Deal, T. E. and Kennedy, A. A., *Corporate Cultures: The Rites and Rituals of Corporate Life*. Penguin, 1982.
Handy, C. B., *Understanding Organisations*. Penguin, 1985.
Harrison, R., 'Understanding your Organisation's Character', *Harvard Business Review*, May–June 1972.
Quinn, R. E. and McGrath, M. R., *The Transformation of Organisational Cultures: A Competing Values Perspective in Organisational Culture*, ed. C. C. Lundberg and J. Martin. Sage Publications, 1985.
Scholz, C., *Organisational Culture and Leadership*. Jossey Bass, 1985.

Organisational development

This term can be attributed to Beckhard (1969). He defined organisational development as a planned, top-down, organisation-wide effort to improve the organi-

Table 14 Charles Handy's categories of organisational culture

Culture	Description
Power	This type of culture is based on trust and good personal communication. There is little need for rigid bureaucratic procedures since power and authority are based on only a few individuals. The power culture is dynamic in that change can take place quickly but is dependent on a small number of key, powerful individuals. This culture tends to be tough on employees because the key focus is the success of the organisation, often resulting in higher labour turnover.
Role	This type of culture tends to be bureaucratic in nature, thus requiring logical, coordinated and rational processes with heavy emphasis on rules and procedures. Control lies with a small number of employees who have high degrees of authority. They tend to be stable organisations, operating in a predictable environment with products and services that have a long lifespan. Not considered to be innovative organisations, they can adapt to gradual, minor change, but not to radical ones.
Task	This type of organisational culture relies on employee expertise. The matrix structure tends to prevail in these organisations, with teams of individuals specialising. They need and tend to be flexible organisations with individual employees working with autonomy, allowing fast reaction to changes in the external environment and having set procedures in place to address this aspect.
Person	This type of culture relies on collective decision-making, often associated with partnerships. Compromise is important and individuals will tend to work within their own specialist area, coordinating all aspects and working with autonomy without the need to report to other employees.

sation's effectiveness and health. He believed that the organisation's process needed a series of interventions in order to improve them.

This was later developed and is now taken as a strategy that has the intention of changing the structure, beliefs, values and attitudes of an organisation. The aim is to allow the organisation to be in a better position to adapt to new challenges, markets and technologies. A more broad approach could encompass anything that is done to improve the running of an organisation, including improvements in systems and planning.

The term is often interchangeable with 'organisational effectiveness', particularly if the initiative is driven by **human resources**.

Beckhard, Richard, *Organisation Development: Strategies and Models.* Addison Wesley, 1969.
Bradford, D. L. and Burke, W. W. *Reinventing Organisation Development.* Pfeiffer, 2005.
Lewin, Kurt, *Group Decision and Social Change.* Holt Rinehart & Winston, 1958.

Organisational structure

Organisational structure is a crucial consideration for all international businesses. Efficient organisational structure requires three main criteria, these are:

Table 15 Deal and Kennedy's categories of organisational culture

Culture	Description
Macho	These types of organisation have to make decisions quickly and adopt a tough attitude towards their employees and fellow managers. There is a high degree of internal competition and the operations tend to be high risk. The majority of these organisations do not form strategies or plan for the long term but are considered to rely on short termism, with a low level of cooperation within the organisation itself. There is a high labour turnover resulting in a weak organisational culture.
Work hard/play hard	This type of culture tends to be associated with sales. The majority of individual employees are sales orientated but the level of risk is low. It is the employees' ability to accumulate sales that is important and the culture tends to encourage team building and social activities for employees. The organisation encourages competition and offers rewards for success, but does not necessarily rate quality as highly as volume.
Company	These types of organisation are often in high-risk areas and operate on the basis that decisions take a long time to come to fruition. Decision-making takes place at the top of this hierarchical organisation and the overall approach can often be old-fashioned. Each new invention or technical breakthrough will pose a threat to the business.
Process	This type of culture operates in a low-risk, slow-feedback environment where employees are encouraged to focus on how they do things rather than what they do. They tend to be systems- and procedures-based, requiring employees to work in an orderly and detailed fashion, attending meetings and work groups. There will be rigid levels of management in the hierarchical structure, but because the organisation operates in a predictable environment, reactions from management are often slow.

- The way in which the organisation is divided into sub-units. This is known as 'horizontal differentiation'.
- The location of the decision-making responsibilities within the structure. This is known as 'vertical differentiation'.
- How the business has established integrating mechanisms.

Arguably, there is a fourth consideration, which is known as 'control systems'. This is taken to mean how the performance of sub-units within the organisation is assessed and how well the managers of those sub-units control the activities within their area of responsibility.

It is essential for organisations which are pursuing a variety of different strategies as part of their international business activities to choose and then adopt appropriate organisational architecture that is responsive enough to implement

Table 16 Quin and McGrath's categories of organisational culture

Culture	Description
Rational	The rational culture is firmly based on the needs of a market. The organisation places emphasis on productivity and efficiency and encourages management to be goal-orientated and decisive. All activities are focused on tangible performance and employees are rewarded on achievement.
Adhocracy	This type of culture is an adaptive, creative and autonomous one where authority is largely based on the abilities and charismatic nature of leaders. These organisations tend to be risk-orientated and emphasis is placed on employees' adherence to the values of the organisation itself.
Consensual	These types of organisation are often concerned with equality, integrity and fairness and much of the authority is based on informal acceptance of power. Decisions are made by collective agreements or consensus and dominant leaders are not often present. Morale is important, as is cooperation and support between employees in order to reach organisational objectives. Employee loyalty is high.
Hierarchical	This type of culture relies on stability and control through the setting of rigid regulations and procedures. Decisions are made logically on facts alone with the management tending to be cautious and conservative. The employees are strictly controlled, with management expecting obedience.

the identified strategies. The organisational structure or architecture of a multinational business organisation will very much depend on whether it is a multi-domestic business, global, or trans-national in its nature. As multinationals spread their interests across the globe they inherently become more complex in nature. In addition to this, they also become less able to change. Nonetheless, the move towards increased **globalisation** of industry has meant that businesses trading internationally must be able to adapt or amend their organisational structure to incorporate new strategy and operations in new markets.

Origin and destination traffic

This travel-related term refers to passengers on a flight who are either boarding or getting off at a particular destination, as distinct from those remaining on the aircraft, bound for another destination. It is commonly known as 'O & D traffic' and is often used by airlines on marginal routes, where stopovers are made to drop off and pick up additional passengers. In effect the system works rather like a bus, with the capacity to stop at various destinations for a short period to enable embarkation and disembarkation.

Outsourcing

The term 'outsourcing' relates to the hiring of another organisation, or its employees, in order to carry out a specific task or activity that would normally be carried out in-house. Examples of such activities are shipping/transportation, computing services or payroll accounting. The main advantages to an organisation of outsourcing are:

- There are economies of scale because the outsourced organisation also serves many other organisations.
- There is little likelihood of the outsourced organisation gaining a competitive advantage.
- The outsourced organisation is more likely to be conversant with current regulations or legislation regarding the task or activity if it is carrying out a similar activity for other organisations.
- The organisation does not have to incur the expense of training its employees to carry out the operation.

O

Pareto Principle

Vilfredo Pareto (1848–1923) was an Italian economist and sociologist, known more widely for his theory on mass and elite interaction as well as his application of mathematics to economic analysis.

The fundamental concept of Pareto Analysis or the Pareto Principle is that a business derives 80% of its income from 20% of its customers. In other words, this 20% of loyal customers are the foundations upon which a business can build its profits and its market share. On the reverse, the remaining 80% of their customers only provide the business with 20% of their income. This is largely due to the fact that these customers are irregular purchasers, and are far more prone to brand switching.

Marketing aims to ensure that the profitable 20% of customers retain their customer loyalty and that gradually significant numbers of the remaining 80% are transformed into loyal customers, thus increasing market share and profitability.

See also **repeat customer.**

Passenger space ratio

Passenger space ratio is a measure that compares the amount of public space that is available on a cruise ship with the passenger capacity of that cruise ship. The result gives the theoretical amount of public space that is allocated per passenger. The higher the passenger space ratios figure, then the more room there is on the ship for each of the passengers. Although cruise vessels are usually rated in terms of accommodation, passenger space ratios and facilities, the passenger space ratio is an overall measurement of the spaciousness of the ship. Most modern cruise ships have a ratio of 35, which equates to 3,500 cubic feet of space per passenger. More luxurious lines may reach 40 or 45. The complete calculation is made by dividing the vessel's gross registered tonnage by the number of passengers. Broadly speaking, below 20 is poor, between 20 and 30 is average and over 50 is excellent.

Passing off

Passing off occurs when a business adopts a similar name to an existing business, with the purpose of trying to use the other business's reputation in order to attract customers and sales. In effect, they are trying to take advantage of the goodwill which has been built up by the original business. In the vast majority of countries passing off, if proved, is an illegal action, punishable by court action.

People 1st

People 1st is the specific Sector Skills Council in Britain responsible for hospitality, leisure, travel and tourism. It covers the fourteen industries that make up the sector, which are:

- Contract food service providers
- Events
- Gambling
- Holiday parks
- Hospitality services
- Hostels
- Hotels
- Membership clubs
- Pubs, bars and nightclubs
- Restaurants
- Self-catering accommodation
- Tourist services
- Travel services
- Visitor attractions

The strategy is to improve communication with employers and to support funded skills training to encourage investment in skills. They also aim to improve communications with employees, particularly related to the acquisition of skills and career development. Their key success measurement is to improve Britain in its international perception.

See also **SkillsActive**.

www.people1st.co.uk

Per-capita cost

This is a calculation that estimates the cost per individual of providing a particular service or facility. A leisure facility may, for example, calculate their total running costs, including any capital expenditure, and then divide that figure by the number of customers or clients using the facility. This will provide them with a per-capita cost. This can be a valuable figure in working out the prices that need to be charged per customer in order to breakeven or produce a profit.

A per-capita cost can also be used as a broad measure of the effectiveness or response rates of marketing initiatives carried out by leisure organisations. Typically they will total the cost of their marketing spend and then divide this figure by the number of individuals who have made a booking or become a customer or client as a direct result of that marketing campaign. They will then be able to see the precise cost per acquired customer or client. It is a useful budgetary calculation, as it will enable the organisation to see how many customers need to be attracted in order to cover the total cost of a project or campaign. From this, **breakeven points** can be calculated.

Per-capita tour

This is a tourism-related term for what is alternatively known as a scheduled tour. Tours may be part of a tour operator's regular schedule of tour departures, but in order to ensure that the tour is profitable it is often sold to the general public. In some instances it is also known as a public or a retail tour. A per-capita tour is also used as a way in which a tour operator or a particular region, or indeed a leisure activity centre, can work out the net average income per user. It encompasses the **direct spending** on the activity or tour itself and any other earnings from the client.

Perceived value

This form of pricing strategy requires a business to have already established perceptions of customers in relation to the benefits or qualities of a particular product or service. Customers will have their own perceptions of whether the product or service offers them value compared to the price demanded by the business. Providing a balance can be established, and that the price and the customers' perceptions of the value of that price are near to equal, then this can form the foundation of a business's pricing structure.

Performance management

This is a broad process that aims to assess an organisation's progress towards its achievement of sets of established goals. It can be used to measure a wide variety of different sets of goals or functions within an organisation, such as financial, sales, skills and management control. It can be applied to a broad range of different organisational situations. It usually involves:

- Planning
- Monitoring
- Developing
- Rating
- Rewarding

In an employee-performance management context, 'planning' would relate to setting expectations, 'monitoring' being the process of continually checking performance; 'developing' would relate to training programmes that aim to improve employees' capacity to perform. 'Ratings' could be achieved through appraisals or feedback mechanisms and 'rewarding' would be related to pay and other non-financial benefits and incentives.

Permission marketing

Permission marketing is also known as 'request marketing' and involves **direct marketing** approaches to customers who have expressed an interest in receiving further information, news and updates from a particular business. Permission marketing is used in several different areas of marketing and across a wide variety of different industries. Conventional forms of permission marketing relate to the continued contact with customers who have requested brochures or sales literature on a previous occasion, but may not, however, have yet purchased products or services from the business. Alternatively, these may be lapsed customers who are still on a business's database.

Permission marketing has developed considerably over the last few years alongside the increased intensity of business use of the internet. It is closely associated with concepts such as opt-in email or other positive customer-initiated contacts with a business. Permission marketing practitioners distinguish their

P

form of marketing from the more intrusive forms, direct mailing or emailing unsought sales messages to customers. Permission marketing, by its very nature, assumes that the customer has a basic form of interest in what the business is offering and that they welcome the periodic contact with the business.

> Godin, Seth and Peppers, Don, *Permission Marketing: Turning Strangers into Friends and Friends into Customers.* Simon & Schuster, 1999.

Personalisation

Personalisation is a growing area of sales and marketing, as it seeks to provide individual customers, or groups of customers, with adapted versions of the basic product. Specific changes or amendments can be made to the standard offering: for example, customers can buy a regular model of a vehicle but determine the colour, the trim and the internal colours and layout. Personalisation has become possible as businesses adopt a more **market orientated** approach and adapt their production systems to produce products and services on demand, rather than stockpiling supplies in the anticipation of sales. Personalisation allows marketing to focus on the individuality of each of the products and the options and choices available to each and every customer.

> Kasanoff, Bruce, *Making it Personal: How to Profit from Personalization without Invading Privacy.* John Wiley & Sons, 2001.

PEST analysis

This concept originally began with just four criteria, with the acronym PEST (Political, Economic, Social and Technological). These forces are seen as being the principal external determinants of the environment in which a business operates. In later years the four forces became five under the acronym SLEPT (Social, Legal, Economic, Political and Technological). The concept has now extended to include seven forces, using the acronym STEEPLE (Social, Technological, Economic, Educational, Political, Legal and Environmental protection).

The purpose of the five forces, or its variants, is to examine or audit where threats originate and where opportunities can be found. In other words, the broader STEEPLE acronym applies to the macro-environment (factors outside the organisation). The main areas of interest within each letter are shown in Table 17.

In more recent times, PEST has been transformed into a broader set of analyses of the internal and external environments in which organisations operate. This has led to the development of the acronym DEPICTS:

- Demographic
- Economic
- Political
- Infrastructure
- Competition
- Technological
- Social

See also **Porter's Five Forces, SWOT analysis.**

Porter, Michael, *Competitive Advantage.* Free Press, 1985.

Table 17   STEEPLE analysis

Letter	Description
S	Social and cultural influences, including language, culture, attitudes and behaviour which affect future strategies and markets.
T	Technological and product innovation, which suggest how the market is developing as well as the future developments in research and arising opportunities.
E (E1)	Economics and market competition, which consider factors such as the business cycle, inflation, energy costs and investments; an assessment is made as to how they will affect the level of economic activity in each market.
E (E2)	Education, training and employment, primarily the trends in these areas which may impact upon the availability of trained labour as well as the potential demands of new generations and probable expectations.
P	Political, which focuses on current and proposed policies which will impact on the business and the workforce.
L	Legal, which focuses on current and proposed legislation; of equal importance is the business's adherence to current laws and regulations.
E (E3)	Environmental protection, which addresses the business's current and future impact on the environment, working on the basis that environmental protection will continue to be a major issue in restricting and amending the ways in which a business operates.

Pioneering costs

The term 'pioneering costs' is associated with the costs and risks facing an international business entering a new overseas market for the first time. In many respects these are trail-blazing organisations that do not have the benefits of knowing how to deal with that overseas country, either from experience or by learning lessons from other international businesses that have come before. Pioneering costs include the time and effort required to learn how the market operates and how that country's government, rules and regulations can have an impact upon the business's ability to be successful. Pioneering costs are borne alone by the first entrant into the market. Later entrants can benefit from lessons and mistakes learned by the pioneer. However, assuming the pioneer has been successful, later arrivals may find it as difficult, if not more so, to establish themselves in the new marketplace.

P

Point of turnaround

Point of turnaround is the terminal destination of an aircraft or other form of transport. In other cases it refers to the final destination of a passenger, who may be undertaking a series of connecting journeys in order to reach their destination.

Port of entry

A port of entry is a place in which an international traveller can lawfully enter a country. The port of entry is set up so that checks can be made on passports, visas and luggage, if required. It can be at an airport, a road and rail crossing of a land border, or a conventional sea port. The port of entry will inevitably incorporate immigration procedures and travellers may only be able to cross the border at designated times. In Europe, for example, once within the European Union there are few ports of entry, which allows individuals to freely travel across the member states. There are, however, exceptions, particularly in relation to Britain, which retains strict port of entry conditions.

Porter's Five Forces

Michael Porter's classic Five Forces model appeared in his 1980s book *Competitive Strategy: Techniques for Analyzing Industries and Competitors*. It has become the standard analysing tool for many businesses.

The Five Forces shape every market and industry and help a business to analyse the intensity of competition, as well as the profitability and attractiveness of the market and industry. The Five Forces can be best explained as in Table 18.

There have, however, been a number of criticisms of the model proposed by Porter, the first of which points to the fact that the model focuses only on the external environment and does not take account of the internal activities of the business; in effect the model does not consider the resources of the business. The second criticism suggests that Porter ignores the possibilities of joint ventures and alliances formed between businesses in order to cope with rivalries and competition. Added to this, the model does not place enough emphasis on the role of competition. The third major problem is far more fundamental. The Porter model is a static one, it does not have the capacity to cope with a dynamic environment in which conditions, competition and relationships are constantly changing. Porter reluctantly took part of this criticism onboard in 1991, but did not fully integrate the dynamic nature of many industries into the model. The fifth key criticism revolves around the fact that the model does not deal with the creative side of problem solving and decision-making. The model suggests that decisions and responses are analysis-based, reactive and not creative or proactive. Critics such as Mintzberg, Ahlstrand and Lampel (1998) suggest that this approach leads to 'analysis paralysis', in which a business or organisation fails to respond in a timely manner to changes and challenges.

In terms of the model's use and application within the leisure industry it still has currency. However, the model needs to be used or applied with a degree of caution, taking into account the key criticisms outlined above. The model is ideal for an 'outside-in' analysis or view of an organisation, but this must be balanced with a clear view of the actual strengths and weaknesses of the organisation and an analysis as to how the organisation is able to respond to the external environment. The model provides organisations with part of the understanding of how they manage to create value for their clients or consumers compared with the competition.

Mintzberg, H., Ahlstrand, B. W. and Lampel, J., *Strategy Safari: A Guided Tour through the Wilds of Strategic Management*. Free Press, 1998.

Porter, Michael E., *Competitive Strategy: Techniques for Analyzing Industries and Competitors*. Free Press, 1980.

Table 18   Porter's Five Forces

Five Forces	Description	Implications
Threat of new entrants	The easier it is for new businesses to enter the industry, the more intense the competition. There may be factors which may limit the number of new entrants, which are known as barriers to entry.	Customers may already be loyal to major brands. Incentives may be offered to customers in order to retain them. Fixed costs will be high and there may be a scarcity of resources. Businesses and customers may find it expensive to switch suppliers and take the attendant risks.
Power of suppliers	This measures how much pressure suppliers can place on businesses within the industry. The larger the supplier and the more dominant, the greater the amount by which it can squeeze a business's margins and profits	In some markets there are few suppliers of particular products as there are no available substitutes. Switching to other suppliers may prove difficult, costly and risky. If the product is extremely important to the buyer they will continue to purchase it. In many cases the supplying industry has a higher profitability than the buying industry.
Power of buyers	This is a measure as to how powerful customers are and what pressures they can apply to a business. The larger and more reliant a customer is, the more likely they are to be able to affect the margins and volumes of business.	There may be a small number of buyers who purchase large volumes of products and services. Buyers may be tempted to switch to an alternative supplier. If a product is not at the core of their business or requirements, a buyer may choose not to purchase for a period of time. The more competitive the market, the more price sensitive the customers may be.
Threat of substitute products	This is a measure as to how likely it is for buyers to switch to a competing product or service. Assuming the cost of switching is low, then this will be a serious threat.	Businesses should be aware that similar products, if not exact substitutes, may tempt the buyer to switch temporarily, at least, to another supplier. If, for example, a supermarket chain is offered considerably cheaper alternatives to plastic shopping bags, they may be tempted to move over to cardboard boxes or paper sacks.

continued

Table 18 (*continued*)

Five Forces	Description	Implications
Competitive rivalry	This measures the degree of competition between existing businesses in an industry. It is usually the case that the higher the competition, the lower the return on investment. Margins are pared down to the lowest levels.	Assuming there is no dominant business, then many of the competitors will be of a similar size. There will also be little differentiation between competitors' products and services. The more stagnant the industry, in terms of market growth, the higher the possibility that competitors will focus on taking customers away from other businesses, rather than attempting to develop the market themselves.

Porter's Four Generic Competitive Strategies

Porter's initial argument with regard to competitive strategies suggests that organisations have two basic decisions to make in order to establish a competitive advantage, these are:

- Whether to compete on price, or differentiation, which justifies higher prices.
- Whether to target a narrow or a broad market.

He suggests that the decision behind these two choices leads to four generic competitive strategies, although there is a fifth, which he does not mention. In essence the choices of strategy are as shown in Table 19.

Table 19 Porter's Four Generic Competitive Strategies

Strategy	Description
Overall price or cost leadership	Theoretically this strategy seeks to appeal to the widest possible market, as products and services are offered at the lowest price. This form of strategy requires ongoing efforts to reduce costs without detrimentally affecting the product or service offered to the consumer. This tends to be an attractive strategy if the products generally on offer in the industry are much the same, or if the market is dominated by price competition. It is also the case that this is a good way forward in cases where product differentiation is difficult and most buyers purchase through the same channels.

continued

Table 19 (*continued*)

Strategy	Description
Differentiation	This strategy rests on being able to offer differentiating features to consumers, who are then prepared to pay premium prices, based on concepts such as quality, prestige, superior technology or special features. Ultimately any sustainable differentiation is derived from the *core competencies* of the organisation. The organisation has to have unique resources or capabilities, or some form of better management of their value chain activities. Differentiation tends to take place when there are many ways in which products and services can be differentiated and the uses or needs of the consumers are diverse. Differentiation is also useful when competitors are not using this strategy and the market, or industry, is one which experiences rapid, technological change or product innovation.
Price or cost focus	This is essentially a market niche strategy which aims to sell into a comparatively narrow segment of the competition, where lower prices are attractive to the consumer. This form of strategy tends to be used when the business lacks either resources, or the capabilities to offer their products or services to a wider market. It is ideal in situations where the consumers' needs are diverse and there are multiple niches, or segments, within the market. To some extent this is a trial-and-error strategy as each of the segments will differ in size, growth, intensity and profitability. It is also true to state that major industry leaders will not see the niche as being critical to their success and will therefore not focus upon it. Generally the strategy only works if few competitors are targeting the same segment.
Differentiation focus	In essence this is a variant form of market niche strategy, but instead of highlighting low prices as being a key feature, the organisation concentrates on creating differentiating features.
Best cost provider	Theoretically at least, this strategy gives consumers a blend of cost and value, as the organisation is offering them products or services which have a relatively high level of characteristics and quality at a lower cost than most of the competitors. In essence this strategy has two elements: low cost and differentiation, and can be successfully used to target value-conscious buyers. Normally businesses operating this form of strategy do not target the broader market, but niches larger than segments. In order to be successful with this strategy the business has to have sufficient resources and capabilities and must have the facility to be able to scale up their production and their fulfilment whilst maintaining lower costs.

P

Day, George S. and Reibstein, David J., *Wharton on Dynamic Competitive Strategies*. John Wiley & Sons, 1997.

Porter, Michael, *The Competitive Advantage: Creating and Sustaining Superior Performance*. Simon & Schuster, 1998.

Porter, Michael, *Competitive Strategy: Techniques for Analyzing Industries and Competitors*. Simon & Schuster, 1998.

Positioning Strategy

Positioning strategy or product positioning is certainly best described using a multi-dimensional scale. A product's position incorporates many different aspects, features and benefits that may be directly or indirectly associated with the product itself.

In the diagram in Figure 6, the various brands marked A–E are plotted on a multi-dimensional scale and placed in positions that **marketing research** has elicited from the perceptions of customers or consumers, probably both users and non-users. A business will use a positioning strategy for each **market segment** it wishes to target. In other words, it will compare perceptions, both implicit and explicit, against each of the key competitors. Positioning a product requires a number of suppositions, these are:

- That the product, service or brand has objective and/or subjective attributes.
- That potential purchasers may consider one or more of these attributes during the buying process.
- That any respondent has actually considered the attributes of each of the competing products and is, in some way, able to state where they would place a specific brand within the parameters established for the positioning process.

Product positioning is also useful in a pre-launch phase and, indeed, during the design of new products and services. Typically a business will seek to identify the prime desired characteristics and attributes of successful brands by using a multi-dimensional scale to product position these **market leaders**. They will then seek, in their development of the new product or service, to replicate the best features, in order to allow themselves to be in an advantageous position once the brand hits the market.

Marketing strategies need to be specifically designed in order to match the perceived product position of a given brand. In other words, the **marketing mix** needs to support the product position and not seek to undermine it.

Feig, Barry, *Marketing Straight to the Heart: From Product to Positioning to Advertising.* Amacom, 1997.

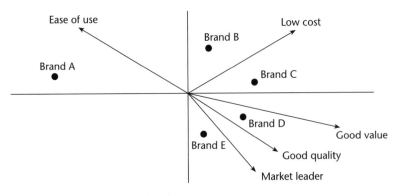

Figure 6 A multi-dimensional scale

Postmodern perspective

Postmodernists view leisure as hedonistic, fragmented and inauthentic. They take the view that self-actualisation is no longer an aspect of leisure. Postmodernists believe that there are few controls over what is and is not an appropriate form of leisure and that institutionalised definitions of acceptable leisure behaviour have all but disappeared.

Preferred supplier

A preferred supplier is an individual or another business or organisation that has a formal arrangement with another business or organisation, with the view to developing a mutually beneficial relationship. The purchasing business will usually have thoroughly checked the supplier to ensure that they uphold specified levels of service, quality and perhaps ethical standards. Increasingly, preferred suppliers have adopted a partnership role, taking on responsibility for the development of new products and services on behalf of their customers, holding buffer stock and supplying expertise as and when it is required. The preferred supplier will not necessarily be the cheapest supplier of equivalent products and services, but will have demonstrated and provided high levels of quality and service. They will be given priority in the selection process when ordering and will in effect be an approved supplier.

Prestige Pricing

Prestige pricing is a pricing strategy which relies on the business, through marketing, to have established a perception in the minds of customers that the product or service has notably superior levels of quality, exclusivity or service. Prestige pricing may also be referred to as 'premium pricing', as products or services have a pricing structure that is often somewhat different from the competitors. The business trades, and relies heavily, on the continued and engrained customer perceptions of the product, for which they are prepared to pay a considerably higher price than for other alternatives available.

Price fixing

Price fixing is associated with businesses or organisations that either individually or collectively conspire to manipulate the pricing of products and services within a given market or geographical region. An organisation that has the sole ability to supply products or services may be considered to be a monopoly if it controls in excess of 50% of the market. Without adequate external control it could therefore charge whatever price it desires, within reason, as customers or clients have no alternative but to make purchases from that organisation. Two or more businesses that collude to fix prices are often referred to as 'cartels'. They secretly agree pricing structures, usually incorporating an agreement or an arrangement that promises not to compete with one another on price grounds, but perhaps to coordinate price-based competition to force other competitors out of the marketplace. In Britain, for example, monopolies and cartels are often investigated by the Competition Commission and can face fines or imprisonment if they are found to be in breach of the competition or enterprise acts.

A very broad range of different leisure-related organisations have been implicated in price fixing scandals. In 2003 in Britain, Argos and Littlewoods were fined

£22.5 million for toy price fixing. In 2006 and again in 2008, British Airways was accused of conspiring with other airlines to fix the price of fuel surcharges.

Price sensitivity

Price sensitivity is a measure of how customers may react to changes in the costs of the products and services that they purchase. It is a term closely associated with price elasticity and it is largely determined by a difference in the perceived value of a product or service or the number of competitors in a market.

Pricing strategies/policies

There are innumerable pricing strategies which can be adopted by business in order to fulfil specific marketing objectives. The most common are summarised in Table 20.

Table 20   Pricing strategies

Pricing Strategy	Explanation
Market penetration pricing	Low prices, particularly when a product is first launched, in order to obtain a significant penetration into the market.
Market skimming	High prices to support heavy advertising and sales promotion. Involves a higher than usual profit margin on each unit sold.
Average price	Basing pricing on the average for the industry.
Product mix	A pricing strategy associated with setting prices along a product line, which successively offers more features or higher quality for a higher price.
Optional	The practice of setting prices according to optional or accessory products that are offered together with the main product.
Captive	Setting a premium price on products that must be used with a popular main product.
Product bundle	Combining several products and offering the whole bundle at a discounted or reduced price.
Discount	Offering a variation in price for those who settle their account quickly, or offering seasonal discounts to encourage customers to buy at times when demand is low.
Discriminatory	Setting the price within a set of parameters, negotiated with each individual customer, dependent upon quantity purchased, location, timescales or product type.
Psychological	Setting prices which appear to be fundamentally better or more appealing to the customer.
Promotional	Offering temporary pricing structures to increase short-term sales, such as loss leaders or prices attached to special events, cash discounts for frequent purchasing or reduced prices for local stockists, where delivery is not a particular concern.
Cost Plus	Setting the price at a set proportion or percentage above the cost of production and all other associated costs.

P

Nagle, Thomas and Holden, Reed, *The Strategy and Tactics of Pricing*. US Imports and PHIPES, 2001.

Primary data

Primary data is information which is collected during **primary research**. It is differentiated from **secondary data** or **secondary research** by virtue of the fact that it has been specifically collected for the purpose of the study which is ongoing. Typical forms of primary data include:

- Customer demographics and socio-economic characteristics.
- Customer lifestyle or psychological characteristics.
- Customer attitudes and opinions.
- Customer awareness and knowledge.
- Customer buying intentions.
- Customer motivation.

Normally primary data is collected using either direct communication with the respondents, verbally or in writing, or by using email, or observation can be used to collect a variety of primary data information.

Sayre, Shay, *Qualitative Methods for Marketplace Research*. Sage Publications, 2001.

Primary research

Primary research is concerned with the collection of **primary data**. By inference the term suggests that any data collected during this **marketing research** exercise should be fresh and hitherto uncollected, collated or analysed information.

Daymon, Christine and Holloway, Immy, *Qualitative Research Methods in Public Relations and Marketing Communications*. Routledge, 2002.

Product differentiation

Product differentiation is also known as 'brand differentiation'. Brand differentiation involves the identification of tangible and intangible benefits or features that can be used to differentiate the brand from competing products or services.

Tangible features or benefits tend to be conscious and rational benefits such as the precise function of the brand and what it achieves or provides to the customer. The intangible benefits tend to be emotional or subconscious features that the business wishes to attach to the brand, such as providing warmth or nourishing food for the family, safety or other physiological needs.

Differentiation strategies include featuring low prices, larger selections, convenient, efficient and rapid service, the latest or most trendy product, prestige or best value overall, and reliability.

P

Productivity

The term 'productivity' can be applied to the broad economy of a nation, region or locality, or a specific organisation, whether this is in the private or public sector. It measures the output in relation to each unit of input. For example, specific productivity measurements can be made in relation to labour, and in this case, each hour worked by employees is an input (and therefore has a definable cost) against the output (again definable, as the output will have a defined value), such as sales price.

Profit margin

A business's profit margin can be calculated in different ways, but essentially it is described as being the profit proportion of a business's sales revenue.

Effectively, the profit margin can be expressed in two different ways; the first uses the following formula:

$$\frac{\text{Profit}}{\text{Selling price}} \times 100$$

If the profit is £100 for an item and the selling price was £500, then:

$$\frac{100}{50} \times 100 = 20\%$$

In this case, the profit margin on the item is 20%. Alternatively, the business could use mark-up as the primary calculation methodology. The mark-up being: the gross profit added by the business to each unit of the product being sold. Using the mark-up method, the following formula is applied:

$$\frac{\text{Gross profit}}{\text{Cost}} \times 100$$

In the same case with the same item, the following calculation can therefore be made, if we assume that the cost (of sales) or direct costs involved are some £400 per unit:

$$\frac{100}{400} \times 100 = 25\%$$

Whilst this figure appears more desirable, it is in fact telling us exactly the same thing, although it has factored in the actual direct cost of sales for that unit, rather than simply addressing the gross profit difference between the sales revenues and profit figures.

Project-based leisure

According to Stebbins (2005), project-based leisure consists of short-term, complex, creative leisure activities that are carried out in free time. This form of leisure requires planning, effort and usually skill or knowledge. It incorporates projects that are followed through until completed, perhaps taking weeks, months or years. Others are of a more intense but shorter duration, such as preparation for a festival, event or celebration.

Stebbins, R. A., 'Project Based Leisure: Theoretical Neglect of a Common Use of Free Time', *Leisure Studies*, 24 (2005), pp. 1–11.

Promotion mix

The term 'promotion mix' describes the combination of two or more elements, which may include advertising, personal selling, public relations, and sales promotion. These four elements are very much the traditional components of the promotion mix. In addition to these, other techniques are now increasingly added to the overall promotion mix. The additional components include:

- Branding
- Corporate image
- Customer service
- Direct marketing
- Exhibitions
- Internal marketing
- Merchandising
- Packaging
- Sponsorship
- Email/internet
- Word of mouth

Proper resource pricing

This is a pricing technique, or approach, that is closely associated with sustainable or **ecotourism**. It involves pricing natural resources at levels that reflect their actual economic and environmental values. It has much to do with ecosystem sustainability and the promotion of cost-effective energy efficiency. It recognises the fact that under-valued resources are often wasted. One such example is clean air. As it has no monetary value it is inevitably wasted in this sense, as it suffers from pollution and is degraded. The conclusion is that if it has no price then it has no perceived value. The European Union has already begun levying energy taxes based on the carbon content of fuel in order to control carbon dioxide emissions.

Pro-poor tourism

Pro-poor tourism is a different approach to tourism development and management. It seeks to increase the linkage between tourism and tourism's contribution to the reduction of poverty in a given area. It seeks to recognise and to develop a direct link between tourism and the poor by incorporating increased local employment into the tourism infrastructure. Clear economic benefits can be enjoyed by regions that can harness the positive aspects of tourism. Employment and local wages, along with training can be improved. Business opportunities can be created. Some local people can offer products and services direct to tourists and others can provide service support. The focus is on increasing the livelihood benefits through empowerment, the mitigation of environmental impact, addressing competing uses of natural resources, managing the social and cultural impacts of tourism and ensuring that tourism income contributes to improvements in services and infrastructure.

> www.odi.org.uk
> www.propoortourism.co.uk

Prospecting

Prospecting relies on the establishment of a comprehensive database which helps identify lists of potential customers. Various criteria are set as to the likelihood of customers wishing to purchase products or services from the business. Customers

P

are ranked in order of their suitability and are systematically contacted by the sales force.

Psychographics

This is a **marketing research** and **market segmentation** technique used to measure **lifestyle** and for the development of lifestyle classifications. The technique relies on measuring customers' AIO (activities, interests and opinions). Psychographic segmentation is a workable means of dividing large markets into smaller groups according to individuals' lifestyles, activities, opinions and beliefs.

Kahle, Lynn R., *Cross-national Consumer Psychographics*. International Business Press, 2000.
Kahle, Lynn R. and Chiagouris, Larry (eds), *Values, Lifestyles and Psychographics*. Lawrence Erlbaum Associates, 1997.

Psychologism

A psycho-logistic approach to the study of leisure, it aims to analyse beliefs, perceptions and motivations of the individual. It tends to ignore any cultural, historical or social contexts. Neulinger (1974) suggested that leisure is a self-enhancing, effective state related to perceived freedom. He suggested that there should be a distinction between intrinsic and extrinsic motivations in leisure, 'intrinsic' being related to an individual's freedom to make leisure choices, whilst 'extrinsic' refers to external criteria that influence an individual to take up a particular leisure activity. Neulinger was of the opinion that individual motivation is the primary driver in individuals choosing particular leisure activities and in this way his approach is similar to that of Iso-Ahola (1989). In this, it is claimed that leisure is identified with freedom and self-determination; leisure experiences revolve around achieving intrinsic rewards and in many cases showing competence at that leisure activity; and also that an individual enjoys mastering a particular leisure activity and individuals will choose a challenging activity that maximises their own sense of fulfilment.

There are links with what is known as 'solipsism', which suggests that the only reality for an individual is their own immediate experience and that nothing exists outside of an individual's consciousness.

Iso-Ahola, S., 'Motivation for Leisure', in E. Jackson and T. Burton (eds), *Understanding Leisure and Recreation: Mapping the Past, Charting the Future*, Venture Publishing, 1989, pp. 247–80.
Neulinger, J., *The Psychology of Leisure*, Charles Thomas, 1974.

Public Liability (PL) insurance

PL insurance covers any awards of damages given to a member of the public because of an injury or damage to their property caused by a business or one of its employees or representatives. It also covers any related legal fees, costs and expenses as well as the costs of hospital treatment (including ambulance costs) that the NHS may claim from the business. Premiums are usually calculated on the basis of the business turnover, the type of business and an estimate of the level of activity of the business. Hotel premiums are usually calculated on the number of beds provided, to reflect the number of guests; likewise a theme park's premium would be based on the average number of visitors, but modified by an assessment of the possible risks (historical or theoretical) that those visitors might face in using the facilities, attractions and rides at the park.

Public relations

The basic function of public relations is to establish and maintain a mutual understanding between a business and its publics. Typically, public relations activities will include the preparation of press kits, seminars, making charitable donations and sponsorships, community relations and lobbying.

Broadly, public relations have the following objectives:

- Establish and maintain the prestige and reputation of the business.
- Support the promotion of products and services.
- Deal with arising issues and opportunities.
- Establish and maintain goodwill with customers, employees, government, suppliers and distributors.
- Deal promptly with unfavourable publicity.

In effect, public relations seek to transfer a negative or null opinion of the business into knowledge or a positive attitude. Public relations can be seen as distinctly different from advertising, as can be seen in Table 21.

Table 21 Public relations and advertising

Public Relations	Advertising
Informative	Informative and persuasive
Subdued messages	Immediate impact
No repetition	Repetition
Credibility	Less credible
Newsworthy	Not necessary
Low cost	High cost

P

Mazur, Laura and White, Jon, *Strategic Communications Management: Making Public Relations Work*. Addison Wesley, 1994.

Pull strategy

'Pull strategy' is a term which is simultaneously related to both distribution and advertising. Literally, as the term implies, advertising and marketing aim to motivate end users to demand a product or service. They then approach the retailer, who is then persuaded to stock the products and services.

As can be seen in the diagram in Figure 7, pull and **push strategy** can be used simultaneously to force products and services through distributors to the end users.

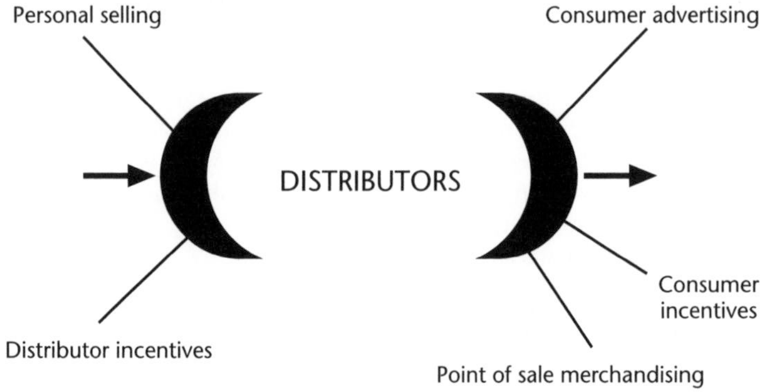

Personal selling

Consumer advertising

DISTRIBUTORS

Consumer incentives

Distributor incentives

Point of sale merchandising

Figure 7 Pull strategy and push strategy

Push strategy

An alternative to, or perhaps used in conjunction with, a **pull strategy** is a push strategy, which aims to provide encouragement to distributors to stock and therefore make available products and services to end users. The principal objective of a push strategy is to offer incentives, usually through personal selling techniques, to distributors to encourage them to stock and display products and services, thus achieving the goal of pushing the products and services through the distribution channel to the end user.

P

Qualitative research

Qualitative research is a **marketing research** approach which largely revolves around interview methods. It is distinct from **quantitative research** in the sense that its sample is far smaller, but the depth of the information is greater. Typically, qualitative research techniques would include depth interviews and group discussions. Qualitative research would be used for a number of different research projects, including exploratory, diagnostic, evaluative and creative work (see Table 22).

Table 22 Strengths and weaknesses of qualitative research

Strengths of Qualitative Research	Weaknesses of Qualitative Research
• Depth and detail on each individual respondent may be high.	• Fewer people studied.
	• Less easy to generalise.
• Openness – respondents tend to be more prepared to be open using a personal approach.	• Difficult to aggregate data.
	• Highly dependent on researchers' skills.
• Can help avoid pre-judgements.	• Setting where respondent is questioned may affect results.

Seale, Clive, *The Quality of Qualitative Research*. Sage Publications, 1999.
Silverman, David, *Interpreting Qualitative Data*. Sage Publications, 2001.

Quality assurance

Quality assurance is attempts by a business to make sure that agreed quality standards are met throughout the organisation, primarily to ensure customer satisfaction. There has been a degree of international agreement about quality, consistency and satisfaction, which are enshrined in the International Standards Organisation (ISO) 9000 series of quality systems standards. If a business meets these standards, it is normally assumed that they have achieved quality assurance.

Quantitative research

Quantitative research is a **marketing research** approach which entails the collection and analysis of data, primarily in numerical form. Quantitative research tends to be the preferred option when a researcher is looking to test the existence of relationships between variables, or looking at specific attributes in a population, which may be based on measurements derived from a sample. Quantitative researchers tend to assume that within a range of probabilities, providing they use appropriate and objective research, a definite anticipated outcome can be established. The key to effective quantitative research is to minimise the possibility of error or bias. In order to evaluate the quality of the quantitative research, usually certain criteria are used, as can be seen in Table 23.

Table 23   Criteria for evaluating quantitive research

Criteria	Description and implications
Construct validity	Does the study actually measure the attributes and variables which were the intended purpose of the survey?
Reliability	Was the data collection methodology sound enough to provide accurate and consistent measures?
Internal validity	Were extraneous variables eliminated and were rival explanations controlled?
External validity	Was a sound sampling strategy employed, given the time constraints and the information accessed?

Creswell, J. W., *Research Design: Qualitative and Quantitative Approaches*. Sage Publications, 1994.
Nardi, Peter M., *Doing Survey Research: A Guide to Quantitative Research Methods*. Allyn & Bacon, 2002.

Queuing theory

Queuing theory addresses how an organisation deals with customers' orders and calls. Typically, queuing theory will attempt to estimate the average performance of the system by investigating various aspects of the time taken to deal with a customer's request. Investigations and estimations will be made of the mean time customers are in the queue before their request or order has been fulfilled. Similar calculations will be made regarding the number of customers in the queue and the number of individual products related to those orders which are in the queue. Queuing theory is useful in understanding the limitations or problems associated with *capacity*, but it does not necessarily take into account the mean arrival rates of the requests or orders, the changeover or set-up periods involved in switching from one customer's order to another, or, for that matter, service and maintenance issues.

Quota sampling

Quota sampling is used extensively in **marketing research**. The basic purpose is to identify the correct proportion of respondents who have the same agreed characteristics as the target research population. Typically, an interviewer will be given quotas of particular groups of people that they are required to interview. If, for example, the research population is known to consist of 70% women, of whom 50% are over 55, then this quota will be explicitly stated to the interviewer. They will be required to interview a proportionate sample in line with the quota sample criteria. There can be complex criteria used in quota sampling, which may encompass age, gender or type of household. The quota sample aims to make the survey as representative as possible and help to eliminate sampling errors.

There is another variant of quota sampling called 'non-proportionate quota sampling', which does not require the interviewer to match the proportion in the research population. Interviewers are simply instructed to interview a minimum number of individuals in each particular identified group.

Barnett, Vic, *Sample Survey Principles and Methods*. Arnold, 2002.

Q

Race and leisure

The study of race at an even broader level than a simple investigation into race and leisure often began with the supposition that individuals from different races are biologically different in some way. Kraus (1994) wrote:

> A race is a statistical aggregation of people who share a composite of genetically transmissible physical traits, such as skin pigmentation, head form, facial features, stature, and the color, distribution and texture of body hair. Since gross similarities are to be noted among human populations, many attempts have been made to classify these people of the world racially. Estimates of racial types range from 3 – Caucasoid, Mongoloid and Negroid – to 30 or more.

However, classifying individuals purely on this biological definition of race fails to explain many aspects that relate race and leisure. It does not incorporate income, wealth, healthcare, education or availability of leisure time. Whilst race can correlate directly to some of these factors but not on a biological basis, it can indirectly relate to leisure activities.

Society is multiracial and undoubtedly whatever physical differences may or may not exist, they do not have a direct impact on an individual's personal decision to become involved in a particular leisure activity, although the state, culture and hierarchy may conspire to either deflect them or block them from participation.

There has been very little investigation into the link between race and leisure. Studies have been more concerned with class and it was not until the 1960s that any particular focus was made on the availability and inequality of leisure services and recreation in respect of race. Much of this derived from the civil rights movement in the United States. Writers such as Roberts (1970) believed that society was moving into a period where there would be leisure democracy, where there would be no attempt by any visible or invisible agency to prevent or inhibit freedom and choice.

Certainly in the past 20 years or so there have been a number of investigations into comparative participation of different races in a wide range of leisure activities, but in the majority of cases they have always separated social class and race, whilst simultaneously looking at combined factors such as social status, gender and age. There has been relatively little research that can seek to explain why particular racial groups may or may not be attracted to particular leisure activities. This is also compounded by the fact that there are clearly different participation rates according to gender.

Kraus, R., *Leisure in a Changing America: Multicultural Perspectives*. Macmillan, 1994.
Roberts, K., *Leisure*. Longman, 1970.

Rack rate

'Rack rate' is a term that is used in the travel and tourism industry to describe the price that a customer would pay if they were to contact a hotel directly instead of operating through a travel agent or an online service. Usually the price charged by the hotel is considerably higher in the rack rate, but this is not necessarily the case as the hotel may take the view that if they are not prepared to negotiate the price then the room will remain empty.

Rack rate is also referred to as 'walk up rate', retail price or actual price. Hotels will inevitably show high rack rates and be prepared to negotiate down to a price that they actually expect for the accommodation.

Random sampling

Random sampling is a **marketing research** technique in which a sample of respondents is chosen to represent the target research population. On the basis that each individual approached by a researcher has an equal chance of being chosen, the likelihood of bias is seemingly reduced.

Reach

The word 'reach' has several connotations related to the leisure and tourism industry. In its most basic form, 'reach' can refer to the catchment area in which a leisure facility can confidently expect to attract potential customers. It can also be related to marketing reach, referring to the ability or range of the leisure facility, in so far as it can publicise its products and services to a broader geographical area and confidently expect, or anticipate, positive responses through bookings and interest. With the ability to market products and services via the internet, theoretically all leisure facilities have an infinite reach, but practically speaking it is about being able to attract paying customers or clients, rather than simply informing potential target markets of the availability of products and services at a specified location.

Reach also implies contacting relatively untapped audiences through social networks, conventional advertising and publicity. Reach, however, is inextricably linked to the ability of the organisation to convert potential interest and enquiries into firm sales and bookings.

Realm of freedom

According to Marx, the realm of freedom is the set of relations that support the free and full development of an individual. Marx believed that these relations could only develop after the removal of the capitalist class and when those who actually produced products and services controlled the means of production. The realm of freedom, therefore, is directly associated with a Communist society, which Marx believed to be the long-term objective in evolution.

See also **realm of necessity**.

Marx, K., *Capital*. Lawrence & Wishart, 1977.

Realm of necessity

These are the obligations of individuals to reproduce themselves. Marx believed that the realm of necessity was controlled by the dominant capitalist class. The capitalist class's wealth was based on the exploitation of all other classes and the using of surpluses. He believed that although capitalism did allow workers time off, their ability to involve themselves in leisure was reduced because they were physically exhausted. Marx wrote:

> Man only feels himself freely active in his animal functions – eating, drinking, procreating, or at most in his dwelling and dressing up, etc. and in his human functions he no longer feels himself to be anything but an animal. What is animal becomes human and what is human becomes animal. Certainly eating, drinking, procreating etc. are also genuinely human functions. But abstractly taken, separated from the sphere of all other human activity and turned into soul and ultimate ends, they are animal functions.

See also **realm of freedom.**

Marx, K., *The Economic and Philosophic Manuscripts 1844*. International Press, 1964.

Receiving agent

A receiving agent is often used in the travel and tourism business and is a contractor, or partner organisation, which provides services to passengers, such as those that have booked tours. Receiving agents are responsible for organising aspects of a total tour package, such as transportation to and from accommodation or the selling, organising and provision of excursions.

Receptive operator

In essence a receptive operator is an inbound tour operator. This is a tour operator or travel agent that specialises in providing services to incoming tourists at a resort or in a region.

Recession

Recession is part of the economic or business cycle in as much as it represents a period when there is a slowing down of demand. In effect a recession occurs when there is a fall in the growth of a nation's gross national product. It is typified by a reduction in the level of investment, poor business confidence and, consequently, a growth in unemployment figures. In financial terms, a recession represents a formidable challenge to businesses as they must continue to operate, perhaps reducing output and cutting back on overheads, whilst remaining ready to take advantage of an upturn in the business cycle.

Serious and long-term recessions are often referred to as depressions, reflecting the fact that demand and business activity are significantly reduced during these periods. Ultimately, the recession will break; but not before imprudent organisations have been driven out of business.

Allen, Roy, *Financial Crises and Recession in the Global Economy*. Edward Elgar, 1999.

R

Recreation

A recreation activity can be distinguished from a leisure activity, as it is primarily an activity that aims to amuse or stimulate. It is perhaps most closely associated with physical activities and therefore has an association with outdoor pursuits. According to Walmsley and Jenkins (2003), recreation has a great deal to do with personal development and aims to bring: 'A degree of balance to spirit, mind and body'.

Recreation can be differentiated from broader leisure pursuits as they tend to provide an opportunity for individuals to involve themselves in activities in different surroundings, perhaps new landscapes and ecosystems. Recreation literally derives from the Latin meaning 'to restore', implying both psychological and physical revitalisation. Whilst the majority of leisure activities are based around the home, or at least around technology of some sort, recreation certainly adding the outdoor element to the definition has become enormously popular. Huge numbers of citizens based in urban environments decamp to visit the countryside and engage in the broadest possible range of recreational activities. Throughout the world, millions of trips into the countryside are made each year. Many of the recreational activities are based on land or water, physical pursuits, from golf to horse riding, rafting, windsurfing, photography and **backpacking**. Increasingly, participation in nature-based recreation has become an important aspect of many individuals' leisure times.

As with many other broader forms of leisure activity, a host of factors, largely socio-economic, affect the level to which different sections of the community involve themselves in recreation. Outdoor recreation studies are a broad and important area of leisure studies and have attracted an enormous amount of academic attention. In some countries it has also come to the fore with governments launching initiatives and programmes in order to encourage greater participation in outdoor recreation. These have become embedded in tourist programmes across the world. As Roberts (1978) argued, the study of recreation is still too narrow:

> Recreation is only part of leisure. Suggesting that the quality of life depends upon sports complexes and fun centres smacks of 'bread and circuses'. The second objection is that the recreation approach is asociological, meaning that it takes too little account of how both supply and demand for recreation facilities are likely to be influenced by the wider social system.

Pigram, J. and Jenkins, J., *Outdoor Recreation Management*. Routledge, 2006.
Roberts, K., *Contemporary Society and the Growth of Leisure*. Longman, 1978.
Walmsley, D. J. and Jenkins, J. M., 'Leisure', in *Encyclopaedia of Leisure and Outdoor Recreation*. Routledge, 2003.

Recreation management

With the increase in interest in outdoor recreation there has been a growing concern regarding the maintenance, management and impact of tens of thousands, if not hundreds of thousands, of people visiting the countryside or wilderness areas. This has brought about a new breed of management concerned with various aspects of resource management. According to Pigram and Jenkins (2006): 'Outdoor recreation is recognized as an important form of resource use and particular attention is given to the adequacy of the resource base to provide a quality environment for sustained use.'

Patmore (1983), whilst focusing on rural areas, also highlighted the fact that leisure and recreation demands on rural areas, the coasts, water resources and other factors needed closer management:

The explosion of leisure activities during the 1960s, and in particular the rapid growth of the use of the countryside for recreation, sparked an academic interest that closely paralleled the practical concern of planners with the phenomenon. Much of this interest came from geographers and led to several papers and texts of note in the late 1960s and early 1970s.

Therefore recreation management incorporates social aspects, access, disability, mobility, travel behaviour, recreational experiences and a host of other elements that combine to ensure that outdoor environments are able to be sustained and protected, both for current users and for future generations.

Patmore, A. J., *Recreation and Resources: Leisure Patterns and Leisure Places*. Blackwell, 1983.

Pigram, J. and Jenkins, J., *Outdoor Recreation Management*. Routledge, 2006.

Refinancing

Refinancing involves the replacement of one loan with another. Typically a business will obtain a new loan commensurate with the size of the outstanding balance of an existing loan and use this new loan capital, probably with the same property as collateral, to eliminate the original loan. This is usually undertaken in order to take advantage of a more preferable interest rate, although there are implications financially regarding the fees for such a refinancing deal.

Businesses also use refinancing to reduce the term of a longer loan, or perhaps to switch from a fixed rate loan to an adjustable rate loan, taking advantage of recent falls in the interest rate.

Refinancing is not always an option for businesses, particularly if there are what are known as pre-payment or early settlement fees attached to the existing loan. These penalty charges often offset the advantages of shifting to another loan under a refinancing package.

Friedman, Jack P. and Harris, Jack C., *Keys to Mortgage Financing and Refinancing*. Barrons Educational Series, 2001.

Regional development agencies

In Britain in 1998 the Regional Development Agencies Act created a number of regional development agencies (RDAs) around England. They were first launched in 1999 and are concerned with the economic prosperity and opportunity in nine different English regions. One of the principal roles of the organisations is to improve levels of education, learning and skills and to support continued enhancement of the environment and the infrastructure. Collectively, since 2002, over 500,000 jobs have been created as a direct or indirect result of RDAs' involvement.

www.englandrdas.com

Relationship marketing

Relationship marketing attempts to develop a long-term relationship with customers on the premise that it is far cheaper to retain existing customers than it is to attract new ones. There are a number of factors involved in relationship marketing, which tend to frame the exact nature of how it works within a given organisation, these are:

- A primary focus on customer attention.
- An orientation towards product benefits rather than product features.
- An emphasis on commitment and contact with customers.
- The adoption of a total quality approach.
- The development of ongoing relationships with customers.
- The deployment of employees at various levels to maintain contact.
- The cultivation of key customers.
- The emphasis on trust, honesty and promise keeping.

Egan, John, *Relationship Marketing*. Financial Times, Prentice Hall, 2001.
Payne, Adrian; Christopher, Martin; Peck, Helen and Clark, Moira, *Relationship Marketing for Competitive Advantage: Winning and Keeping Customers*. Butterworth-Heinemann, 1998.

Remote ticketing

Remote ticketing means that a travel agent or a website can allow a customer to make a reservation at one location and then generate a ticket at another location. Many businesses will use proprietary software, such as Amadeus, in order to print documents and issue document print commands. It uses a system of branch and remote offices, which can send print requests. Satellite offices usually have limited access to the remote ticketing functions. Ticket delivery offices are usually located at airports or city locations and print the travel documents on behalf of accredited agents. Remote ticketing provides an extremely convenient service for the travel industry. Individuals can order their travel through an agency and then either pick up their documents at the ticket printing location, or have them forwarded to them by conventional mail.

www.amadeus.com

Repeat customer

'Repeat customer', associated with the concept of customer retention, is a marketing term used in relation to activities designed to ensure that customers remain customers and are not lost to the competition. Customer retention can measure the degree to which a business loses its customers and suggest reasons why they have been lost. Remedial activities are then put in place to stem this trend and, in the longer term, activities and policies are created in order to prevent similar loses. Data is collected regarding lapsed customers through customer-retention focused market research, which seeks to identify reasons why customers are no longer purchasing from the business.

Murphy, John, *The Lifebelt: The Definitive Guide to Managing Customer Retention*. John Wiley & Sons, 2001.

R

Research and development

New product development and the bright ideas associated with such an endeavour must be tempered with the practicalities of production. Whilst many good ideas appear to be workable on paper, the realities of the situation may mean that the product cannot be produced in a cost-effective and efficient manner.

An organisation has to assess whether it is looking for a new product that its current production process is capable of producing. It would serve no purpose for an organisation to develop an idea for a new product only to discover that the actual production process has to be carried out elsewhere, possibly by subcontractors or business partners. After all, one of the key considerations in developing new products, regardless of their design, is that the organisation should make full use of its production facilities.

The design of new products is often changed gradually as the organisation becomes aware that the actual design presents problems. This process, although not enjoyable for the designer, needs to be considered in terms of efficiency and overall benefit to the organisation. Whether the design process is undertaken by the organisation itself or by external organisations, the business must ensure that it carries out feasibility studies. These are undertaken at the earliest possible stage to ensure that resources are not wasted in the development of a new product design when there is no likelihood of that product being produced in a cost-effective way. This screening process needs to be rigorously enforced to make sure that the business does not invest funds in product designs that are impractical and will never come to fruition. The development of new products can be not only time consuming but expensive. The desire to develop new products should be tempered by an awareness that many small businesses fail as a result of over-investing in new product development. However, the success of new products is central to the long-term success and growth of the organisation. It should be noted that only a small percentage of new products are ever successful. It is imperative for an organisation to plan its new product development using the following steps:

- Allow an initial screening period in which an investigation is carried out to assess how the product fits in with current products and services.
- Investigate whether the new product could be produced using current production methods.
- Test the production process.
- Fully cost the production process.
- Carry out the necessary market research.
- Produce a test batch of new products and test market them.

Resource audit

A resource audit seeks to identify and value all of the resources that are available to a business, organisation or indeed a destination. Some of the resources will be owned, but others are available through supplier arrangements, **joint ventures** or partnerships. One of the most common types of resource audit is a human resource audit, which looks at an organisation's policies, procedures and practices and aims to create a comprehensive system that effectively adds value.

Responsible tourism

Responsible tourism has close ties with sustainable or **ecotourism**. However, responsible tourism tends to be more closely linked with the tourists' choice of destination and mode of transport to that destination. Others take the view that responsible tourism should generate economic benefits for local people and involve local people in decision-making that will directly affect their lives and life chances. Responsible tourism should also minimise the social, economic and environmental impact on particular regions. It also stresses that tourism needs to be culturally sensitive and make a positive contribution to the conservation of cultural and natural **heritage**, and to respect diversity.

www.responsibletourismpartners.org

Retail Price Index (RPI)

The Retail Price Index (RPI) is the UK equivalent of the Consumer Price Index (CPI) in the US. The RPI represents an index of prices of products and services aimed at the consumer market (in other words, regularly purchased by average householders). The shifts between years are calculated by selecting a base year, which is given a value of 100. In subsequent years, the change in the price of the *basket* of products and services is expressed as a percentage change from that base figure. If, for example, the base year was set in relation to 1995, then the RPI could be expressed in the manner shown in Table 24.

Table 24   Retail Price Index

Year	RPI	% Change from Index
1995	100	–
1996	108	8%
1997	110	10%
1998	112	12%
1999	114	14%
2000	118	18%
2001	120	20%
2002	125	25%
2003	128	28%
2004	130	30%

In this fictitious case, the RPI shows that the basket of products and services is 30% more expensive in 2004 than it had been in 1995.

Retail Sales Index

R

The Retail Sales Index is a US monthly figure which measures products sold by retailers. Each month a sample of retail outlets of varying types and sizes is chosen in order to calculate the volume of trade undertaken in the previous month. The Retail Sales Index is widely believed to be a prime indicator of consumer confidence. It is released in the middle of each month and relates to data collated from the previous month. The report only deals with products and not services, and therefore does not cover the entire range of consumer purchases in a given month. Nonetheless, many businesses and government agencies consider that the Retail Sales Index is an indicator of great value, showing in which direction the economy is currently moving.

Revenue management

'Revenue management', as the term implies, relates to managing or maximising revenues or profits, usually for fixed, perishable resources, such as hotel rooms or airline seats. It is also often referred to as either 'data management' or 'yield management'. It is particularly important in the airline industry, in hotels, car rentals and transportation, as the resources that they sell are all perishable.

See also **yield management**.

Right-wing politics

The term 'right wing' is used to describe organisations, parties or individuals with a tendency towards conservative or reactionary positions. The term is believed to have derived from the period of the French Revolution, where those that supported the monarch sat on the right in the parliament. Right-wing political groups tend to be supporters of forms of capitalism and can be nationalistic, traditionalist and pro-religion. There are of course many different types of right-wing politics around the world, from the centre or centre-right to more extreme ultra-right parties. They are usually implacably opposed to those that are broadly referred to as left-wing.

See also **left-wing politics**.

Risk management

Risk management is an integral part of managerial responsibility. Risk management does not just apply to managers in senior positions, as it takes place on a daily basis at various levels of risk. There are no tried and trusted methodologies of risk management, but there have been several attempts to create standard model, as can be seen in the diagram in Figure 8.

This is, however, a rather simplistic means of assessing risks and dealing with the risk management procedure, since it suggests that each risk can be addressed

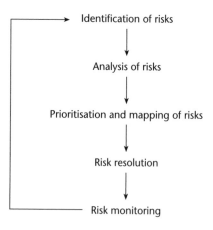

Figure 8   Standard Risk Management Model

one-by-one, and in fact risk management often involves dealing with several risks simultaneously. Therefore a more complex risk management model, such as the diagram in Figure 9, may be employed.

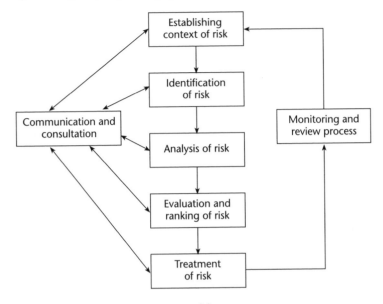

Figure 9 Complex Risk Management Model

Other businesses prefer to take a more proactive approach with regard to risk management and may well evaluate the probability of risks and its impacts prior to the risk even taking place or threatening to take place. These forms of proactive risk management can be exemplified in the model shown in Figure 10.

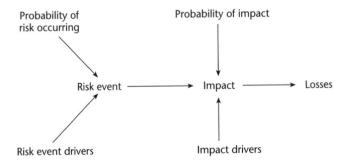

Figure 10 Proactive Risk Management Model

Smith, Preston C. and Merritt, Guy M., *Proactive Risk Management*. Productivity Press, 2002.

Romantic organicism

Gellner (1998) suggested the ethic of cognition. He saw this as an individual's right to scrutinise rules, precedent and hierarchy even though in challenging them it could result in punishment. In essence it underpins criticism and innovation and implies the sweeping away of obedience. Gellner believed that individual choice comprised two models:

- Atomistic individualism – where the judgement of the individual is paramount and individuals strive to become self-sufficient through their own efforts, and even though they may need to cooperate with others it is individual enterprise that develops a coherent world.
- Romantic organicism – this suggests that the community is paramount and that the individual is subservient and subject to its laws. An individual is there to contribute to the continued improvement and development of society and, in order to have social membership and belonging, cooperation is imperative.

In essence, romantic organicism views an individual not as a solitary being but as part of a community. The community's values have a single culture that is hostile to pluralism and to diversity. In this respect, any leisure activities undertaken by the individual have to reflect the central values of the group.

On the other hand, atomistic individualism takes the view that individuals, whilst being members of a community, will only enjoy satisfaction if they pursue their own self-interests. Pluralism and diversity are celebrated and freedom to be involved in any form of leisure practice that contributes towards innovation or development, either at an individual or a cultural level, is desirable. Atomistic individualism is therefore linked to **voluntarism**, **psychologism** and pluralism, whilst romantic organicism is linked to moralism, socialism and determinism.

Although these two differing approaches are necessarily theoretical, there are parallels in real-life experiences. It is possible that some societies are organised along romantic organicism lines, such as Germany during the period of Nazi rule, or the Soviet Union as exemplified by the brand of Communism of Stalin. Stepping out of line or defying values in both instances were met with the full force of the state.

Gellner, E., *Language and Solitude*. Cambridge University Press, 1998.

R

Sales margin

A margin can be applied either to the total business carried out by an organisation, or to a specific product, range or service. In its more general use, 'margin' is expressed as the gross profit as a percentage of the turnover of the business. When applied to specific products, it refers to the difference between the total costs (including overheads) attributed to the product, compared with the selling price of that product. In this respect, 'margin' is not dissimilar to the term 'mark-up' which may be based on a fixed percentage addition to the costs of a product in order to ensure a sufficient profit margin.

Scheduled flight/tour

Most major airline operators will run a scheduled timetable. Flights are set to leave at a particular time on certain days each week and will fly, regardless of the number of seats sold. Some of these scheduled flights are seasonal and cater specifically for the package tour market. Many of these are ad hoc to some extent and will depend on bookings and capacity usage. They are not scheduled flights in the broadest sense of the term, as they are only peak scheduled services. All other types of flight used for passenger traffic are known as charter flights. These are one-off services, put on according to demand.

Seasonal relative/factor

Seasonal factors are used as a more accurate means by which an organisation can estimate demand in a given period. Typically, the organisation will calculate the average demand across the year, giving it a base line to work towards in each month. Many businesses experience fluctuations in demand as a result of seasonal influences. They will therefore calculate a weighting and apply it to specific months which match recognised fluctuations in demand. Therefore an organisation which produces products for the Christmas period may weight the months preceding the critical months with a larger factor than months after the critical period has passed. For example, a business may weight October to December as 3.0, whilst they may weight January to March as 0.5. Using the average demand across the year, the factor is then applied to that average demand in order to calculate the required number of finished products to be ready by that month.

Second tier airport

A second tier airport is a subsidiary airport that is distinct from the central hub for international and domestic flights in a given region or city. Many of these major airports are reaching or have reached maximum capacity in terms of their ability to handle flights. Consequently, second tier airports are used to cater for additional traffic which needs to connect with that specific destination. In many cases the second tier airports are used by low cost carriers, as an alternative that is often cheaper than flying direct into the main hub. There has been considerable debate as to whether it is ethically sound for an airline to claim that they are flying into a specified city location when in fact the aircraft actually terminates at a location 50 or more kilometres from the international hub.

Secondary data

In **marketing research**, secondary data, or **secondary research**, is seen often as a viable alternative to **primary data** or **primary research**. Typically, secondary data can be described as being either internal or external sources of information. Internal data includes information which is already held by the business commissioning the marketing research study and may include sales invoices, customer records and warranty cards, etc. A vast amount of other secondary data is, of course, available external to the business in the form of published or commercially available data. Typical examples would include a government census or a set of syndicated research findings.

Secondary data certainly has an advantage in terms of cost and time. However, it is often the case that the available secondary data does not match the research design in terms of its objectives. It may also be the case that the data has aged to the extent that it is no longer relevant and that it would be foolish to base any decisions on that data. It is also notoriously difficult to verify the accuracy of secondary data, particularly if it has been republished and it is not clear how the information was initially gathered. There is often no indication as to the degree of error that may have crept into that research.

There are, however, several ways of evaluating secondary data, these are:

- Is the data specifically useful for the research study?
- How current is the data?
- Is the data dependable and has it been verified?
- Is there any bias?
- What methodologies and specifications were employed?
- What was the objective of the original data collection?
- What is the nature of the data available in terms of variables, measurement and categories?

Secondary research

Secondary research involves the gathering of **secondary data**. Secondary research is usually concerned with the scanning and collection of relevant publications, literature and other data sources. It is usually accepted that secondary research is an easier form of marketing research to manage than **primary research**.

Stewart, David W. and Kamins, Michael A., *Secondary Research: Information Sources and Methods* (2nd edition). Sage Publications, 1993.

Security surcharge

Even before the terrorist attacks against targets as diverse as New York, Bali and London, airlines and airports were levying security charges on passenger tickets that passed through specific hubs. In 2006, for example, the British government announced that they were considering adding a fresh surcharge to flight tickets in order to offset some of the tens of millions that were being spent on security staff, training and upgraded equipment. This was largely at the request of the British Airports Authority (BAA Ltd), who in the run-up to 2006 had spent £14 million in additional security costs.

Self-regulation

Self-regulation is either a private agreement or a set of standards which have been agreed by members of an industrial sector. These self-regulating standards may be either substantive or procedural. Although it is not always the case, self-regulation may mean the absence of government regulation. However, many governments enter into an agreement with the industry and may provide a safety net.

Theoretically, self-regulation reduces, but perhaps does not eliminate, the need for government regulation or involvement. Self-regulation can be more flexible than government regulation as it can be changed to reflect the impact of new technologies. Self-regulation is also valuable in establishing a dialogue between customers and the industry and establishing trust between them.

Self-regulation, however, is less transparent and potentially subject to manipulation or collusion by the industry. Equally it may be the case that customers and the government may lack the means to enforce industry compliance. Self-regulation is appropriate in some circumstances, but not in cases where there is a monopoly provider.

Semiotics

Semiotics is the science of signs. There are three key branches: semantics, which refers to the relationship between signs and what they refer to; syntactic, which is the relation of signs to each other; and pragmatics, which is the relation of signs to those who use them. It has been applied to the study of leisure in MacCannell (1999) in his study of markers, and Gottdiener (1997) in his work on the theming of consumer and leisure cultures. MacCannell took the view that a sign seeks to represent something to someone else and that signs narrate. Some signs may have complex meanings, such as the Statue of Liberty, symbolising hope and freedom.

Gottdiener, M., *The Theming of America*. Westview, 1997.
MacCannell, D., *The Tourist*. University of California Press, 1999.

Serious leisure

Serious leisure is taken to be an amateur hobby or unpaid activity that is founded on a disciplined approach to the acquiring of knowledge and skills. In effect the individual organises this leisure activity rather like a career, **benchmarking** their progress. It also incorporates a considerable allocation of time and money and a strong identification with the area in which the activity lies. Typical examples

S

revolve around self-enrichment or in the enhancement of self-image, whilst others are related to social integration. Prime examples include membership of drama groups, creative writing classes, wargaming or chess clubs. The concept was originally suggested by Stebbins (2001) when he made the distinction between serious and casual leisure practices.

Stebbins, R., *New Directions in the Theory and Research of Serious Leisure*. Mellen Press, 2001.

SERVQUAL

SERVQUAL was created by Parasuraman, Zeithaml and Berry and is used consistently in industry, particularly by those in the service sector. It measures the difference between customer expectations, and perceptions after they have undergone a customer service experience with the organisation.

SERVQUAL assists an organisation in obtaining feedback from customers on the following five dimensions of customer service:

- Tangibles – the organisation's physical facilities, its equipment, and the appearance of its personnel.
- Reliability – the organisation's ability to perform the promised service dependably and accurately.
- Responsiveness – the organisation's and its employees' willingness to help customers and provide them with a prompt service.
- Assurance – the organisation's and its employees' levels of competence, courtesy, credibility and security.
- Empathy – the customer's ability to access the organisation and its information, and its employees' ability to communicate with and understand the needs of its customers.

Despite criticism from some academics, SERVQUAL is used extensively in the service industry. One of the main criticisms is that service quality may not be a function of the gap between a customer's expectation and the actual service they receive, but that it is a function of the value that is delivered to the customer.

The SERVQUAL scale was developed by Parasuraman, Zeithaml and Berry, and their development work has been replicated by several researchers and many have recommended that the scale be adapted to suit each particular service setting.

Parasuraman, A., Zeithaml, Valarie A. and Berry, Leonard L., 'A Conceptual Model of Service Quality and its Implications for Future Research', *Journal of Marketing*, Vol. 49 (Fall 1985), pp. 41–50.

Short haul

'Short haul' is a term that is associated with the length of an airline flight. They are usually domestic or may involve a short trip across a state boundary. Normally they are taken to be no more than 800 km or around 1.5 hours in duration. They are almost exclusively non-stop flights. Some larger tour operators classify any flight under 3 hours as being a short haul flight.

See also **long haul.**

Shoulder season

A shoulder season is a period between high and low seasons. They are increasingly heavily marketed by tour operators, as they often provide many of the advantages of high season, whilst avoiding the lack of facilities often experienced during low seasons. The prices of many of the hotels, flights and holidays are reduced in order to tempt passengers to travel during shoulder seasons. Ski resorts, for example, will cite early December as being a shoulder season, and in the Mediterranean late March and April, avoiding Easter, is a shoulder season, as is late September and early October.

Simple random sample
See **random sampling.**

SkillsActive

SkillsActive is one of the twenty-five Sector Skills Councils in Britain. SkillsActive focuses on the active leisure and learning industry. It identifies five sub-sectors:

- Sport and recreation
- Health and fitness
- Playwork
- The outdoors
- Caravans

The organisation provides employers, training providers and policy makers with advice on skills development and training. It is a government-funded organisation, which aims to involve more employers and their workforce in best-practice training and development programmes. The primary aim being to improve productivity and reduce skills gaps and shortages, it aims to take a strategic lead in the development of demand-led, flexible learning and skills development. It is also part of a broader EU-wide strategy where there is also a focus on workforce development.

www.skillsactive.com

Social capital

'Social capital' is a term that is used to describe a positive social structure that aims to have all of the ingredients necessary for sustained economic development. Positive social capital therefore implies that there is a high level of skills in the workforce (vital for the knowledge-based economy) and that there is widespread engagement with networks across the country. Equally, there will be a high level of interdependence of activities in a complex society.

There is often a key distinction made between a group's internal social capital (such as being a distinctive ethnic group) and its external social capital (focusing on the informal links it has with wider networks). In this respect, social capital is often used as the opposite of **social exclusion.**

See **social cohesion.**

Social class

Social class or socio-economic measures or classifications are often used in **marketing research**. There are several different varieties of social class and grades. The National Readership Survey (UK) identifies the categories listed in Table 25.

Social cohesion

The term 'social cohesion' is usually attributed to the Ouseley, Cantle and Denham reports which were produced in the aftermath of the riots in Britain in summer of 2001. The term was originally used to analyse and criticise attempts which had been made to reduce the level of **social exclusion** which had focused on building internal **social capital** without paying any attention to the importance of dealing with external social capital. The phrase that describes the state of affairs which was assumed to have led to the riots was 'parallel lives' (Cantle Report).

See **social capital**.

Denham, J., *Building Cohesive Communities: A Report of the Ministerial Group on Public Order and Community Cohesion*. Home Office, 2002.

An online copy of the Ouseley Report can be found at www.bradford2020.com
An online copy of the Cantle Report is at www.oldham.gov.uk

Social exclusion

'Social exclusion' refers not only to poverty, and low income, but to some of the wider causes and the consequences. The British government defines social exclusion as:

> What can happen when people or areas suffer from a combination of linked problems such as unemployment, poor skills, low incomes, poor housing, high crime, bad health and family breakdown. (Cabinet Office 1999)

In Britain, child poverty had trebled in the period 1979–95. In the decade to 1996 the number of drug addicts had quadrupled and on average over 2,000 people were sleeping rough on the streets of London alone.

Table 25 Social class and grade structure

A	Upper middle class (higher managerial, administrative or professional), which comprises about 3% of the population.
B	Middle class (intermediate managerial, administrative or professional), which comprises approximately 10% of the population.
C1	Lower middle class (supervisory, clerical, junior administrative or professional), containing around 25% of the population.
C2	Skilled working class (skilled manual workers), comprising around 30% of the population.
D	Working class (semi- and unskilled manual workers), or around 27% of the population.
E	Lowest levels of subsistence (state pensioners with no other income, widows, and casual and lowest-grade earners), forming the remaining 5% of the population.

Table 26 Charities and social exclusion

Organisation	Main activities
Association of British Credit Unions	Tackling financial exclusion.
British Urban Regeneration Association	Promoting best practice in regeneration.
Department for Communities and Local Government	Facts and figures from the Index of Deprivation.
Groundwork	Environmental regeneration charity, involves people at a community level.
Joseph Rowntree Foundation (JRF)	From poverty indicators and neighbourhood renewal strategies to employment and drugs research. Briefings and reports on a range of social policy issues.
National Evaluation of Sure Start	Research into the impact and cost-effectiveness of the 260 Sure Start programmes in England.
Neighbourhood Renewal Unit	This sets out the government's vision for narrowing the gap between deprived neighbourhoods and the rest of the country.
New Economics Foundation	Community schemes, timebank initiatives and environmental projects.
Oxfam	Focuses on neighbourhood renewal strategies.
Sure Start	A programme that promotes the physical, intellectual and social development of pre-school children, particularly those who are disadvantaged.
UK Social Investment Forum	Promotes ethical investment, green investment, shareholder activism, social banking and community finance.

When New Labour came into power in 1997, they set up the Social Exclusion Unit to analyse the reasons behind these trends. It was part of a broader strategy by the government to encourage not-for-profit and other enterprises to invest in deprived communities (spearheaded by the Social Investment Taskforce, led by the then Chancellor of the Exchequer and later Prime Minister, Gordon Brown, in 2000).

In more recent time, a number of charities, organisations and enterprises have become directly involved in trying to combat the negative effects and consequences of social exclusion, as can be seen in Table 26.

See **social inclusion.**

The following references refer to specific writings on social exclusion and inclusion related to sport.

Bryant, P., *Social Exclusion and Sport: The Role of Training and Learning*. Sport England, 2001.

Leisure Futures, *Active Communities – A Review of Impact and Good Practice*. Sport England, 2002.

Sport England, *Making English Sport Inclusive: Equity Guidelines for Governing Bodies*. Sport England, 2000.

Social imaginary

This is a perspective that has been used in the study of popular culture. It looks at the facts and values of different leisure practices and considers them in terms of the way that they enrich or satisfy. The imaginary itself, according to Bromley (2000), is narratives for a new belonging. The social imaginary approach poses a set of challenges about how individuals recognise culture and leisure. It is not necessarily a theory as such but an individual's idealised view of how life and society should be. Leisure is seen as an important agent in generating social imaginary ideals, such as in popular theatre and sport, musical events and demonstrations, where people can visualise the way in which there might be a better future.

Bromley, R., *Narratives for a New Belonging*. Edinburgh University Press, 2000.

Social inclusion

Identifying the fact that an individual or a group's brilliance is no longer a sufficient basis for success, social inclusion aims to provide a framework that supports inclusion. These are structured, systematic approaches and processes that aim to support and to achieve full diversity and inclusivity. They aim to challenge discriminatory and oppressive practices that contribute towards social exclusion.

Typically, a social inclusion policy would encompass:

- making a positive contribution towards the economic, social and environmental well-being of the local population;
- reducing inequalities of opportunity and poverty;
- increasing tolerance of difference and celebration of diversity.

The term is now used as a positive one to describe a range of policies aimed at:

- equality of opportunity
- maintaining **social cohesion**
- building **social capital**
- minimising **social exclusion**

The main political driver is the postwar consensus that governments should provide a minimum quality of life (this is a moving standard). Annually, the British government spends around £400 billion on social security and by adding in costs of health, law and order, education, housing and the environment, around half of the annual government spend is related to socially inclusive areas.

Social exclusion is more profound at times when the economy is in difficulty; government spending at these times tends to focus on productive spending rather than 'sticking plaster' spending.

The term 'social economy' is also used in this respect. This term is used to describe the economic activity that is not accounted for by the private or state sectors. Therefore, this includes the activities of:

- the not-for-private-profit sector
- voluntary and community organisations
- charitable organisations
- mutual societies
- cooperatives
- social enterprises
- development trusts

It is important to appreciate that the boundaries between the social economy and other sectors is constantly shifting. There is a focus on investigating the work of these organisations and their service delivery to groups as well as to geographical areas where levels of social exclusion are considered to be too high.

Social responsibility marketing

'Social responsibility' in marketing refers to situations where a business responds to consumerism and environmental concerns and incorporates them into their long-term strategy. In essence, there are five different approaches, which are summarised in Table 27.

Social systems approach

The sociologist Talcott Parsons (1902–79) was at the foundation of the Cheek and Burch (1976) social systems approach to leisure. They defined leisure as a social

Table 27   Social responsibility

Socially responsible approach	Description of approach
Consumer orientation	The business considers its actions from the point of view of the customer.
Innovative marketing	An approach which aims to produce a genuinely useful, no frills product or service that breaks new ground.
Value marketing	A longer-term aim which seeks to make a gradual impact by growing a solid base of loyal customers sold on the fundamental concepts of the product or service rather than trying to stimulate shorter-term sales and profits.
Sense of Mission marketing	An organisation which looks at the wider implications of what they do and how they produce it rather than focusing on the products themselves in a more narrow sense.
Social marketing	Combining the needs and wants of the consumer with those of the business, society and the environment for all parties' longer-term benefits.

S

institution and stressed that it helped to improve the stability and growth of society. Not only that, but also it supported solidarity and reaffirmed the social order. For them, the main group was the family, which socialised individuals and gave individuals the opportunity to find a leisure activity that was natural or appropriate to them. The job was taken up by schools, which emphasised role models and helped to reinforce identities. They did not ignore voluntary behaviour as part of the system by which individuals select their ideal leisure activity.

> Cheek, N. and Burch, W., *The Social Organisation of Leisure in Human Society.* Harper Rowe, 1976.

Societal marketing

The societal marketing concept is, in many respects, similar to the marketing concept itself; the crucial difference is that it also takes into account society's well-being.

The concept was developed against the backdrop of increasing consumer and governmental concerns regarding the environment and as a result the fundamental marketing concept was challenged as being inadequate to consider wider issues such as waste, resource shortages and environmental impacts.

Societal marketing therefore encompasses the traditional marketing concept in terms of identifying and fulfilling the needs and wants of consumers in an effective and efficient manner, but goes a stage further in its determination to do this without detrimentally affecting society. Profit is not put aside in order to do this; simply the business seeks to find alternative methods of production and delivery of its products and services which minimise the harmful effects of that process. Organisations which adopt this marketing approach believe that consumers will respond favourably towards them if they are seen to be making strides in addressing societal concerns, and unfavourably if they are seen as being responsible for environment problems. It is thus the case that organisations such as The Body Shop (eliminating animal testing, using recyclable materials, etc.) and McDonald's (using recyclable and environmentally friendly packaging) can gain additional market share as they are seen to be making positive pro-environmental efforts. Other organisation such as Exxon or Shell, who have consistently denied their involvement in pollution through oil spillages, receive a negative response as they are perceived to be less concerned with the environment than with profit. Ultimately, societal marketing can be seen as giving the organisation a competitive edge over its rivals.

Solidarity

Hobbes (1651), whilst believing that life was nasty, brutish and short, and believing that individuals are constantly engaged in a struggle against everyone else to accumulate as much as they can for themselves, believed that life does provide three useful aspects related to the analysis of leisure. He believed:

- that life was competitive and that it always focused on the struggle for power;
- that resources are always scarce and it is scarcity that makes individuals competitive;

- that solidarity allows individuals to agree the basic rules which govern the way in which the struggle for scarce resources is carried out.

Undoubtedly this view still has connotations because there is always a degree of limit in terms of the time and resources to pursue leisure activities, and the fact that these limitations are enforced upon individuals by third parties.

Hobbes, T., *Leviathan*. Penguin (reprint), 1651.

Species needs

Species needs, or species-specific needs, are related to structural and cultural distinctions in human relations. The assumption is that all humans have shared species-specific psychological and physiological needs. Clearly they have a set of basic needs, including companionship, sleep, food, drink and clothing. However, the way in which these are acquired or desired differs across the world, according to diverse cultures. The needs of a tribesman in Africa, even at a basic need level, will be markedly different from those of someone working and living in a major city. It is important to remember that even though there are cultural differences there are other factors at play, including the way in which the individual is perceived by others and an individual's own self-image.

Split ticketing

Split ticketing is a practice found in the travel industry where the purchase of two single-journey tickets is made in order to obtain a lower fare compared with a standard return.

Stakeholder

A stakeholder is an individual or a group that is either affected by, or has a vested interest in, a particular business. Stakeholders can include customers, managers, employees, suppliers and the community, as well as the organisation itself. Each business places a degree of importance against each stakeholder and will attempt to understand what its stakeholders require of it. They will take these views into account when making decisions.

Rahman, Sandra Sutherland; Andriof, Jorg; Waddock, Sandra and Husted, Bryan, *Unfolding Stakeholder Thinking: Relationships, Communication, Reporting and Performance*. Greenleaf Publishing, 2003.

S

Stakeholder analysis

'Stakeholder analysis' refers to a range of tools and activities which aim to identify and describe the **stakeholders** of a business under the following criteria:

- their attributes;
- their inter-relationships;
- their interests related to given issues;
- their interest and influence over given resources.

Stakeholder analysis takes place for a variety of reasons, including:

- To empirically discover the existing patterns of interaction and inter-relationships.
- To improve interventions.
- To provide a management approach to policy making.
- To provide a prediction tool.

In essence, stakeholder analysis attempts to identify the key 'actors' in the system and assess their respective interests in the system. In another sense, stakeholder analysis therefore helps a business understand what can often be a complex and potentially turbulent business environment. There is also a notion that the management of the organisation has a desire to, in some way, manage a stakeholder relationship. Typically, stakeholders are described as either internal or external, as can be seen in Table 28.

There are also groups which straddle the divide between internal and external, and could include the following:

- Customers
- Vendors
- Suppliers

Stakeholder analysis seeks to identify the following features of stakeholder groups:

- The relative power and interest of each stakeholder.
- The importance and influence of each stakeholder.
- The multiple interests that they have, or indeed, multiple roles.
- The networks and coalitions to which they belong.

A flexible set of steps to accomplish stakeholder analysis would therefore include:

- An identification of the main purpose of any analysis.
- A development of the organisation's understanding of the stakeholder system and decision-makers in that system.
- An identification of the key stakeholders related to the organisation.
- An identification of stakeholder interests, their characteristics and their sets of circumstances.

Table 28 Stakeholder groups

Internal stakeholders	External stakeholders
Management (both direct and functional).	Government (regulators, legislators, legal systems, courts, political parties).
Employees (groups, teams and unions).	
Sponsors.	Competitors.
Owners (stock or shareholders, board of directors, venture capitalists, finance providers).	Community (special interest groups, local population).
	Media (radio, television, internet data services and newspapers)
Functional departments (accounts, HRM, engineering, marketing, etc.)	

- An identification of any patterns of interaction between stakeholders.
- A definition of any options for the organisation.

In order to assess the relative power and participation of any potential stakeholders, a model of stakeholder involvement can be constructed, as can be seen in the diagram in Figure 11.

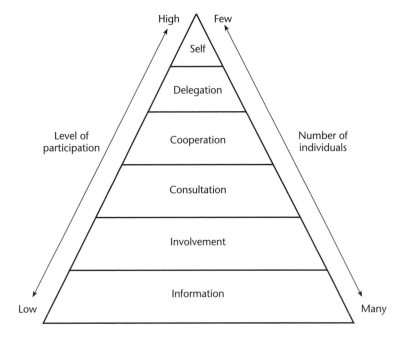

Figure 11   Model of stakeholder involvement

This model reveals that the larger groups (consumers etc.), although significant in numbers, are not overly involved in an organisation, whilst those stakeholders fewer in number (such as the board of directors) are closely involved.

The diagram in Figure 12 suggests that there may be as many as nine different perspectives upon which to begin any form of stakeholder analysis. On the proactive side, stakeholder analysis is relevant when there is no immediate crisis between the stakeholders and the organisation. On the reactive side, there may be conflict which prompts the stakeholder analysis.

See **stakeholder mapping.**

Hemmati, Minu; Dodds, Felix; Enayati, Jasmin and McHarry, Jan, *Multi-Stakeholder Processes for Governance and Sustainability: Beyond Deadlock and Conflict.* Earthscan, 2002.

Scharioth, Joachim and Huber, Margit (eds), *Achieving Excellence in Stakeholder Management.* Springer-Verlag, and GmBH, 2003.

S

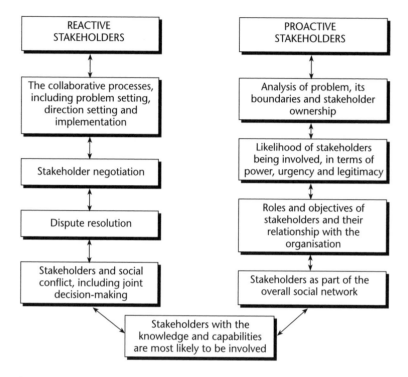

Figure 12 Stakeholder analysis

Stakeholder mapping

Stakeholder mapping is a process that is used to categorise, through the creation of diagrams, the position of stakeholders of an organisation. One such mapping method was devised by Gardner, Rachlin and Sweeny (1986). It cross-referenced the power of stakeholders with their dynamism. It was used to ascertain where the effort of an organisation should be in relation to its stakeholders. Each of the two measures was stated as being either low or high, therefore creating four distinct groups, A to D, as can be seen below:

- A – low power and dynamism, offering the organisation few problems, which are easy to deal with.
- B – high dynamism and low power. These are unpredictable, but manageable.
- C – high power and low dynamism. These are powerful but predictable, so their expectations can often be quite easily met.
- D – high in both measures. They offer the greatest dangers or opportunities to the organisation. Their opinion is often unpredictable and organisations tend to deal with them by testing out new strategies with them first, before making a final decision.

There are various other stakeholder mapping models, such as Mitchell, Agle and Wood (1997). They identified power, legitimacy and urgency as the key characteristics of stakeholders and were able to identify seven different groups based on a combination of these three characteristics.

See also **stakeholder analysis.**

Gardner, J. R., Rachlin, R. and Sweeny, H. W. A., *Handbook of Strategic Planning.* John Wiley & Sons, 1986.

Mitchell, R. K., Agle, B. R. and Sonnenfeld, J. A., 'Who Matters to CEOs? An Investigation of Stakeholders' Attributes and Salience, Corporate Performance and CEO Values', *Academy of Management Journal*, October 1999.

Mitchell, R. K., Agle, B. R. and Wood, D. J., 'Toward a Theory of Stakeholder Identification and Salience: Defining the Principle of Who and What Really Counts', *Academy of Management Review*, 22:4 (1997), pp. 853–86.

Strategic alliances

Strategic alliances are either short-term or long-term alliances between two businesses with the purpose of sharing resources. Strategic alliances may include **joint ventures**, but in general they are a business relationship in which the two businesses pool their strengths, share risks and try to integrate their business functions for mutual benefits. As opposed to any other form of close cooperation, both business entities remain independent throughout the arrangement. Strategic alliances are an important way of being able to break into new markets, to acquire new technical skills and improve on the business's competitive position. Firms may create a strategic alliance in one of the following four ways:

- Through internal growth
- Through merger and acquisition
- Through spin-offs
- Through strategic alliances

The alliance strategy is particularly attractive to international businesses that wish to operate in foreign markets which are relatively politically stable, or in developing countries which have free market systems (and are not usually suffering from high inflation or high private-sector debt). Strategic alliances can be used to offset many of the risks associated with **pioneering costs** as the risks are spread.

There are, in effect, six different ways in which a strategic alliance could assist international businesses in entering a foreign market, these include:

- Exporting – which has all the advantages of avoiding the set-up costs of manufacturing in an overseas market, but may have the disadvantage of higher transport costs and potential trade barriers. A strategic alliance could be used to form an association with a marketing subsidiary in the host country.
- Turnkey projects – this allows an international business to become involved in an overseas market where there may be prohibitions related to foreign direct investment. In essence, the international business exports only their process abilities and understanding, but this may inadvertently create a competitor in the longer run.

S

- Licensing – this involves framing a strategic alliance on the basis that a host country's industry undertakes to manufacture products in accordance with the trademarks and patents of the international business. The international business may risk losing control over its licences and will be passing on technological know-how to a potential long-term competitor.
- Franchising – this involves a strategic alliance with a host-country business, which will bear the risks and the costs of opening up a new market. There are often problems of dealing with quality-control issues with distant franchisees.
- Joint ventures – this involves establishing a strategic alliance based on the sharing of costs and risks and the gaining of local knowledge and perhaps political influence. Again the international business may lose a degree of control and protection of their technologies.
- Wholly-owned subsidiary – whilst the international business will have to bear all of the costs and risks in opening up the overseas market, a wholly-owned subsidiary offers tighter control of technology and other aspects of the business operation.

In order to make strategic alliances work, both businesses need to have sophisticated formal and informal communication networks and take steps to build trust between one another. Both parties need to take proactive steps in order to learn as much as they can from the operations of their partners.

Doz, Yves and Hamel, Gary, *Alliance Advantage: The Art of Creating Value through Partnering.* Harvard Business School Press, 1998.

Strategic plan

A strategic plan is an overarching series of activities which aim to implement and develop a new concept, deal with a problem or establish the foundation of the business's objectives in the coming period. There is a close relationship between the implementation and the strategic development process.

Strategic planning should be a continual process, with the monitoring and control procedures providing the information for the development of the strategic plan and future strategic plans.

Stress management

'Stress management' is an increasingly common term which most employees consider is relevant to their job role. Research has shown that the majority of individuals consider that their job is stressful. However, in-depth research by an organisation into the considered levels of stress within the workforce could result in an adverse effect on productivity. Research surveys have discovered that 70% of managers know that their employees are suffering from stress, 60% of absenteeism is stress-related, and 100 million working days are lost annually, resulting in costs throughout the UK in excess of £1.5 million. Continued stressful situations that are not dealt with can lead to burnout.

There are innumerable reasons why stress can occur, including:

- Meeting deadlines and targets that have been set to a tight schedule.
- Inadequate or uninterested management.

- Inadequate resources.
- A conflict of values, either within **groups** or with management and colleagues.
- Frustration.
- Change within the organisation.

Stress management has become an increasingly important area for the **human resources**, and certainly employee assistance programmes, which provide the employee with a counselling and mentoring service, have been in existence in the US for a number of years. Many UK organisations are now also adopting these programmes, although research carried out by Marie McHugh has identified six issues that managers still need to address:

1 That stress is costly to an organisation.
2 That stress-related costs have to be reduced.
3 That often they are not aware of employee stress levels.
4 That often they have no solution to managing stress.
5 That often they under-value employees and do not see the need for counselling and support.
6 They do not see the link between employee stress and organisational success.

McHugh and Brennan concluded that the concept of a cross-organisational *total stress management* approach should be considered, as shown in the diagram in Figure 13.

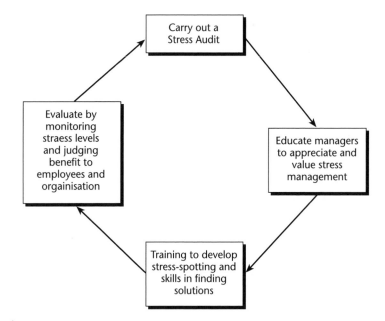

Figure 13   Stress management

All individuals have differing stress thresholds, which represent how they cope and when they reach the stage where they are unable to cope. Several researchers have discovered that the majority of individuals fit into one of two different categories, either *Type A* or *Type B,* as shown in Table 29.

Table 29   Stress thresholds

Type A characteristics	Type B characteristics
Subject to pressures of time and responsibility.	Do not find pressure in time and responsibility.
Work hard and are competitive, but can appear aggressive and impatient.	Work hard but are calm in their approach, with little need to be self-praising.
Subject to physical stress symptoms.	Do not show signs of stress, either in their approach, or physically.
Extrovert and neurotic.	Introvert and calm.

Friedman, M. and Rosenman, R., *Type A Behaviour and Your Heart.* Knopf, 1974.
McHugh, Marie and Brennan, Shirley, 'Managing the Stress of Change in the Public Sector', *International Journal of Public Sector Management,* 7:5 (1994), pp. 29–41.
Newstrom, W. and Davies, Keith, *Organizational Behaviour: Human Behaviour at Work* (9th edition). McGraw-Hill, 1993.

Sub-culture

A sub-culture is a clearly identifiable group of individuals within a broader culture who have features about them that differentiate them from the dominant culture. Sometimes they are referred to as a 'counter culture'. They will have their own conventions, rituals and values. Sometimes they may have negative views of the dominant culture, or at least be ambivalent to it. They may have stylistic behaviours. Typically, 'sub-culture' is used to describe groups such as punks, skateboarders, Goths and others. Maffesoli (1996) described sub-cultures such as these as being urban tribes.

Maffesoli, M., *The Time of the Tribes: The Decline of Individualism in Mass Society.* Sage, 1996.

Suggestion scheme

Many organisations find the honest and constructive suggestions made by employees as to the efficiency of the organisation's processes and procedures to be invaluable. So much so, that they provide the employees with a straightforward way of presenting these suggestions by the use of a suggestion scheme. A committee of managers would filter through the suggestions and select those considered to be appropriate, having investigated the implications and possibilities attached to each.

Suggestion schemes have a number of advantages and disadvantages, as can be seen in Table 30.

Table 30 Merits of suggestion schemes

Advantages	Disadvantages
An improvement in procedures and methods for the organisation and the employees.	Interest in the scheme may deteriorate if management do not encourage employee participation.
A safer working environment.	Maintaining the scheme can be expensive in terms of money and time.
Increased and widened channels of communication because the employees feel able to express their opinions.	
Innovative and creative employees can be encouraged, often by receiving a reward for a successfully implemented suggestion.	
Increased employee job satisfaction.	
Benefits to the organisation, through the suggestion scheme, that eliminate the cost and time considerations.	

Superstructure

In Marxist economism, the economic base of society is seen as determining everything else in the superstructure (the make-up or elements of society). This includes all of the consciousness of individuals and groups in relation to political, social and intellectual matters.

Marx's own view was that the economic relationships determined social phenomena (also known as materialist theories or historical materialism). Economism is also related to technological determinism (how far technology does or does not affect social change).

Stuart Hall and other so-called culturalist Marxists reject the concept of the base and superstructure. They argue that there is dialectic between what Marx intended to be understood by social being and social consciousness.

> Curran, James, Gurevitch, Michael and Woollacott, Janet, 'The study of the Media: Theoretical Approaches', in Michael Gurevitch, Tony Bennett, James Curran and Janet Woollacott (eds), *Culture, Society and the Media*. Methuen, 1982.

Supplemental carrier

A supplemental carrier is an airline or air carrier that does not usually operate scheduled or routine services, but offers its carrying capacity to other airlines or tour operators in order to assist them in periods of high demand for travel.

Supply chain

The 'supply chain' is simply a generic description of the processes and organisations involved in converting raw materials to products bought by the end user. The supply chain may involve organisations which extract raw materials, others which carry out a basic form of process upon these raw materials, which are then passed on to a manufacturer who will turn them into usable parts. Parts are then converted into components, which in turn are assembled or processed into a form of finished goods. These finished goods may then pass through the hands of distributors and retailers, before reaching the end user. Supply chains may involve several suppliers, several more manufacturers and a related distribution system. In other words, the supply chain incorporates all the costs, time, transportation and packaging that may be associated with the various stages of the process of conversion. Increasingly, supply chains take into account the return journey which many finished products undergo after having spent a considerable time with the end user. Therefore a reverse supply chain is often in operation alongside the standard supply chain. This reverse system incorporates replacement parts and their flow, as well as the disposal and recycling of parts, components or whole products.

Supply chain management

The supply chain management approach involves the integrated managing and control of the flow of information, materials, and services from the suppliers of the raw materials, through to the factories, warehouses and retailers to the end customers. The benefits to an organisation involved in supply chain management should be lower inventory costs, higher quality and higher customer service levels. These benefits will only be gained, however, if all those involved in the supply chain are conforming to the standards set.

Martin, Christopher, *Logistics and Supply Chain Management.* Financial Times, Prentice Hall, 1998.

Support vendors

Support vendors are essentially **outsourced** business services who increasingly provide specialist assistance to a business in order for the business to concentrate on its core activities. Support vendors are external to the organisation and have their own employees. They can provide a wide range of support services to the organisation, such as managing the mail, dealing with warehousing and shipping or providing technical support. This is particularly useful to businesses who have neither the skills, finance or inclination to develop their own support services and it is especially useful for businesses which operate with low profit margins.

Surcharge

A surcharge is an additional fee that may be added to another fee or charge. In recent years both fuel surcharges and security surcharges have been added on top of other charges to airline travellers. Surcharges can also be made by businesses if customers choose to pay by electronic money services, such as credit or debit cards, reflecting the fact that it costs them more to process the payment.

Sustainability

Sustainability can be applied to the broadest possible areas of leisure and tourism activity. It implies a level of use that does not seriously impact on the ecological processes, biodiversity, functions or infrastructure of a particular location or region. It is broadly applied to oceans, land, and resources such as energy, water and food. It aims to prevent environmental degradation and the securing of the area in question for future generations.

Sustainable development

The term 'sustainable development' is often criticised as it is so vague. Broadly it is meant to mean that resources can be used to the extent to which they meet human needs but preserve the environment. This presupposes that a carrying capacity for these natural systems can be worked out and that a limit of growth in the use of a resource can be set. Sustainable development can be differentiated from green development in as much as the latter values the sustainability of the environment over any economic or cultural considerations, whilst sustainable development attempts to balance all three.

Sustainable tourism

See **ecotourism** and **responsible tourism**.

SWOT analysis

SWOT analysis is a very useful technique in looking at the overall future of an organisation, as well as in considering the launch of a new marketing activity. SWOT analysis covers the following aspects, of which the first two considerations look at the internal workings of the organisation.

- Strengths – What is the organisation or business good at? What are its key advantages over the competition in terms of its products and services as well as its facilities, customer service and the expertise of its employees?
- Weaknesses – What is the organisation not good at? Where does the business fall down in terms of the ways it does things? Are the products and services good enough? Is the marketing good enough?
- Opportunities – What is happening OUTSIDE the organisation that offers it some opportunities? Has the transport system in the area been improved? Has a major competitor closed down?
- Threats – What is happening OUTSIDE the organisation that could threaten it? Are there more competitors?

Figure 14 is a common SWOT analysis grid which helps to place all of the considerations in the right position. The marketing function would need to consider all of these strengths, weaknesses, opportunities and threats before they made any major decisions.

Dealtry, Richard, *Dynamic SWOT Analysis – The Developer's Guide.* Dynamic SWOT Associates, 1994.

Synergy

Synergies are the benefits which can result from combining different aspects of an organisation, rather than allowing them to act separately. In other words, organisations will seek to group complementary activities in situations where there is a

Strengths	Weaknesses
Opportunities	Threats

SWOT analysis

Figure 14   A SWOT analysis grid

strong possibility of collaboration. This means that a mutual benefit can be enjoyed, particularly when common work or activity form the basis of the alliance.

Synergies can also be enjoyed between organisations where complementary skills or production processes, or indeed knowledge of a specific market, can be brought together in order to achieve far more than the two organisations could possibly have hoped for individually. Synergies can either bring about short-term project-based alliances between businesses, or may well prove to be the foundation of a longer-term relationship.

'Business synergy' is a term often applied to **franchise** operations, in as much as when individuals purchase a franchise they become part of a larger 'family'. All of the members of the family work together and the most effective ideas are shared.

S

Target market

A target market or a target audience is a group of individuals or businesses, usually identified during a **market segmentation** exercise, arising out of **marketing research**. The members of the group have common characteristics, attributes, beliefs and possibly buying habits. A target market is the prime objective of a business's advertising and marketing activities. A business may well have identified a number of different target markets and will have prioritised them in terms of their potential and profitability. The terms 'target market' and 'target audience' are largely interchangeable. However, there is an inference in the term 'target audience' which suggests a willingness or receptiveness on behalf of those who belong to the group to respond positively to messages promoting products, services or brands.

> Webber, Harry, *Divide and Conquer: Target Your Customers through Market Segmentation.* John Wiley & Sons, 1998.

Tariff

A tariff is, in its simplest form, a tax on products, raw materials or commodities which have been produced abroad; it is imposed upon them by the government of the country into which they are being exported. Governments will set the level of tax in accordance with their own tariff schedule and it may indeed be applied to goods entering or leaving the country. Tariffs are primarily levied in order to protect domestic industries from imported goods, as tariffs inherently make the imports more expensive. Tariffs are also used as a primary source of revenue for the government.

Increasingly, many countries have reduced their tariffs, as part of the continuing process of freeing up world trade, but have not wholly dispensed with them.

A tariff schedule is a comprehensive list of products, goods and commodities that a country is prepared to allow to be imported. The tariff schedule not only details all of these different products, goods and commodities, but it also details the relevant import duties which are applicable to each of them.

> Jackson, John H., *The World Trading System: Law and Policy of Economic Relations.* MIT Press, 1997.

Teamwork

Many organisations have gradually come to the realisation that teams represent a proven means by which productivity and performance can be assured. Various industry surveys, particularly in the manufacturing sector, seem to suggest that over two-thirds of all organisations actively encourage teams. The actual nature of the team is of prime importance and their creation is of particular relevance to **human resources**. Essentially there are three different types of team, all of which have a degree of authority, autonomy or **empowerment**.

Empowered teams are usually given the authority to plan and implement improvements. Self-directed teams are virtually autonomous and are mainly responsible for supervisory issues. Cross-functional teams are more complex as they involve various individuals from different departments who are working towards a common end.

Training needs to be provided to teams both before and during their creation in order to assist the members in establishing their relationships with one another and understanding their new responsibilities. It is also essential that teams are given clear instructions and, above all, support from management in order to carry out their tasks. Once a team has been established and a degree of authority is delegated to them, management and human resources need to step back and allow the team to develop and learn how their new working practices will operate.

The team itself, management and human resources retain the responsibility of monitoring and motivating the teams and their members. This requires effective communication skills and a feedback system which enables teams to request additional assistance should be it be required.

Telemarketing

'Telemarketing' is an alternative term which is used to describe telephone sales. Telemarketing uses the telephone as its primary means of contacting potential customers. Clearly, the purpose is to obtain orders from the customer without the need to visit the customer personally, or their premises. Telemarketing has become an increasingly valuable tool and an integral part of direct marketing. Telemarketing enables a business to streamline its distribution channels in such a way as to allow it to cut out the intermediaries it formerly used to rely upon in order to provide products and services to the end users.

Increasingly sophisticated technology is being employed in order to assist tele-marketing exercises, such as software which can flag recommended intervals between sales contact with a customer, as well as storing aged data on all trans-actions, conversations, complaints and queries associated with that customer.

Rowson, Pauline, *Easy Step-by-Step Guide to Telemarketing, Cold Calling and Appointment Making*. Rowmark, 2000.
Schiffman, Stephan, *Cold Calling Techniques*. Adams Media Corporation, 1999.

Terrorism

The link between terrorism and the study of leisure may not be immediately apparent; however, Kelly (1987) suggested that the reality and the threat of terror-ism has impacted on individuals' 'freedom to be'. In the US, Britain and other primary targets for terrorism, the security forces and the police have stepped up their vigilance with regard to transport links and public spaces. Terrorists have for many years targeted locations associated broadly with leisure. Public houses were targeted in Birmingham by the Irish Republican Army in 1974 and in the same year there was an explosion at the Tower of London, a major tourist site. Terrorists have also targeted commercial properties associated with shopping and culture, such as Harrods in London in 1983, Warrington in 1993 and Manchester in 1996. Across the world, terrorists have targeted tourist areas and specifically places where leisure activities are designed to ensure that visitors feel as relaxed as possible and free to do as they please. Bali was hit in 2002 and before that there were attacks in Cairo in 1996 and a year later at Luxor, also in Egypt. More recently there have been attacks in Kenya in 2002 and in Mumbai in 2008. Other terrorists have targeted transportation systems. The Tokyo underground was attacked in 1995, Madrid's main railway station in 2004 and the underground and bus network in London in July 2005.

With terrorism as a constant threat it has serious implications for leisure and recreation. It is a global risk and it should not be ignored in the broader investigation into leisure.

See also **security surcharges.**

Kelly, J., *Freedom to Be: A New Sociology of Leisure.* Macmillan, 1987.

Theming

The theming of parks, shopping malls and other leisure and tourist environments not only aims to present a symbolic version of a particular narrative or vision, but it also seeks to create an environment that symbolises something that is not, or perhaps has never been. It is sanitised, sometimes sentimental, lavish in design, extravagant and in its own way it represents a counter culture. It is a counter culture in the sense that it does not reflect any prevailing culture in society, but instead tries to project some form of idealised environment. Shopping malls, for example, in terms of both their design and their construction, are created to reflect luxury and refinement and to encourage consumption.

Extreme examples of theming can of course be found in the theme parks run by Disney and by dozens of other corporations. They are commercial environments full of myths, echoes and a fairytale vision. Whole areas of cities can likewise be themed, such as Las Vegas, and it can also be applied to areas of cities that have been deconstructed and then recreated to form the backdrop for major sports events, such as the Olympics. This is certainly the case with the wholesale removal of houses and businesses for the Beijing Olympics in 2008 and the London Olympics in 2012. To some extent these latter two examples will at least provide a legacy in terms of leisure and recreation. However, as Ritzer (2004) suggested, the design styles of many of the malls and even more practical structures, such as underground systems and travel hubs, are dominated by architectural styles and values that are never applied to any other area of building. Ritzer suggested that they were fake and referred to it as 'the globalization of nothing'. This is echoed by the fact that many town and city centres and squares, not to mention malls, are virtually indistinguishable across the world. They have similar architecture and layout and are full of very similar commercial features, with global brand names forever prominent. Ritzer called these 'non-places'. They are standardised, themed around money and not under local management but multinational management.

Auge, M., *Non-Places.* Lawrence & Wishart, 1995.
Ritzer, G., *The Globalization of Nothing.* Pine Forge, 2004.

Therapeutic recreation

Therapeutic recreation is seen as a means of purposefully utilising or enhancing leisure as a way in which an individual's health, well-being and quality of life can be achieved. Typically, those involved in this aspect of recreation are known as recreational therapists, or activity therapists. What distinguishes therapeutic recreation from many other therapies is that it combines social, emotional, cognitive and physical activities that are freely chosen by the individual. They are structured activities, such as organised sports, outdoor activities or creative arts. They are designed to be enjoyable and personally rewarding.

Robertson, T. and Long, T., *Foundations of Therapeutic Recreation*. Human Kinetics, 2007.

Throwaway

A throwaway is a leaflet or a pamphlet that is given out by an organisation, or placed in a dispenser for selection by individuals, which is likely to be discarded after it has been read. Throwaways may seek to perform a number of functions, from straight advertising and promotion, to announcements and other information. The term 'throwaway', however, has now acquired negative connotations and has close links with the more undesirable aspects of consumerism. It implies over-consumption, excessive production and short-lived, disposable items. Increasingly, organisations will seek to minimise the amount of disposable marketing information that they generate, or at least try to mitigate its production by using environmentally friendly paper and printing techniques and requesting that the individual, after having read the throwaway, recycles it.

Tiered pricing

Tiered pricing enables an organisation to offer the same product or service to different types of customer at different prices. Typically, a leisure organisation might have a tiered pricing system for children, adults and the retired. Alternatively they may have a tiered pricing system that matches the busy and quiet periods of the day, week or year. Other organisations may have a tiered system related to educational use, bookings by **not-for-profit organisations**, or corporate users. Tiered pricing may also apply to the number of individuals booking an activity at the same time, with lower prices per head for larger groups.

Total quality management (TQM)

The concept of total quality management (TQM) has been stimulated by the need for conformance by organisations with regard to quality levels. This need has been brought about in essence by an increased demand by customers and suppliers for higher quality products, parts and components. The fundamental principle behind total quality management is that the management of quality is addressed at all levels of an organisation, from the top to the bottom. Improvements are made on a continuous basis by applying the theories and approaches of management theorists in an attempt to improve quality and decrease organisational costs. The emphasis, primarily on quality, is also very much on people and their involvement, particularly with regard to suppliers and customers. The fundamental principles of TQM are summarised in Table 31.

Table 31   Fundamental principles of total quality management

TQM Principle	Description
Committed and effective leaders	A commitment to and a belief in the principles of TQM by those key decision-makers at the top of the organisational structure is essential. They have to portray this commitment to the lower levels of management in an effective style of leadership by providing resources to make changes happen.
Planning	It is imperative that all changes are planned effectively, particularly as the TQM approach may be fundamentally different from the approach currently adopted by an organisation. All planned changes must be integrated throughout the whole organisation with cooperation throughout all levels and functions. With quality, or improved quality, as the key dimension, a longer-term strategy will be adopted throughout the whole of the organisation's functions, from new product design through to getting the product to the end user.
Monitoring	A continuous monitoring system will be put into place so that the process of *continuous improvement* can be supported and developed. Problem identification and the implementations of solutions will be sought.
Training	Without education and training, employees and management will lack the expertise and awareness of quality issues. It will be difficult to implement changes in organisational behaviour unless there is a comprehensive and effective educational scheme which not only seeks to provide the initial information and understanding of techniques, but constantly updates those techniques in order to reinforce understanding. Without this investment, short-term TQM benefits will be difficult to achieve, as will the long-term impact of TQM through conventional measurements, such as increased efficiency and general growth.
Teamwork	The development of empowered cooperative teams is an essential prerequisite of TQM. Under the system, teams are encouraged to take the initiative and often given responsibilities which would have formerly been management roles. Without the involvement and **empowerment**, TQM is almost impossible to implement as it requires both the participation and the commitment of individuals throughout the whole organisation.
Evaluation and feedback	It is imperative that individuals within the organisation see the fruits of their labour. There should be an integral system which not only provides positive feedback but also rewards for achievement. The evaluation and feedback of TQM will invariably involve the measurement of achievement in both internal and external targets, notably through **benchmarking**.
Long -term change	As TQM becomes embedded and very much a fact of life in the ways in which employees think and processes are carried out, there is a permanent change to the way in which attitudes, working practices and overall behaviour are approached.

T

Bank, J., The Essence of Total Quality Management. Prentice Hall, 1992.
Oakland, J. S., *Total Quality Management*. Butterworth-Heinemann, 1993.

Tourism typologies

Murphy (1985) identified two categories of tourist typologies: interactional and cognitive–normative. An interactional tourist typology considers the interactions that take place between the tourists and their destination area. This can, of course, be refined, creating subdivisions of tourist typologies based on the degree to which interaction takes place. It can investigate travel behaviours, interests and opinions. Cognitive–normative tourist typologies tend to focus on the travel motivations of tourists. Plog (1972) and Smith (1990) identified the following:

- Allocentrics – adventuresome individual travellers.
- Mid-centrics – individual travellers to destinations that have facilities.
- Psycho-centrics – those that visit popular destinations on package holidays.

Cohen (1979) looked at tourists' motivations and suggested that they travel for experimental, experiential, existential, diversionary or recreational reasons. Tourist typologies are criticised on the following grounds:

- The generalisations of a typology have been derived from a relatively restricted amount of data.
- They are methodologically inconsistent, and from theorist to theorist the same tourist categories are called different things.
- Questionnaires have tended to be the most common way of gathering data and there has been a lack of extensive case study research.
- Motivations and activities of tourists are often far too complex to try to squeeze into rigid categories.
- The typologies do not reflect changing tourist types over time, and some may therefore not be relevant over generations.
- Few have been empirically tested and most are still theoretical in nature.

Cohen, E., 'A Phenomenology of Tourist Experiences', *Sociology*, 13 (1979), pp. 179–202.
Murphy, P., *Tourism: Community Approach*. Routledge, 1985.
Plog, S., *Why Destination Areas Rise and Fall in Popularity*. Travel Research Association, 1972.
Smith, S. L. J., 'A Test of Plog's Allocentric/Psychocentric Model: Evidence from Seven Nations', *Journal of Travel Research*, 28:4 (1990), pp. 40–3.

T

Tourist Information Centre (TIC)

In Britain and in many other countries there are tourist information centres, or tourist information points. In Britain, covering England, Scotland, Northern Ireland and Wales, plus the offshore islands of Guernsey, Jersey, the Isle of Man and the Isles of Scilly, there is a network of Tourist Information Centres (TICs). They provide information about what is going on in the local region, how to get around, ideas for what to do, where to go and where to stay. They tend to be funded by local authorities and located in popular tourist towns, cities and resorts. Many Tourist Information Centres also sell tickets to local events.

In order to remove the sometimes negative connotations related to the word 'tourist', some attractions have adopted Visitor Information Centre as their preferred description. Indeed some theme parks consider the term 'tourist' to be so negative that they have substituted it with the word 'guest', which is the derivation of the American preoccupation with guestology.

www.britainexpress.com

Town twinning

Town twinning is the creation of sister cities or towns. They are often also referred to as 'partner towns'. The purpose is to foster closer relationships between towns or cities in different geographical or political areas of the world. In many cases the towns or cities will have similar histories, demographics and other characteristics. It is an extremely popular concept across Europe and is supported by the European Union. There are at least 1,300 such projects across the European Union. These are supported by the Council of European Municipalities and Regions. The idea is to bring two or more communities together to bring mutual benefits. It allows the twinned towns or cities to share in one another's development and experience the art and culture of the twin.

Twinning has become more universal in recent decades, with towns and cities in the US, Mexico and other locations entering into twinning partnerships. Twinning is often criticised on the basis that it is an unnecessary and expensive relationship and makes little contribution to economic or cultural development.

www.twinning.org

Tracking study

This is a type of research methodology that seeks to measure the same variables over a period of time, in order to determine their changes. Usually they are used to consider attitudes, awareness and buying habits.

Transformational change

Transformational change is a root and branch change process which seeks to fundamentally improve the way in which a business may operate. It requires considerable planning, coupled with an overarching strategy and commitment across the entire organisation. There are some seven steps which are associated with transformational change:

- Defining the change strategy – which assesses the need and readiness for change, the best change configuration and how the process of change will be controlled.
- Management commitment – this entails developing a sense of ownership amongst the management and working towards a strategic vision for the change, as well as identifying how that vision relates to each manager.
- Creation of the change strategy – creating a change strategy that will be meaningful to all employees and defining the way in which the vision can be communicated to all **stakeholders**.
- Building employee commitment – the creation of the means by which the change can be 'sold' to the employees and the identification and management of resistance to that change.

- Development of a new culture – incorporating the development of new values for employees and new behaviours which are aligned to the vision, including the regular review of support required.
- Reconfiguration of the organisation – redesigning roles, competences, structure, and the identification of appropriate individuals who will assume those roles.
- Managing performance – the creation of a new working environment with relevant performance measurement and the alignment of business performance to individual objectives.

Anderson, D. and Anderson, L. S. A. (eds), *Beyond Change Management: Advanced Strategies for Today's Transformational Leaders*. Jossey-Bass Wiley, 2001.

T

UNESCO

UNESCO, or the United Nations Educational, Scientific and Cultural Organisation, is an international United Nations agency founded in November 1945. It has a broad remit and aims to create dialogue between countries to share values, civilisation and culture. It has specific aims, which include:

- Halving the world population that lives in extreme poverty by 2015.
- Achieving universal primary education worldwide by 2015.
- Reversing the trend in the loss of environmental resources by 2015.
- Eliminating gender disparity in education by 2015.

Clearly it has responsibility and impacts on culture, communications, education, natural sciences, as well as human and social sciences. It has permanent delegations in all 182 United Nations member states.

www.unesco.org

Unique selling point (USP)

'Unique selling point', or 'unique selling proposition', is a marketing term which is used to identify a specific product or service benefit that is only available to that product or service. It is not a feature which can be clearly associated with any of the competitors' products or services. In effect, this unique feature allows the business to create a unique selling proposition. In other words, this single feature becomes the focus of the advertising message and any other associated marketing or selling activities.

At its very core, the unique selling proposition, assuming it has a meaningful significance to the target market, is the basis for brand differentiation.

> Forte, Alessandro, *Dare to be Different: How to Create Business Advantage through Innovation and Unique Selling Proposition.* Forte Financial Group, 2002.

Utilisation rate

'Utilisation rate' measures the maximum or optimum usage rate of a facility or service compared with its actual or average usage rate. In this way an organisation can calculate how well it is using its resources and whether it needs to make adjustments or, indeed, whether or not it needs to try to attract additional users. Utilisation rates can be calculated across lengthy periods of time or they can be calculated on smaller time-specific periods for comparison purposes.

VALS

The VALS framework is a proprietary **market segmentation** system of SRI Consulting Business Intelligence. It measures two dimensions: the primary motivation, and resources, and identifies eight segments based on responses received from large samples of consumers, using questionnaire-based **marketing research** (see Figure 15).

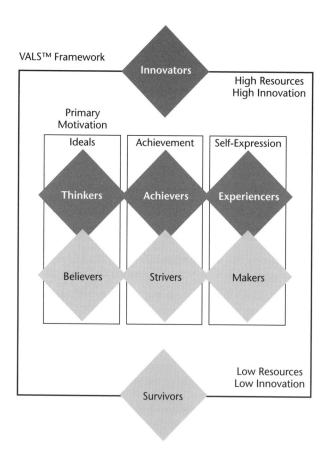

Figure 15 VALS framework

The two criteria can be best described as follows:

- Primary motivation – this criterion examines what exactly it is that motivates a consumer to purchase specific products and services. Typically, factors such as a sense of achievement and self-expression are coupled with utility and value.
- Resources – the VALS system considers resources in a rather unique way, as it recognises that all purchases are necessarily made in relation to a consumer's ability to pay for them. Key personality traits may determine factors such as impulsiveness, vanity, self-confidence or innovativeness. This criterion, therefore, measures not only the resource constraints but also a person's tendency to ignore them.

The eight key segmentation groupings are described in Table 32.

Table 32   Segments of VALS framework

Segment	Description
Innovators	This is a category which was formerly known as 'actualisers'. They are individuals with a high level of self-esteem, abundant resources, who are receptive to new ideas. They are active consumers and tend to buy up-market, niche products and services. Their purchases are an expression of their taste, personality and independence. They enjoy variety and the finer things in life.
Thinkers	A category that was formerly known as 'fulfilleds'. Thinkers tend to be mature, comfortable and satisfied, have a good level of knowledge and are responsible. They take a well-ordered approach to decision-making and are open to new ideas. Their level of income allows them to look for value, functionality and durability in the products and services they purchase.
Achievers	Achievers have essentially goal-orientated lifestyles; their lives revolve around their families and career. They are fairly conventional and prefer stability to risk. They are active consumers, however, and look for established, well-known products which, in a sense, show their level of success to those around them. They are particularly interested in time-saving products and services.
Experiencers	Experiencers are generally young and impulsive consumers who are very much inclined to purchase fashionable products and follow trends. They search for variety and are not frightened to take risks in their purchases. They are conspicuous consumers primarily in fashion and entertainment.
Believers	Believers have some factors in common with thinkers, as they are conventional and traditional. They have set routines, usually focused around the family and home or other social organisations to which they belong. As consumers they are fairly predictable and will tend to choose familiar and established brands. They are possibly one of the most loyal types of customer.

continued

Table 32 (*continued*)

Segment	Description
Strivers	Strivers are motivated by achievement and seek the approval of others. Financial rewards to them allow them to buy brands with style in order to replicate other groups to which they aspire to belong. They seek to demonstrate their ability to purchase products and services to their peers and, within certain constraints, are fairly impulsive.
Makers	Self-expression is the primary motivator, rather like experiencers and achievers. They are constructive and largely self-sufficient. They tend to live a fairly traditional life and are unimpressed by those who conspicuously consume. They tend to buy basic products as they have a preference for value and utility rather than luxury.
Survivors	Survivors were formerly known as 'strugglers' as they have few resources. They focus on meeting immediate needs rather than striving to attain their desires. As consumers they are cautious, but they are loyal to their favourite brands, particularly if these are being offered at a discount.

VALS is a very flexible system that has not only been applied specifically to the US, but also to a number of other different countries. VALS is directly applicable as it provides geo-demographic information for a number of different marketing activities, including **direct marketing**, sales analysis, retail site location, merchandising and media analysis.

www.sric-bi.com

Value added

Value added, or added value, is an increase in the market value of a product, part or components which excludes the cost of materials and services used. In other words, this is a cost-plus-profit concept, defining 'value added' as either the difference between the cost of producing a product and the price obtained for it (the selling price), or an additional benefit offered to a purchaser in order to convince them to buy. Added value is the key concept in both the internal and the external accounting systems of an organisation and is a useful means of identifying the relative efficiency of a business. It should be noted that the value-added concept looks at the internal input costs in such a way that they are not confused with the external output costs, which may be beyond the control of the organisation.

The value of the goods or services supplied may depend on a number of different variables. Obviously, if the organisation is processing raw materials into finished products and is responsible for all stages of the production process, then it has a relatively high degree of control over the level of added value involved. Organisations which buy in components or part-finished products do not have this depth and length of control. They purchase products which have had value added to them already. The supplier will have gone through a similar set of calculations prior to selling the components or part-finished products on to the organisation, which in turn will continue their processing. In the final analysis, the level of value added to the goods or services supplied is directly related to the price the customer is willing to pay. An organisation may decide to add value which would raise the price beyond that which the average customer is willing to accept. In such a case, the supplier would have either to accept that it cannot receive the price it expected, or to drastically reduce its costs, which have contributed to the end user price.

The most common definition of value added is profit. Before the profit is realised, however, it is necessary to be able to cover the directly applied or over-head costs of the organisation. If the organisation is able to cover the various costs, then it has gone a considerable distance towards being able to breakeven. It is only when added value exceeds the breakeven point that the organisation moves into real profit. It is, perhaps, this part of the value-added concept that is most important. Profit means a number of things to an organisation: for example, additional investment potential, expansion, reorganisation or acquisition. The nature of value added has a tendency to push up the end user price from the moment the raw materials are extracted. In stages, some more dramatic than others, added value will be heaped upon the product. Each layer of the supply chain will demand its rightful profit in handling the product or service. Consequently, if an organisation is not involved in the total extraction, processing and sale of a product or service, then it may not be able to curb unnecessary levels of added value elsewhere in the trading cycle.

Value Added Tax (VAT)
Effectively this is a consumption tax, which is levied on value added. It is distinct from a sales tax, as VAT is levied at every point at which value is added in the supply-chain process. VAT systems are used across the European Union and in the US state of Michigan, along with most of the Nordic countries, and in India, Mexico, Australia, Canada and New Zealand. VAT rates differ from country to country and are subject to fluctuation in order to stimulate or to depress consumption.

Value-based pricing
Value-based pricing means that a business, rather than setting their prices according to the costs of products or services provided, using historic prices, competitors' prices or the market price, set their price on its perceived value to the customer. In this way the organisation aims to set prices according to the value delivered by that service or product. This also allows them to offer differentiated, or **tiered pricing** for different groups, based on differing perceived value. In theory value-based pricing should make an organisation more competitive and profitable. However, it relies on the organisation fully understanding how customers actually measure value. This is usually achieved by bringing in a feed-back system or survey.

Variable cost
Variable costs are expenditure which varies directly with changes in output. In other words they are inextricably linked to the level of activity. Variable costs

would include raw materials, components, labour and energy, which would vary according to the degree of production.

Variance report

A variance report is essentially an efficiency measure. It aims to compare forecast or expected levels of performance with actual levels of performance. In this way an organisation could compare predicted visitor figures with actual figures, predicted income with real income, or costs that had been budgeted with the actual costs incurred. Clearly the actual figures will be either more or less than the budgeted figures in the majority of cases, unless of course the budgeted figures prove to be extremely accurate. If costs are actually higher than predicted or income lower than predicted then this is known as an adverse variance, meaning that it is not desirable. If costs are lower than predicted or income higher than predicted then this is a positive variance, which means that the organisation performed better than was expected.

Venture capitalist

A venture capitalist is an individual who invests money in a start-up company. Many venture capitalist organisations are run as part of investment banks. The venture capitalist provides the funding for fledgling businesses which lack the financial muscle to put their ideas into the marketplace. The venture capitalists often retain a controlling share in the business and, should the business prove to be successful, then their initial investment is hugely rewarded by future returns.

Gompers, Paul and Lerner, Josh, *The Venture Capital Cycle.* MIT Press, 2002.

Virtual leisure

The term 'virtual leisure' incorporates both computer and internet technologies. Virtual leisure therefore includes games software, music and video software, internet gambling, simulation technologies and virtual tourism.

VisitBritain

This is the official travel and tourism website for Britain. It incorporates destination and city guides and maps, and has Britain's largest online accommodation directory. The information and practical travel advice is made available in a wide variety of languages.

www.visitbritain.com

Visitor interpretation

The term 'visitor interpretation' is used to describe the way in which a visitor location seeks to convey content, features and attractions using a range of text, visual, audio-visual, guides and role play features. Often they are designed to educate visitors and give them a taste or experience of the site or attraction, by providing insights into its historic, environmental, and natural or other features. They are the ways in which visitor attractions can add value to the visit, improve customer satisfaction and attract repeat business.

The National Association for Interpretation is a **not-for-profit organisation** that focuses on heritage interpretation. It has 5,000 members across North America and in thirty other countries around the world. It advises on giving talks and tours, allowing visitors to interact with exhibits, and enhancing educational programmes.

www.interpnet.com

Voluntarism

Voluntarism is the opposite of determinism in the study of human behaviour. Whilst determinism involves constraint through structured behaviour, compulsion and external force, voluntarism focuses on free choice, with no constraint, encompassing flexibility and spontaneity. In reality, of course, human behaviour is often at some point between these two extremes. A prime example is support for a football club. An individual may show voluntarism in selecting a particular club to support, purely out of individual choice. However, that voluntarism may in fact have been influenced by peer group pressure, which implies a degree of determinism.

According to Parker (1983), individuals possess a degree of freedom, choice and self-determination. But involvement in leisure activities is rather more complex than this, as a decision to be involved in an activity may be blocked because of other commitments. Equally, the free choice of how to spend non-work time can be inhibited by a lack of funds, or by the fact that, due to the individual's age, they are unable to be involved in that activity. There is therefore a complex interdependency between voluntarism and determinism, which is not always easy to unravel.

Parker, S., *Leisure and Work*. Allen & Unwin, 1983.

Wait list

A wait list, as the term implies, means that a customer, client or traveller has been placed on a waiting list in case an opening for the activity or for the flight they want becomes available. The organisation will usually prioritise those that have registered an interest first, giving them the first option if an opening becomes available. The organisation, in admitting an individual to the waiting list, is not guaranteeing them an opening. Airlines, for example, will usually only put passengers on a waiting list if they believe, from their computer modelling of past booking and cancelling behaviour, that there is a reasonable chance that a seat will become available. This is particularly true if flights historically have a high proportion of business passengers, as they are the most likely to cancel their booking close to the departure date. In comparison, holiday flights usually cannot be changed or cancelled without a penalty and they are less likely to be cancelled at the last minute.

Web promotion

Web promotion aims to increase traffic to a particular website. Key to web promotion are strategies aimed at ensuring that search engines select the website on the first page of a search result. This is achieved by using a combination of meta tags, keywords, titles, as well as banner and link exchanges. It may also include participation in news groups and ensuring that the website is on directory listings.

> Inan, Hurol, *Measuring the Success of your Website: A Custom-centric Approach to Website Management*. Pearson Education Australia, 2002.

White paper

This is an informal name that is used to describe a report or proposed piece of legislation. White papers provide details on new legislation, although they do not necessarily suggest that the government intend to push the new legislation into law. They are derived from green papers, or may in fact be a document that has been developed external to the parliamentary system. The term 'white paper' also refers to business documents which focus on particular solutions or outline the benefits of products and technologies. In this way they are used as an internal and external marketing tool. They are used to generate sales leads and establish the business or organisation as a key mover in the development of business knowledge. They can also be used for educative purposes.

> *See also* **green paper.**

Will call/will call window

These two terms refer to the process and the location where a customer can pick up tickets or other documents that they have already ordered. They can usually be found in terminals, lobbies, theme parks and other venues, such as theatres. Usually the 'will call window' of a theatre opens around 90 minutes before the performance.

Work and leisure

A major area in the study of leisure is the balance or trade-off between work and leisure. They both compete for an individual's time. Work imposes a responsibility on individuals, which is often not flexible, and in many cases individuals will choose to work longer hours in return for additional pay. For a time there was a focus on the belief that increased mechanisation and technology, coupled with rising productivity and wages, would lead to reduced working hours and provide individuals with longer periods of time to consume leisure goods and services. However, despite legislation and regulation on the maximum permitted working hours in various countries, actual working hours per week for full-time employees still hovers around forty hours. Clearly, if an individual spends more time at work or physically and mentally recovering from work this reduces the amount of time that they can engage in leisure activities. Some suggest that those that have extremely demanding work, with a lack of free choice about hours, would display signs that leisure was declining as an integral part of their lives.

See also **Work–life balance.**

Work ethic

This concept is based on the Puritan or Protestant beliefs of Calvinists and Lutherans. The term 'Protestant work ethic' was coined by Max Weber. Work ethic suggests that work is a duty and that it benefits both the individual and society. It is not just a Protestant-based belief and is equally applicable in countries such as Japan, China and South Korea, each of which has strong work ethics. It makes a distinction between individuals who see work as being the cornerstone of their lives and those who have a rather more relaxed view and are, perhaps, less materialistic. There are some inferences that work ethic is a capitalist construct, focusing on the desirability of hard work.

Work–life balance

Increasing pressure on employees to commit to longer working hours and sublimate their home life for work has become a considerable concern in many countries over the past few years.

In March 2000, for example, the British government launched a scheme through the Department of Trade and Industry with the following objectives:

Its aim is twofold: to convince employers of the economic benefits of work–life balance, by presenting real-life case studies; and to convince employers of the need for change. The campaign focuses on three areas:

1 Tackling the long-hours culture
2 Targeting sectors with acute work–life balance problems
3 Providing support and guidance

The Work–Life Balance campaign is situated within the Department for Trade and Industry (DTI), where it sits alongside policy and legislation on employment rights.

This includes maternity rights, paternity and adoption leave, time off for emergencies, parental leave and part-time work.

www.dti.gov.uk/work-lifebalance/

More recently, the campaign has gained additional support amongst certain employers, leading to the formation of the Employers and Work–Life Balance part of the Work Foundation.

www.employersforwork-lifebalance.org.uk

World Heritage Site

As of 2008 to 2009 there were just fewer than 900 properties that were considered to be key cultural or natural heritage sites. All had been chosen by the World Heritage Committee as having irreplaceable and universal value. World Heritage Sites are identified as part of UNESCO's general global strategy. In order for a site to be considered it must meet one out of ten key selection criteria. There is a distinct list process in which potential sites are submitted and then considered. The site is then nominated, independently evaluated, and then the World Heritage Committee makes a final decision.

www.unesco.org

World Summit on Sustainable Development

This event took place in Johannesburg, South Africa, in 2002 and is also known as the Earth Summit 2002. It took place ten years after the first Earth Summit in Rio de Janeiro. Arising out of the summit was the Johannesburg Declaration, which proclaimed an agreement to focus on:

> The worldwide conditions that pose severe threats to the sustainable development of our people, which include: chronic hunger, malnutrition, foreign occupation, armed conflict, elicit drug problems, organized crime, corruption, natural disasters, elicit arms trafficking, trafficking in persons, terrorism, intolerance in incitement to racial, ethnic, religious and other hatreds, xenophobia and endemic communicable and chronic diseases.

www.un.org/events/wssd

World Tourism Organisation

The World Tourism Organisation was created in 1974 and is closed associated with the United Nations. It aims to operate as a clearing house for the collection and analysis of tourism information and also offers national tourism organisations the opportunity to enter into international discussions and negotiations. It also aims to promote and develop tourism as a component part of sustained economic development.

The World Tourism Organisation has 7 strategic priorities, in order to attain sustainable travel and tourism development. It therefore recommends to nations the following:

- To have a clear vision of the future of travel and tourism
- To measure and promote the economic importance of travel and tourism.

- To put forward a positive image of the travel and tourism industry as both career and job opportunities.
- To encourage free access, open markets and removal of barriers to growth.
- To improve infrastructure in proportion to customer demand.
- To provide access to capital resources and technological advancement in the travel and tourism field.
- To promote responsible travel and tourism in terms of the preservation of natural, social and cultural environments.

www.world-tourism.org

World Travel and Tourism Council (WTTC)

The WTTC is designed to be a forum for the travel and tourism industry and it aims to raise awareness of the industry, which employs in excess of 230 million people worldwide and generates around 10% of world gross domestic product (GDP). The organisation was established in 1990 and its three original main issues were:

- Promoting the recognition of the economic contribution of the travel industry.
- Ensuring that markets expand in harmony with the environment.
- Reduction of barriers to growth.

www.wttc.org

Worldwide Fund for Nature (WWF)

This is one of the leading environmental organisations. It was founded in 1961 and is active in over 100 countries. The WWF is renowned for its practical experience, knowledge and credibility. It is therefore considered by many national governments to be the first point of contact for advice and consultation on a broad range of environmental issues.

In Britain, for example, WWF-UK has some 300 staff. WWF-UK works closely with government at different levels, business and communities both in Britain and around the world to ensure that people and nature receive their fair share of natural resources. In 2007–8, WWF-UK spent £42 million on operational work (largely funded by membership fees and supporters' donations).

WWF-International is based in Switzerland.

www.panda.org/
www.wwf.org.uk/

Yy

Yield management

Yield management is real-time demand forecasting, which is also known as revenue management or real-time pricing. It is used by organisations to calculate the best pricing policy for optimising profits. Yield management is based on real-time modelling and forecasting of demand behaviour per market segment.

This methodology was first adopted by the airline industry in the early 1980s as a means of comparing supply and demand to differentiated pricing and control of the inventory for each price category. The concept rests on the premise that the producer gains in increased turnover and revenue, whilst the customer enjoys lower prices for the same quality of service.

Yield management is a tactical weapon which aims to ensure profitability of manufacturers in a competitive environment. From the early 1990s the concept began to penetrate other sectors of activity, initially in the United States and then in Europe.

Youth culture

Youth culture is a particular aspect of examining an element of **sub-cultures**. Youth culture clearly focuses on the study of adolescent groups and in the past has examined groups as diverse as mods and hippies. As with any aspect of leisure studies, there have been radically different ways in which youth cultures have been examined, through longitudinal studies, participative research, observation and the examination of literature and images related to each of the youth cultures. Youth cultures, as with sub-cultures, reflect a degree of solidarity and distancing from the dominant cultural types within a society. The youth cultures create their own boundaries, where individuals are either inside or outside the group. There are inevitable tensions with law enforcement and with the mass media, and particularly elements of the media that either demonise or stereotype the groups without focusing on the realities of the situation, or even investigating the roots behind the youth culture.

See also **sub-cultures.**

Index

Page numbers in **bold** indicate definitions